Solly's Girl

A memoir

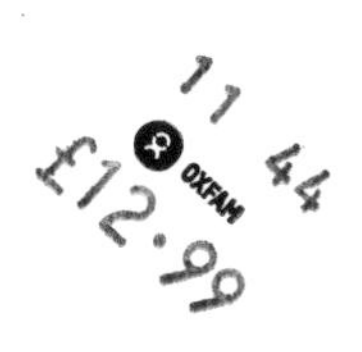

Solly's Girl

A memoir

Ros Collins

The Write Your Story Collection ~ Book No. 124

---

www.alanandroscollins.wordpress.com

First issued by Makor at Lamm Jewish Library of Australia 2015
www.ljla.org.au

National Library of Australia Cataloguing-in-Publication entry
Creator: Collins, Rosaline, author.
Title: Solly's girl : a memoir / Ros Collins.
ISBN: 9780992514129 (1st edition [Makor] paperback)
ISBN: 9780994388605 (1st edition ebook)
ISBN: 9780994388612 (2nd edition paperback)
Subjects: Collins, Rosaline.
Collins, Alan, 1928-2008.
Jews--Australia--Biography.
Women librarians--Australia--Biography.
Male authors--Australia--Biography.
Dewey Number: 305.89240922

Production: Inklink Advertising Pty Ltd

Cover photograph by Nigel Clements

WRITE YOUR STORY is a cultural activity of Makor at Lamm Jewish Library of Australia

---

In honour of Sadie and Solly

In memory of Alan

With love for our family

And remembering Sophie

CONTENTS

Introduction 1

Chapter 1: She's Got a 'Ticket to Ride' 3

2: Isinglass Windows 12

3: The 'Gulag' 20

4: Go West, North or South – Anywhere but East! 33

5: Mostly Romantic 55

6: The Thirties 67

7: 'I'll Shoot You First' 75

8: Working Girl 85

9: 'My Country, Right or Wrong' 95

10: Advance Australians 101

11: Afternoon Tea 111

12: Toby Toys 117

13: Leon 125

14: Going Back 132

15: Green Door 137

16: The Age of Aquarius 143

17: Golden Summers 152

18: 'What's in a Name?' 163

19: Five Tickets to Dachau 182

20: [A] Rose Is a Rose Is a Rose Is a Rose 188

21: Digital 198

22: The Community 206

23: 'Lullaby of Broadway' 215

24: Author, Author 223
25: All the Initials: NT, WA, US 234
26: Kadimah 242
27: U.K. Bye, Bye 256
28: Five Seagulls 264
29: Year One 272
30: Year Two (2009–2010) 279
31: Merry Widows 286
Epilogue 291
Acknowledgements 292
Map of the places our families knew in Europe 295

FAMILY TREES

1: Ancestors of Rosaline Fox 296
2: Descendants of Rosaline Fox 298
3: The Leimseider/Gilbert Family 300
4: The Schlesinger Family 302
5: The Green/Samuel Family 304
6: The Collins Family in the Netherlands 306
7: The Collins Family in England and Australia 308
8: The Cortissos Family 310
9: The Davis Family 312

AUTHOR'S NOTE

Modern transliterations of Yiddish do not always conform to traditional usage; i.e., *matse*, not *matzo*, *Shabbes*, not *Shabbos*. German spelling is not acceptable in contemporary Yiddish usage; for example, *yortsayt* is correct but *yahrtzeit* is not. When a foreign-language word has entered into contemporary English usage, italics are not used in the text; for example, bar mitzvah and kibbutz. I have given translations in brackets after a foreign word in italics when it seemed appropriate. Variant spellings were unavoidable and I have compromised. For example, in Chapter 4 I have left the Yiddish names of my father and his sisters as he wrote them in his memoir, although modern linguists would spell them otherwise.

INTRODUCTION

'Let me entertain you' is how the song goes.

But I'm wary of the Jewish memoir genre. So many authors have suffered such unspeakable torments; it seems almost flippant for me to want to be entertaining. I didn't spend time hiding in an attic, living on turnips or freezing in Siberia. I'm not a witness.

My husband Alan, an author, was fond of saying: 'Leave your mind alone!' and I've never quite understood what he meant. He was a natural storyteller and his books are significant contributions to Australian literature; I'm just fossicking through my memories, teasing out what was funny, romantic or sad – and perhaps provocative. (Alan's memoir, *Alva's Boy*, is very different from *Solly's Girl*, but maybe they are complementary.)

So, in the spirit of *zachor* (remembering) and with the vanity of wanting to say 'I was here', let me tell you some stories …

CHAPTER 1
SHE'S GOT A 'TICKET TO RIDE'

Ah, Lambretta! Not one of your Verdi heroines, all camellias and consumption. It was Innocenti in Milan who created her and, despite a bit of a cough, she was destined to work the streets. Her name was *La Cigale* (the cicada) and we rode her home after our wedding because the Suez Crisis meant a petrol shortage. Wearing a Pierre Balmain copy, and clutching a bouquet of freesia and French mimosa, I took the pillion seat and wrapped my arms around my skinny Australian as we set off into the icy London night. It was February 1957.

The bland and boring fifties were coming to an end, and everyone seemed poised for change. I too needed to get away. I was fifteen when the war ended, and since then had spent a decade experimenting with life. Sex and religion, dependable markers of teenage angst, were major obstacles that hung around until well into my twenties. I was an only child and, for one side of my family, an only grandchild. Against all conventions I'd managed to leave home unwed, which in those days provoked much gossip and family friction. But a bed-sit, in what was at the time 'bohemian' Hampstead, wasn't a long-term future. Society paused, whilst London braced for the swinging sixties. I was at a cross-

Alan riding La Cigale in London, 1956

roads too. The Beatles hadn't quite arrived on the scene when I got my 'ticket to ride'.

I stayed at secondary school until 1948 when I was eighteen, and then set about exploring the cultural scene with enthusiasm. Sinatra played the London Palladium, but I soon threw him over for Olivier in tights. I visited theatres, art house cinemas and concert halls, and discovered museums and galleries. Bookshops were a great attraction. My cousins and childhood friends went to youth clubs and dances, progressing from dates to engagements and suburban domesticity, but this didn't seem to be the path for me. Television was still a novelty. We listened to *The Goon Show*, Doris Day sang *'Que sera, sera'*, and *Oklahoma!* was showing at the cinema. There was trad jazz and a dreadful hybrid called skiffle. I wore clothes made with extravagant amounts of material designed to show that 'Britain could make it', that at last we were in post-war recovery, and I smoked Black Sobranie cigarettes.

Ros outside her parents' house in London, 1956

Modern Israel was eight years old and engaged in her second war, the 1956 Sinai campaign against Egypt. As a Jew I should have been at the very least interested, but I wasn't. The US civil rights movement, freedom buses and the desegregation of schools should have stirred me, but it didn't. South African apartheid hardly registered. London was the centre of my world. It was great to be English, and I would have given anything to be able to claim British ancestry, preferably back to the Tudors

Heading back to Hampstead on *La Cigale* (which bravely flew the Southern Cross flag) my thoughts were all of packing and emigration. I was to be a 'Ten Pound Pom', a subsidised migrant to Australia and was booked to sail with my new husband on the

SS *Stratheden* within a matter of weeks.

The 'whingeing Pom', one who complains that the tomatoes in Australia 'don't taste the same' and the Great Barrier Reef is 'not a patch on Blackpool', is an epithet loaded with scorn. I did yearn for the concrete jungle of London for many years, and to this day am terrified of the bush, but nobody ever has called me out for whingeing. Australia has been the making of me. I'm reminded of the younger sons of the aristocracy who were 'sent to the colonies' when they went off the rails. Here I found a freedom that never would have been mine in the family and community I left behind.

But let's return to Hampstead. Looking back, I find I am now honouring my father and mother far more than I ever did when we lived together, or at any other period in my life. Sadie and Solly Fox reacted to my unexpected wedding in the most astonishingly civil manner. It was just three weeks since they had learned I wanted to marry and their behaviour was exemplary. I can speak as a mother and grandmother, and know exemplary when I meet it. However, my extended family were almost unanimous in condemning me for deserting my parents whilst approving, with a sigh of relief, that at least I was marrying a Jew, and thus no longer constituted a worry for them all. The fact that Alan appeared to have no family to speak of, was stony broke and reduced to working at a London rail terminus shifting mailbags with a West Indian crew – all this was of lesser importance to them than his religion.

La Cigale had courageously battled the fearful London fog and sleet to get Alan and me around to visit most members of my family prior to our marriage. 'It wouldn't be right for your aunts and uncles to come to the wedding, not having met the bridegroom first,' said my mother. With barely three weeks in hand before sailing away, we did our best. Sometimes it all went horribly wrong, like the dreaded dinner at Uncle Will's. We were commanded to arrive at 7.25 pm – not 7.15 or 7.30 or 7-ish. I was marrying a man given to insubordination, so it was a red rag to a bull. We circled the streets of upper-crust Hendon for half an hour before ringing the bell. Aunt Ray was 'posh' and the only member of my family to have a maid; her name was Muriel. Will and Ray had one child, my cousin Michael, a rather gentle young man reduced to hanging out of his bedroom window if he needed a smoke.

Alan was wearing corduroy pants and hiking boots (just about all he owned) when we navigated the minefield of plush furniture and expensive ornaments that was their drawing room. My aunt's face was a study as he brought out a tobacco tin and papers to roll his own cigarettes. She rushed to encircle him with cut-glass ashtrays he managed to miss every time he flicked the ash. Dinner, served by Muriel, was a disaster since Alan had no idea of the etiquette relating to maids.

Uncle Will was the only rich one of my mother's siblings, all of whom deferred to him in regard to financial matters. I know he was very generous to members of the family who fell on hard times. He had a sort of advertising business selling space in magazines and newspapers. My mother and I sometimes visited his office and he'd take us out for lunch. He was a kindly soul and once took me to a pub so I might understand how to order a drink.

After Aunt Ray died, Uncle Will became increasingly frail. He suffered with dementia and ended his days in a nursing home. Allegedly, he wandered off one night and was discovered in a dubious club from where an understanding cop rescued him. (Years later Alan wrote a great short story based upon this episode.)

During my years in Hampstead I always felt constrained to go back home to Ilford on Friday night or for lunch on Saturday. Jewish guilt. After I met up with the Australians, all students hanging out for a meal, I took to bringing a visitor with me. It was a *mitzvah*, a good deed. Once I brought a chubby bloke (who later became an eminent doctor) and several times I took Alan, who was very thin and forever hungry.

The decision to marry crept up on us unexpectedly. We were living together in a chilly attic bed-sit and Alan, longing for home, suggested we take *La Cigale* on an extended road-trip to the southern hemisphere. We had no money, but we huddled in bed poring over a map of the world. He was working at Paddington Station, and I was a trainee buyer in the nightdress department of Marks and Spencer at their head office in Baker Street. I wore high heels and a black suit with a cinched waist – the High Street version of Dior's 'New Look', and anticipated a sophisticated career with the company.

Alan met me from work one day with a cable from his Melbourne employers, Rockmans Stores, advising him his year's leave without pay was up and he was needed back at work to produce their new mail-order catalogue. If he didn't get home quickly his job would be lost. 'We must leave immediately,' he said. Without hesitation I replied, 'If "we" are to go, then I think my parents will be happier if we marry here first.' We found a phone box and spoke to my father, who was at work where he designed ladies' fashions. I asked if he recalled the Australian I'd brought home and he asked, 'The fat one or the thin one?' 'It's the wraith,' I said, and explained that we wished to marry within three weeks and leave soon after for Melbourne. Solly was remarkably calm and merely said Alan and I should meet him and Sadie for a meal that evening. My dear mother ('never arrive empty-handed') brought a beach towel from Debenhams, probably all she could think of that might relate to Australia. The four of us then sat down to discussion and a fish-and-chip dinner (strictly kosher).

The marriage was very nearly cancelled. Particular about lineage, Jewish Orthodoxy needed proof, the real deal and in writing, that Alan was indeed a Jew and had no other wife. At a time when faxes, let alone emails, were some boffin's dream, we had to produce evidence from the Great Synagogue in Sydney. The rabbi booked to conduct our wedding was adamant: no cable, no ceremony. The piece of paper arrived the day before our marriage, which could then take place at my parents' synagogue in Beehive Lane, Ilford, Essex.

In July 1956 the Suez Canal was closed and the politics in the Middle East critical. There were shortages all round and we had a complicated situation. No one would contemplate planning a wedding in such a short time, let alone a Jewish one for an only daughter. Solly was booked to go for a week to Paris for the fashion shows, where he would concentrate on absorbing new trends for the mass market; hiring a reception hall would be difficult; and I still needed to complete the documentation to qualify as a Ten Pound Pom. Alan was a returning citizen, but had no money for his fare as he'd spent that on *La Cigale* back in Milan. Australia House would have to find us berths on a ship, preferably the same ship, and get us back to Melbourne in time for Alan to rescue his job. And the rabbi needed his piece of paper.

The advertisement in the *Jewish Chronicle* was startling:

> … the engagement is announced … the wedding will take place … the young couple will sail immediately for Australia …

Not a soul believed I wasn't pregnant. One Saturday afternoon, Solly and Alan were to have one of those 'serious' man-to-man conversations during which my mother insisted she and I go shopping. When we returned the two of them were dozing happily in armchairs by the fire. Apparently my father had merely asked Alan if he was 'alright'. Al replied that he was fine, except that he had no money to get home, so Solly said he'd pay the fare and that was pretty well that. My father always said he knew a good man when he met one, and the pair of them never exchanged a cross word. Beautiful blokes, both.

Determined to be difficult, I wanted to be married in a National Trust type English mansion, where I would be dressed in red velvet at a candle-lit ceremony. Quite rightly, Solly and Sadie said there would be a traditional Jewish wedding in their synagogue, with a

Alan and Ros at their wedding in London, 17 February 1957. Photograph by Marti Friedlander

proper wedding breakfast afterwards, in keeping with their modest means. Still determined, I insisted on a dress with no frills or lace. Pierre Balmain had designed a short white grosgrain wedding dress and jacket that was the last word in simplicity, and Liberty's in Regent Street made me a copy. Manor Hall, Chigwell, out in what was then semi-rural Essex, was able to accommodate us, and Sadie, left to make a lot of the arrangements on her own whilst Solly was in Paris, chose the menus. Ostwinds, a famous old Jewish family bakery in the East End (long since gone to make way for the much more colourful Bangladeshis) did the catering.

There were plenty of guests for me, but Alan had not one family member to support him. The Aussie students came to the rescue. Dad's sister Sally and her husband, Dave, stood in for Alan's parents. Gerrard, a dentist from New Zealand, and his wife, Marti (now one of that country's most illustrious photographers), were best man and matron of honour. Marti provided us with the best of photographs: un-posed, casual and perfectly matching the unconventional circumstances. Solly, wishing to do his very best to please the Australians, ordered a great deal of beer (he'd heard it was a popular drink) but they chose hard liquor instead. For years afterwards, every time Alan and I visited London, Solly produced a bottle of what must by that time have been pretty stale lager.

I'm told that getting Alan to the synagogue involved a few pauses for 'heart-starters' *en route*, and I think the actual ceremony remained forever hazy for both of us. I do remember how important it seemed to Alan that French mimosa, as close to Australian wattle as we could get, should be in my bouquet and in the men's buttonholes. He also chose freesia, which I now plant in my garden as a memory. By the time he had to make his wedding speech he was completely *shiker* (drunk), but the Australian contingent gave him a resounding cheer and sang 'Waltzing Matilda'. My bemused family, mostly conservative to their backbones, must have found the whole business very odd. However, in the photographs Sadie and Solly look happy – and I hope they were. We never talked about it, or the fact that I was to live so far away.

Other bridal photos show diamonds, but my engagement ring, bought after the wedding from an antique shop in central London, is a Victorian band with a garnet and tiny seed pearls. The dainty gold

L-R: Sadie, Alan, Ros, Solly, 17 February 1957.
Photograph by Marti Friedlander

filigree wedding ring is also antique. I didn't own diamonds until I'd been married for forty years, and am never keen to wear the tiny earstuds Alan bought me in the 1980s. I don't think diamonds are my best friends.

Ros on board the SS Stratheden, March 1957

We didn't know much about each other, Alan and me. His appalling childhood and unhappy youth were mysteries to be unravelled over many years. His books reveal much but I'm still getting to know him. I can only guess what he was thinking in 1957: probably that he was about to have a real home and family for the first time in his life. I had adjustments to make too.

The *Stratheden* sailed from Tilbury. As Sadie, Solly, Alan and I stood on the deck Alan said he didn't want to leave without Sadie and me resolving some of the difficulties in our relationship. And so we did. I don't recall feeling sad at quitting Britain and was not devastated because I was leaving my parents. In my grey, army-surplus duffel coat I was all set to go to Australia. I had my 'ticket to ride'.

CHAPTER 2
ISINGLASS WINDOWS

We were given a tiny cabin below the water line. Alan was a paying passenger and entitled to reasonable accommodation, whereas I, a Ten Pound Pom, should have been in a dormitory. But the man at Australia House was a kindly romantic who viewed the journey as our honeymoon. As we progressed towards the Canary Islands the weather became warmer and my seasickness eased. We sat on deck with Alan's little portable Olympia on our knees, typing blue airmail letters back to London and forward to Melbourne. Sadie and Solly kept every one we sent, and I brought them back to Australia after they died.

The Suez Crisis had affected shipping routes, so our voyage was longer than normal, as we had to travel around Africa. Cape Town did more to awaken us to the realities of apartheid than all the leaflets distributed in London could ever have done, and the signs permitting white – but not black – kids to use the swings in a scrubby little playground near the docks in Durban were enough to raise our staunch socialist consciences. No amount of beautiful Dutch colonial architecture compensated for our anger. Fremantle was a disappointment. All I saw were grain stores and warehouses, and I thought it the most desolate place on earth. After a five-week voyage we steamed through the entrance to Port Phillip Bay, and apprehension took over. My introduction to Melbourne, my sponsor, Alan's friends, and a new life were upon me and I was completely unprepared.

We had learned little about Australia at school. I probably knew the names of two or three capital cities, and was familiar with produce such as wool, dried fruit, lamb and cheese. Alan had not been very forthcoming about his country and its culture, so unlike most of the other English migrants, who had made considered decisions to become Australians, I was quite ignorant. As St Kilda, the roller coaster at Luna Park fun fair, and the Palais Theatre came into view, Alan became excited. 'You'll like it, really!' he said. 'We'll go on picnics and visit the Dandenongs. It'll be just great.' I imagined some Mr and Mrs Dandenong, not a Jewish-sounding name. I didn't know he meant mountains.

We arrived at Station Pier in April 1957 and it was raining. My all-important British passport (navy blue, stiff board covers – none of this burgundy EU rubbish) had been impounded. I, like Esau, had perhaps 'sold my birthright for a mess of …' what? As a Ten Pound Pom I was legally obliged to stay in Australia for two years. Demonstrating the spirit that had got us through the Blitz, I set off bravely in my best Jaeger dress, smartened up with a white hat and white gloves, all ready for the introductions.

I had seen just one Australian film, and looking over the rail I searched for blokes like the actor Chips Rafferty, on horseback and wearing large hats. Chips was nowhere in sight but there was a little group of men, all wearing identical grey raincoats. It seemed they were our welcoming party. Instead of horses they brought 'utes' (utility trucks), serviceable vehicles for transporting goods and equipment; and instead of Akubras they wore soft-brimmed fedoras. There was a casual air about them, a complete lack of formality and a laid-back approach that had great appeal.

The authorities needed to be assured that no migrant would be sleeping rough on the pavements, so a sponsor was necessary. Alan's old friend Phil had gone guarantor for me. When he announced that 'Anna is expecting us for lunch in Caulfield' I assumed Caulfield was the name of his property, rather like Tara in *Gone with the Wind*. At last I would see the real Australia, with sheep and horses and all that Chips had introduced me to. Phil and Anna's tiny house in Alfada

Street, South Caulfield, was something of a letdown. A sheep station it wasn't. A huge unopened crate stood in the back yard: *La Cigale* had been shipped out separately. Whilst Anna and I sipped tea and made polite talk, Phil and Alan went to unpack the crate. Motor scooters were a novelty in Australia, and ours was one of the first to appear in Melbourne. Alan wanted to show Phil how it worked and took *La Cigale* out on to a sloping, newly gravelled road for the demonstration. The petrol had been drained for the journey but there was just enough left for the motor to kick over and for Alan to have no choice but to jump on board. He missed and flew over the weather guard, cutting his nose and landing face down in the gravel. Hours later, Phil returned to take me to the Alfred Hospital where Alan was being repaired. I think he was apprehensive I might be a nervous English lady likely to become easily distraught, but I was fast learning to expect the unexpected in my life with Alan.

Phil offered to drive me through Melbourne and show me some of the sights. Beyond the city I became anxious about the vastness of the southern sky and the sense of a huge empty land somewhere 'out there'. When he dowsed the car lights so I might see the stars, they were in the wrong arrangement for me. I was frightened by it all and longed for the density of London.

We had arrived in Melbourne with ten shillings between us, so it was imperative for Alan to get back to work and for me to find a job. We had a tiny studio flat at Poets Corner, Elwood, not far from the beach, and where many of the surrounding streets are named for English authors: Milton, Tennyson, Southey, Dickens and Thackeray. The area still retains memories of its 1920s Art Deco flavour, despite the ravages of developers. This is where Alan and I returned to in 1987, after twenty-eight years in an outer suburb, and it's where I hope to see out my life.

It was 1957 – strange city, strange climate, no money and it was *Pesach*. Nursing the convalescent Alan, I was immensely grateful to the friends who brought us matzo (unleavened bread) and wedding gifts.

It was a relief when Alan was able to resume his work as advertising manager for Phil and Norman Rockman, owners of Rockmans chain stores. Armed with a glowing reference from one of the directors of Marks and Spencer, I too went there looking for a job. However, in those days the Australian clothing industry was poorly regulated, and my M and S training in quality control far too sophisticated for the rough and tumble of the local scene. Next, I tried advertising, as my prior career in London had been in that world. This might have turned out well, but pregnancy intervened and my working life in Melbourne was on hold for the next ten years.

During the winter of 1957 we took a short trip to Canberra, the national capital, and to Sydney for me to meet Alan's father, Sampson (Sam). The Rockmans, who were the souls of kindness, lent us a delivery van for the journey. Since there was only one seat (for the driver), I perched on one of those tiny gold-lacquered chairs used in fashion showrooms, anchored to the floor with rope.

Sampson (Sam) Collins and Ros in Sydney, 1957

Sam Collins was strange. I didn't know what to make of him, for he was nothing like any Jew I'd ever met before. I am reminded of Jewish characters and caricatures in nineteenth century English novels – though Sam's accent was broad Australian rather than Cockney. He'd obviously done his best to smarten up for my benefit, although his clothes had seen better days. He was all over me 'like a rash' and held my hand very tightly. It must have been excruciating for Alan, but at that time I didn't know their history.

La Cigale sat outside the block of flats at Poet's Corner. We had a problem because Alan did not possess a motorbike licence, and local regulations required one. No matter how domesticated we made ourselves look – shopping basket, me in a headscarf like the Queen – the cops lay in wait for us along the beach road and sprang out from their hiding places in the tea-trees. They really only wanted to have a look at *La Cigale*, but it was unnerving.

As the months went by it became evident we'd have to buy a car. All we could afford was £20 for a 1927 Chevrolet, and although I have no real attachment to vehicles this one captured my heart. Alan had owned a Baby Austin before leaving for Europe and had never driven a thirty-year-old car with such basic controls, but the Chevy did us proud, and we loved her as much as *La Cigale*. The musical *Oklahoma!* was a favourite of Alan's, and when Curley sings to Laurie about the 'Surrey with the fringe on top' and the 'isinglass curtains you can roll right down', the Chevy's mica windows, wooden floorboards and real leather upholstery always come to mind.

La Cigale and the 1927 Chevy in Elwood, 1957

In December 1957 we took summer holidays and drove to Sydney. We camped on the way, and Daniel was probably conceived at mosquito-infested Lake Tyers. I encountered Aboriginal people for the first time, the genesis of Alan's short story 'The Camp'. We travelled along the coastal highway, the weather so hot that cars were banked up beside the road with their radiators boiling. But Alan was a real DIY man who always had something handy, 'just in case' – in this instance, some baling wire he used to tie back the sides of the Chevy's bonnet so the breeze cooled the engine – and we left all those modern cars for dead as we chugged up the Bulli Pass toward Sydney. That's when I became convinced of Alan's potential as a saviour. If we were ever going to be in a jam I was certain he'd have a rescue plan: a widget or gadget, a wire or a string, a box or a bolt that would surely save us. He was rather like Maxwell Smart but without the shoe-phone.

By the time we got back to Melbourne in early 1958 the pregnancy was confirmed, and as spring approached the idea of parenthood took hold. In those days the minutiae of childbirth were not so well known by young people. My mother, Sadie, was far too shy ever to have discussed such intimate details with me, and Alan, who had no family experiences to call upon, took all his information from lurid novelettes in which hapless women boiled water for sterilisation and tore strips off sheets to mop up the blood. However, I did have an obstetrician and was booked to give birth in a big city hospital, so we hoped for a good outcome.

As Alan introduced me to the surrounding areas, my homesickness grew. For many years I referred to Australia as 'lotus land'. Place names with all the wrong connotations: Chelsea was a sleepy beachside suburb, quite different from the 'swinging' Kings Road in its London namesake; Sandringham in Melbourne was nothing like the royal holiday hangout in Norfolk; and Brighton, Victoria, with its *nouveau riche* mansions right down to the soft squeaky sand, was a world away from Brighton, Sussex, with its Regency pavilions and pebbly British beach. I wept for England and asked to see the local equivalent of London's Soho, hoping vainly for something racy and exciting in prim and proper 1950s Melbourne.

By August, in preparation for the coming baby, we had moved from our studio to a third-floor flat in neighbouring East St Kilda. Key money, a rip-off on the part of landlords, was legal at the time; we struggled as well to find the exorbitant price demanded for a second-hand settee and two armchairs. A bed for us, a bassinet for the baby and an enormous television console bought on hire purchase completed our home in Inkerman Street (naturally, adjacent to Balaclava, Crimea, Alma and other reminders of wars past). It was the beginning of our retreat from Alan's beloved beachside.

When my waters broke on 31 August Alan called desperately for help. At the time I didn't realise how much his mother's death in childbirth was behind the panic. Our dear friend Beryl, a week short of having her second child, arrived, sized up the situation and sent him off to hang out some washing and make a cup of tea, a bit of a let-down when he was all prepared for the sheet tearing.

Daniel was born on 1 September 1958, the first day of spring. The obstetrician did not turn up for the event, and capable midwives looked after me. He also failed to turn up for Peter's birth the following year, and just made it for Toby in 1962. This was before the freewheeling sixties with home birthing in a water bath, prenatal meditation and yoga classes. Rigid routine was the order of the day. Fathers did not attend births but sat at home waiting for a phone call. When at last Alan and I were allowed to see and touch our baby, we failed our first test. Daniel was brought ceremoniously to the ward tightly bound in a bunny rug in an arrangement that could only be mastered after much practice. Once alone with this bundle, we wanted to see for ourselves that all the right bits were present and correct, so we undid our parcel to have a look and, of course, were unable to reassemble it.

Our second failure was to take Dan home in a basket placed on the floor of the Chevy, the doors of which had no locks and might easily have swung open. Fumes came up through the wooden floorboards and we almost suffocated him. We were so incapable, I was sent to a maternity unit for a week where they showed me how to hold, bathe and feed our child. Finally the three of us were at home in the Inkerman Street flat. The only immediately available help came from Cookie, Mrs Cook, the widow next door. She was rather Dickensian, with a cleft palate, a lovely disposition, and a firm belief that rubbing Dan's damp nappies over her face would preserve a soft complexion.

Our freedom days were over and it was time to act like a serious family. The Chevy, no vehicle for a baby, made way for a tiny Morris and *La Cigale* was sold to a farmer. We kept the brass cicada mascot Alan had bolted onto her front mudguard, and today it sits next to his photograph, together with his ALP membership card and a little container of sand inscribed ironically for his childhood haven: 'the sacred sands of Bondi'.

The late 1950s were boom time in Australia. Anyone with just a smidgen of get-up-and-go could make a buck, start a business or get a job. Migrants were building the Snowy Mountains hydroelectric complex, and mining towns like Mount Isa were thriving. In the Melbourne Jewish community you'd have to have been a real dummy not to get ahead, but Alan and I were never serious contenders in the upwardly mobile stakes. We needed money but could never find the single-mindedness, the toughness, to be in business; with no capital or family support we were far behind the pack. If you weren't making it in commerce or manufacturing, that left the professions or an academic career, and we had friends busily acquiring degrees in preparation for professorial positions, rooms in Collins Street, or a place at the bar. Unconsciously, we continued along the path set in Alan's early life – that of outsiders. Not that people were unkind; they were quite the opposite, but we didn't match the Jewish norms of the day. Our ambitions and expectations were different.

CHAPTER 3

THE 'GULAG'

It's a tribute to Dan that he survived us as parents and grew very bonny. We were so pleased with having made one baby, we wanted to see if we could manage a repeat, and by early 1959 I was pregnant again.

This time the morning sickness was unending. Alan was anxious; I was ill; the three flights of stairs were difficult, particularly with the huge pram sent out from England, and we were throwing good money away on rent. Buying a house by the beach, Alan's ideal, was impossible on our tiny budget. We were so desperate, he contemplated taking a job as publicity director at Mount Isa Mines over 2,500 kilometres away in Queensland. It would have given us a better income, and in a few years we might have saved for a house deposit. The company flew him up for an interview, but when he told me of the summer temperature (over 40° C), the rudimentary housing and limited social life, I suggested we discuss the idea with my father. When Solly, with difficulty, located Mount Isa in an atlas he was appalled by the huge empty spaces all around. I was unwilling to take Dan and have a new baby in such a remote town, so Solly said he'd help us financially if we could find something in Melbourne.

The Rockman brothers were very kind. One day Norman (or it might have been Phil) wanted to know why Alan's face was so sad. 'A house? Why didn't you tell me? I've got houses. I'm building out in Box Hill North. Go take a look.' We drove over on a dark, wet night and saw an almost-completed cream brick-veneer house. It was at the end of an unmade road with no streetlights and adjacent to a small natural bush park. We agreed to buy it for £4,250 and 22 Currie

22 Currie Street, Box Hill North, c1959

Street, Box Hill North was to be home for the next twenty-eight years, a period Alan uncharitably referred to as 'living in the gulag'.

In retrospect, I think the constant morning sickness was due in part to apprehension. Alan was at work and Daniel and I were alone all day. Adjusting to Australian life was as hard for me as for any migrant with language problems. The neighbours were kind enough, but we didn't live in each other's pockets. Emergencies were another matter. Frank-next-door drove me to the hospital for a false alarm when the vomiting became uncontrollable, and it surprises me that thalidomide wasn't prescribed.

Peter was born on 22 November 1959 – like Daniel at St Andrew's Hospital, Melbourne. No obstetrician. Once again I was doped up with painkillers and knew very little about the birth. When Alan came in to see his new son he brought a bunch of herbs from the garden he was trying to make in Currie Street. Flowers would have been too expensive and I loved his gift. Peter was a very beautiful baby and lay quietly in our arms like an exquisite porcelain doll. As we had no relatives in Melbourne, it was Freda, his godmother, who made the little party, the *l'chaim* to celebrate his *brit*. Daniel's circumcision had been performed by an old rabbi who produced an appalling tin box of equipment from his dusty black coat. Dan got an infection. For Peter we knew better, and a doctor did the job. In those days new mothers often stayed in hospital for as long as a week, and I celebrated 30 November, St Andrew's Day, in bed enjoying Scottish shortbread biscuits in tartan wrapping paper.

Two little boys, fourteen months apart, a barely furnished house in an outer suburb that had a mixture of war-service homes, built by the government for returned soldiers, and brash new brick-veneer houses such as ours, created out of orchard land by developers like the Rockman brothers. There were no pavements or streetlights and just a little strip of local shops. Or else one took the bus to Box Hill proper. Alan was not entrepreneurial, but he was willing to 'have a go' to get us on our feet. At night we made sheepskin slippers, similar to Ugg boots, to sell to markets and city shoe shops. A friend in far-off Caulfield, the heart of the Jewish community, had a tannery in Footscray and we bought the skins cheaply. This little enterprise lasted for only a year or so because the hole punch for the thread made our hands so sore. We flirted with the thought of buying a milk bar. Many young couples were doing this and working themselves into heart attacks from the long hours. We didn't have the capital anyway, so that idea lapsed.

Another piece missing from our suburban jigsaw was family. A small group of very dear friends became, and still are, surrogates for the aunts, uncles and cousins that Alan didn't have and that I'd left behind in Britain.

Freda and Martin were among the closest and took a keen interest in our well being, particularly in regard to Jewish matters. Their kindness knew no bounds. They lived in Kew, not impossibly far away. Raising four children did not prevent Freda from becoming an academic and teacher, one of the new breed of working wives much derided by Martin.

Whilst I was in hospital having Peter, an advertisement appeared in the local paper inviting Jewish families in the Box Hill area to get in touch if they cared to socialise with Joyce and Henry. By the time I returned home we had already formed a friendship that will endure until the end. Henry was the complete German *yekke*, precise, accurate and serious, whilst Joyce was the free spirit, artistic and adventurous. They were hilarious opposites and although he has gone now, her joyfulness remains one of my pleasures.

Over the river in St Kilda, the beach area Alan missed so much, our friends Simon and Beryl and Phil and Anna were raising kids too. A third couple, Mark and Norma took the plunge and made their way to a suburb even more 'outer' than Box Hill where Mark started a pharmacy and Norma presided over the neatest home I ever saw. These were all friends Alan had known before our marriage – some, like Phil, even back in his Sydney teenage years. Unlike us, most of them had extended families in Melbourne, and there were many parents, aunts, uncles and cousins who made us welcome as if we too were relatives.

One of Alan's best short stories, 'The Value of a Nail', echoes this period of our lives, and we were proud to see it published in a prestigious literary journal. It's about Ernst, a Jewish migrant who moves from St Kilda to an outer suburb where he becomes a passionate amateur carpenter, forsaking synagogue for the mecca of the Aussie hardware store. Some affluent friends from the other side of the river come to visit. They are patronising about his homemade furniture, but Ernst is proud of his achievement and finds the visitors shallow and pretentious. It never occurred to me to link all this to Alan, to see in Ernst's pride a reflection of his

Alan painting, Currie Street, c1960

own. I used to tease him because all he could make in his little under-the-house workshop was an endless series of bookshelves, and we soon ran out of walls. Finally, he enrolled for an evening class at Box Hill Technical School to learn the rudiments of carpentry. With profound joy, he gradually made the furniture I still use today.

Making his home, quite literally with his own hands, was a catharsis, not just a hobby. I didn't know then that as a child his stepmother had banned him from the house and made him sleep on a camp bed outside. I didn't know then that he ate his meals from a tin plate he rested on the copper; that the simple dinners I produced were banquets in his eyes. At the time I never understood that the protective wall he constructed around us would have a push-pull effect on our relationships with the Jewish community. Alan's neglected childhood left deep, buried scars he never discussed. They only emerged when he wrote *The Boys from Bondi* in 1987, and *Alva's Boy* in 2007. In 1960, he just wanted to look forward.

Whilst Alan was clearing the unhappy past from his mind, building furniture and planting potatoes to break up the heavy clay soil, I was doing battle with the local council. Our street had open drains in which water rats from the creek in the park could occasionally be seen. Fired with indignation, I wrote to the mayor and said I was not prepared to have our little boys 'at risk of typhoid' and that their British grandparents were horrified! The council took note; the priority list was adjusted, and a team of migrant Italians set to work building pavements. It wasn't entirely smooth sailing. One day I was shocked to find a swastika in the wet concrete outside our house. There was no question of diplomacy or going through channels. I found the foreman, lost my temper and demanded the offence be removed immediately – which it was. But we never discovered who made the marks or why. Alan and I presented as the typical young Aussie family with no money, two kids and a dog. How was it that we should be targeted in this raw, new suburb?

The dog in question was a corgi named Sugar. Freda's uncle had bought two dogs, a poodle and the corgi, but this was impractical as he lived in a flat. Whilst I was in hospital for Peter's birth, Alan was given the choice of which puppy to take, and from that time on our family has never been without a dog. Sugar fitted in well and became protective of the children. A hot summer's day brought a snake from the creek into the front garden where the boys were playing. Sugar was brave enough to attack it and warn me of danger. When our neighbour took a spade, did what had to be done, and hung the creature over our fence as a warning to others, it was the first time I saw a typical Aussie male deal traditionally with such a problem. This sort of thing was a far cry from life in London, where I might have met lounge lizards but certainly not venomous brown snakes.

Sadie and Solly made a very uncharacteristic decision, completely against all their principles of frugality. Two unseen grandsons were more than they could bear, and they were going to 'fly now, pay later'. A visit to Melbourne was planned for the English summer holiday period, a time when we would be deep into the Australian winter. I find it poignant to think of all the holidays my parents went on by themselves after I'd left. It's not that I *would* have accompanied them; it's the aloneness of it all. I have their photograph albums with memories of Tenby ('bracing'), Portugal ('exotic'), Sicily ('bit scary') and Norfolk Broads ('an adventure'). Whilst we were too busy with our small family to take proper notice, they grew older and more frail. Walking sticks appear in the pictures.

My parents made that first trip to Australia in 1960. Solly's employer, the 'Guv'nor', grudgingly allowed him extra holiday time (unpaid) over and above the usual two weeks, and plans were finalised. Solly's sisters, known collectively as 'the girls', were scared their principal male support figure might decide to stay in Australia. But Solly had a strong sense of duty towards these shy, unmarried women, and figured that as I had Alan and the boys, my need was not so great. I think he was wrong. Our family would have benefited enormously from the presence of grandparents, whilst the orphaned 'girls', who were timid and socially inept, cruelly undermined Sadie, who had taken away their only brother.

They flew via Sydney, and Alan went there to accompany them on the final leg to Melbourne. I had a driver's licence but had never made the long trip from Box Hill to Essendon Airport. I pored over Melway maps marking the route, packed up the Morris with Daniel on a seat, Peter in a carry-cot and, for good measure, the corgi as well. In those days airport security was quite lax, and staff helped me position the family right on the tarmac – Dan holding one hand, the carry-cot in my other, and Sugar's lead hooked on my finger. It was only three years since I'd emigrated, but my new life was to be a revelation to Sadie and Solly.

Invitation for our friends to meet Sadie and Solly, 1960

Currie Street probably shocked them. At that time the pavements were not yet made and the muddy clay made walking difficult. Perhaps it was with memories of their own arrival at 36 Ashurst Drive in Ilford, a similarly unmade suburb in 1927, that my parents first saw our home. They were always very polite, and if they disapproved they never said. Naturally, they adored their grandsons, and maybe Sadie reflected on the two little boys she miscarried. One of their main concerns was that portmanteau of a concept: *yidishkayt* (Jewish culture). Box Hill North was certainly very lacking in this regard. Apart from Joyce and Henry in the neighbouring suburb, and Freda and Martin in Kew, we knew of no other Jews in our area. We returned to the 'ghetto' in St Kilda for synagogues, smoked salmon and bagels. Sadie and Solly were completely at home in that environment, where the families of Simon and Beryl and Anna and Phil lived.

I think my parents might have come to stay permanently had we also remained in St Kilda. Then, of course, life for all of us would have been quite different. I suppose we could have found a tiny semi-detached house with no garden in that area, but Alan had dreamed himself into the traditional Australian quarter-acre block, playing cricket in the backyard with the kids, far away from a prying Jewish community that perhaps made him feel inadequate. I'm guessing. Sadie and Solly returned to England full of tall stories about kangaroos roaming along Collins Street and the necessity of never being without a canvas water bag in case of dehydration. An astonished family would have been entranced, listening to descriptions of the strange country to which their black sheep had gone.

Family portrait, 1960.
L–R, back row: Alan and Solly; front row: Ros, holding Dan; Sadie, holding Peter

In 1961 we went to Sydney for the last interstate holiday we were to have for some years. I was six months pregnant and tired from the strain of pretty well everything: marriage, emigration, new house, two small children, not much money, and no idea of my own direction in life. We stayed with Sam and Leon. Leon, Alan's half-brother, was the child of Sam's fourth wife, the stepmother who had treated Alan so cruelly and then deserted the family to run off with a fur-

Sam Collins in Sydney, 1961

niture salesman (see Family Tree No. 7). Sam and Leon lived together, on and off, for many years and at this time they were renting a run-down house in Coogee, a hilly beachside suburb. I never had a meaningful conversation with Sam. Looking at the holiday photographs, it's clear he was not a happy man. Life had not been much good for him. He was in 'reduced circumstances' that were to become even more 'reduced' by 1962 when he lived alone in a room above a pub in Bondi Road. Leon was a taxi driver employed by one of the big companies; he worked hard and eventually acquired the plates for his own cab. The holiday was disastrous from start to finish. In the pictures it's obvious that I'm not in good shape. Alan and Leon do not appear together as brothers, and Alan and Sam are quite pointedly not communicating. The little boys were the only ones having fun.

We had decided that four children would make a family, but the third pregnancy was debilitating and I was quite run down when Toby was born at St George's Hospital, Kew, on 26 March 1962. However, this time around I was conscious for the birth; I was able to hold the baby and have a very British cup of tea almost immediately. It seemed to me that from the very beginning Toby laughed. That's how he's always been – the comic.

Our lack of relatives was brought home to us very sharply with this birth. Alan was forced to ask the local council for assistance with caring for Dan and Peter whilst I was in hospital. It was also our most difficult time financially. Toby's *brit* was a case in point. Moss Cass, who later became a minister in Gough Whitlam's government, was a doctor who specialised in research projects, not general practice. As an old friend he did the procedure free of charge. It must have been a good job, for Toby has three healthy sons of his own. Freda once again made the little party afterwards, notable, I'm told, because there were differences of opinion between Martin and another friend, Shimon, over the correct religious observances.

None of our children was named after any ancestor, a break with Jewish tradition, and we didn't give any of them a middle name. Daniel and Peter were simply names that seemed to go well with Collins – nothing fancy or fussy. Tobias was another matter entirely. Alan had known Richard and Jeanne Pratt when they had all been young, long before the Pratts became public figures. One afternoon during the pregnancy they came to visit. Jeanne suggested that Tobias would be a good, flexible kind of name. She said that if our boy became famous, say a Governor-General, then 'Tobias' had suitable *gravitas*; if he turned out to be a regular Aussie, then 'Toby' would sound friendly and engaging. And so it was.

The years 1962 to 1966 were tough, with holidays reduced to day trips in the Morris. In May 1962 Sam Collins was knocked down by a bus in Taylor Square, Sydney. He refused surgery. 'Son, don't let them take the knife to me!' and the result was that a perfectly simple fractured leg that might have been repaired was immobilised in traction and, of course Sam got pneumonia. Alan took Dan, aged three and a half, to Sydney to say goodbye to his grandfather, who died shortly after. The legalities were handled with much kindness by Leslie Caplan, who, with his wife, Sophie, was a good friend from Alan's youth. Sam's final years must have been very lonely, and his effects were pathetically few. There was a tiny notebook with some anniversaries recorded, a hawker's licence and a couple of hundred pounds, just enough to pay for the funeral. Alan arranged it all whilst I stayed home with the children. We couldn't afford to erect a headstone. The graves of both Sam and Alva, his third wife and Alan's mother, remained unmarked in Rookwood Cemetery for many years.

I found domestic life very demanding, mainly because I demanded so much of myself. My mother's insistence on cleanliness and routine must have affected me subconsciously, as I engaged in a ridiculous struggle for order against the little boys who wanted a more freewheeling Aussie lifestyle. It was lonely out there in Box Hill North. We may have scoffed at the claustrophobia of the St Kilda Jewish community, but there's no denying we cut off our noses to spite our faces in running from the security blanket it offered. At one stage we had three children under five, and the long days on my own with no supportive network were hard. I have a vivid memory of a Freudian moment when I put myself and my sewing machine inside the playpen to escape the boys and the dog, all prowling around outside the bars.

In 1963 Betty Friedan published *The Feminine Mystique,* which I read with growing awareness of the social changes around me. Freda in Kew was always something of a guru in these matters. When we first met in 1957 she asked me – no, instructed me – to meet her on the steps of the State Library for an introduction to Australian culture. I was still making fashion errors with my white hat and gloves, and found Freda's old raincoat and obviously casual attitude to clothes confusing. She was a graduate, intellectually aware and determined to have a career beyond child raising. I had no idea where I was heading, but I was certain I'd never again read women's magazines.

My sexual education had been quite negligible. Naturally, there were no discussions with Sadie, or even a sympathetic aunt. When I finally fled home for the anticipated freedom of that bed-sit in Hampstead, it didn't really live up to my expectations. Romantic encounters were quite sparse. There'd been a young Jewish German refugee in Cardiff I met through my cousin, very sweet, very earnest and aiming to settle in Israel. I said I couldn't possibly go with him because the only place I'd be happy, other than London, was Paris. Such a snob I was! Then there was the Marks and Spencer store manager, ambitious, brash, and full of get-up-and-go. I wrecked that by breaking a wine glass and cutting my foot *en route* to bed. A graphic artist who illustrated some well-known books took my fancy, but I didn't take his, so that didn't go far.

They were all Jewish and, in one way or another, symptomatic of a community I found stuffy, conservative, snobbish and very dull. By the 1950s my desperate family were trying hard to fix me up with distant cousins, uncles by marriage, and friends of friends – anyone at all. I was not willing to mortify Sadie and Solly by marrying out and gave up on the whole idea. I thought a single life with the occasional affair – Jewish or not wouldn't much matter, and they didn't need to know – was a compromise. I saw myself as a modern 'blue stocking', a little like Aunt Rachel, whose history was discussed among the family in hushed tones. The breath of fresh air that Alan and the rest of the young Australians brought into my life was an irresistible call to freedom. I'd never realised there was a different kind of Jew in Australia.

This was no preparation for married life. With my ignorance and inhibitions, Alan's memories of his father's marital disasters, and his own sexual insecurities, we were a fine pair. Throughout his life Alan needed a maternal figure to replace his lost mother, but he also wanted a partner in love. The classic male dilemma, not new, but in his case provoking a particular sadness I should have been better able to understand. I did my best, but I don't think it was good enough. We never had serious conversations in which our past dreams, disappointments and disasters might be shared. Alan suppressed his pre-marriage life totally, until it all came pouring out in *The Boys from Bondi* and *Alva's Boy*. Friends have said he had a chip on his shoulder, that his socialist principles were a kind of reverse snobbery, that his humour often had a bitter edge. He embarrassed me on many occasions. But it cut both ways. My basket of inhibitions exasperated and saddened him. It was hard for us to communicate honestly and our problems were always masked by humour. Today there's no-fault divorce, a 'get-out-of-jail' card tucked away just in case, but I think this diminishes the idea of growth in a relationship. I hung on hopefully to a deepening sense of love for a man I hardly understood, whilst in his mind Alan created a fantasy goddess out of a confused and rather lonely young woman.

Alan with Dan and Peter at Williamstown, c1964

The photographs of our life in the early sixties show Alan very happy in his role as provider, whereas I often look exhausted. He had no good memories to call on and had to find his own way into fatherhood. We were slowly building a life with three children, a mortgage, a little car and a dog. We were a suburban family, not particularly Jewish, hanging on by a thread to the community in far-off St Kilda.

CHAPTER 4
GO WEST, NORTH OR SOUTH – ANYWHERE BUT EAST!

It surprises me that Great-Aunt Berthe's visit to Box Hill North in 1960, a meeting that must have lasted a mere hour or so, has left such an impression and triggered so much history. Most of what I know about her comes from my father's lovingly put-together, handwritten memoir of his family, *As Far as I Remember* (1968). Solly also made us a family tree using the stiff brown paper on which he drafted patterns. In each corner he has drawn a symbol representing our family's origins, and each symbol is superimposed upon a *Magen David*, a Star of David: there's the Austrian eagle, the cross of St George for England, the Prince of Wales' feathers with the motto *Ich dien* (I serve), for Sadie's Welsh upbringing, and for us, in the bottom right-hand corner, a kangaroo with a joey. I too have constructed family trees as appendices to this memoir; they are digitally precise but, sadly, lack Solly's artistry.

Kangaroo symbol from Solly's family tree, 1968

Berthe Schlesinger was my father's aunt, his mother's sister, and my great-aunt (see Family Tree No. 4). She married (Abraham) Adolf Ambor from Andrichau, a town in Galicia in Eastern Europe, not far from Bielitz (now Bielsko-Biala in Poland), where the Schlesinger family lived. They looked to the West for opportunity and culture and moved to Austria, where they became wealthy cosmopolitan

Viennese. There were three children: Joseph, Erna and Humbert. In the late 1930s, Berthe, fearing war, sent Humbert and his wife Anne for safety to Australia and they settled in Melbourne, where their son Leslie was born. He tells me his parents came via London and sailed on a Blue Star Line ship on New Year's Eve 1938. The horrors of Europe had already left their mark: Anne's parents had been shot and Humbert's brother Joseph was interned. In Australia they would start afresh: Humbert became Bernhard (Bern) and the family adopted the Christian faith of their new neighbours. They would never speak of Austria again, and Leslie believed he was the only child in the world called Ambor.

The situation in Europe would have troubled Berthe's sister, my widowed grandmother Regina in London's East End. Her brothers had been taken away to camps, the nature of which was still not fully known. Her nephew Joseph, a cinematographer, had been released, but with a number on his arm. The *Anschluss*, Hitler's annexation of Austria in March 1938, put the Ambor family at grave risk. They needed to leave.

The Ambor/Schlesinger family. L–R, back row: Adolf Ambor, Joseph Ambor; front row: Great-Aunt Berthe Ambor (née Schlesinger), Grandmother Regina Gilbert (née Schlesinger)

My cousin Gina told me that her mother, my aunt Sophie, 'knocked on many doors' seeking visa assistance from Jewish families with film industry connections, but we do not have details of the escape. According to my father, Solly, the struggling little family, who lived in very down-market Bow Road in London's east, were taken by surprise when Berthe, Adolf, Erna and Joseph, their sophisticated relatives from Vienna, arrived one day in March 1939.

He wrote that they came 'with a fair amount of personal belongings and furniture, and in amongst some bedding, hidden from the Nazis, were the first wide-screen cinemascope cameras and lenses'. I was curious enough to search for more information, and found that in 1919 my great-uncle was a founder of Listo, one of the oldest film studios in Europe.

The sisters, Berthe and Regina, had not seen each other for twenty-eight years, and the reunion was emotional. But the joy was to be short-lived, for Regina died three months later, in June 1939.

The Ambors came to my grandmother's house with gifts: for me, a beautiful little round pigskin sewing box with a red velvet lining. I was stood up on the dining room table and presented to the newcomers as the next Shirley Temple. Maybe the family thought that with their connections Uncle Adolf and Joseph might launch me in a film career. My father observes that 'with the typical thoroughness of the continental' the newcomers soon moved out of the East End: it's an odd comment and leaves me wondering how these cultured émigrés from baroque Vienna adjusted to life in Bowes Park, a London suburb of no particular historical importance.

In 1960 Solly wrote that Berthe was coming to Melbourne to see her son and his family and would pay us a visit. We were instructed to make her welcome, ensure the little boys behaved 'nicely', and in general not to shame him. By this time, my great-aunt was the family matriarch. Think Lady Bracknell or Queen Mary of England. Humbert (Bern) must have driven her over to Box Hill North. She sailed into our modest brick-veneer home like a stately barge, ran a white-gloved finger along our furniture (checking for dust?) and sternly refused an armchair, saying that straight-backed seats were better for one's posture. It was all very unnerving, and I was relieved when she left.

The Schlesinger history mirrors that of so many European Jewish families. The lines come to abrupt endings with the murders of my great-uncles in the Holocaust. The names of Nettie and Julie appear on Solly's chart, and maybe they married in America and raised Jewish families – maybe not. Berthe's family has survived and is researching the Ambor line. Regina married Morris Gilbert, and their only grandchildren are my cousin Gina and I. Since Regina was still alive when I was born, I was probably named Röslein or 'little Rose' (Anglicised to Rosaline), after my great-grandmother Rosa (Knoebel). Gina (Regina) is named for our grandmother. We are both mindful of our obligations to remember.

Box Hill North, Victoria, Australia – I couldn't have been much further away from the lives of my grandparents. Many of Alan's forebears were Sephardim, Jews who arrived in London in the 1700s from Spain via Holland. They were very Anglicised by the time they migrated to Sydney in the 1830s and 1840s. Mine came from Eastern Europe, they were Ashkenazi Jews who fled to England just before the turn of the twentieth century to escape the pogroms. It was the time of mass migrations of Jews to America, but my family was probably short of the extra fare.

Borders have changed. Their homes might have been in Poland, or Ukraine, or Greater Russia or a piece of the Austro-Hungarian Empire. Wherever they built their *shtetl* (village) houses, like Sholem Aleichem's Tevye the milkman, they lived and breathed Jewish tradition, a small compensation for not enjoying freedom, democracy and enlightenment. I reflect upon our familiar Australian quarter-acre block, my right to vote, my free university education and raise a silent cheer to the grandparents who chose to leave the greatly overrated *alte heym* (old country). The Eurovision Song Contest will never persuade me otherwise.

Apocryphal stories have survived, though records are minimal. Both my grandfathers forsook military life: my mother's father abandoned the army of Tsar Alexander III of Russia, and my father's father left the Ulanan barracks in Bielitz, where the cavalry of Emperor Franz Joseph of Austria were stationed. Neither of these rulers did much to protect their Jewish citizens from discrimination and anti-Semitism. A book published in 1903, written by Michael Davitt, *Within the Pale: the true story of anti-Semitic persecutions in Russia* (London: Hurst and Blackett) is the report of an investigation by a British committee who visited Russia to see for themselves. My grandparents came from countries where women could be jailed for selling milk or lighting *Shabbes* candles. The earnest Brits concluded in their report that if something weren't done to save these Jewish communities it would be one of the greatest blots on European history.

Mother's father, Nathan Samuel (born Nathan Chwall; also known as Nukhim Zevelev Khvul, or Nukim Seidelowitz Kwul), came from Ignatovka (now Hnativka), twenty-one kilometres east of Kiev in Ukraine. (Sholem Aleichem's Tevye came from fictional Anatevka.) He was born in 1862 and, according to his military pass dated 1890, was the son of a retired soldier. Young Jewish boys were often conscripted into the army, where they were forced to serve for many years, and perhaps this is also my grandfather's history. Nathan's pass gives him permission 'to reside in those places of the Russian Empire where Jews are allowed to live', namely specific towns within the Pale of Settlement, for three months. At the end of this period he is to return to the town hall in Ignatovka, 'otherwise he will be dealt with according to the law'. He was a young man. It's tantalising not to know why he wanted the pass and where he was going. Maybe he had a girl to visit in Kiev?

In 1923 representatives of the American Jewish Joint Distribution

Committee (The Joint), a welfare organisation, visited Ignatovka. Their one-page report gives me a clue as to what Nathan left behind, and what might have happened to his family. Before World War I, 1,300 Jewish people occupied 140 houses in the town. There were two flour mills, two millet mills, a brewery and a tannery. By 1923 peasants had demolished 120 of the houses and destroyed the industries. In 1917 the Jews, along with the rest of the population, received equal rights. Many migrated to Kiev. By August 1919 there were only 900 left in Ignatovka. That same month General Denikin's troops led a pogrom, and forty Jews were murdered. The remaining families fled to Kiev. The committee's report ends with the sad observation that 'Ignatovka no more resembles a town'.

Nathan had courage. He took his pass, bid farewell to his family and just kept going until he left (Russia? Ukraine? Poland?) and landed at London docks. I don't know the route he took, where he embarked, nor how he felt. He was twenty-eight years old and spoke only Yiddish and Russian. He never did learn English in all the time he lived in Britain, so he and I were unable to have a conversation – a pity. I wonder about his arrival in London. The docks were busy places in those days, and I imagine Nathan walking up from the port, perhaps with his belongings wrapped in a cloth like a Jewish Dick Whittington. The authorities there probably gave him the new surname of Samuel, because indeed Chwall/Khvul was quite impossible. He would have made his way to the heart of the Yiddish-speaking migrant community in the East End. He told my cousin Gerald, who knew him well, that men were on the docks recruiting the newcomers, the 'greeners' (as in 'green as grass') to work as machinists in sweatshops. That's how he got his first job. I guess he had a few names and addresses of people from nearby his hometown who would give him a bed and a meal and maybe a little money to get on his feet. In his memoir my father describes the working conditions of that time. Many migrants came from tiny villages where lighting was by means of a paraffin lamp or candles; they had never seen gas burners. In the sweatshops, unscrupulous employers would tell the workers to 'carry on until the oil in the lamp is used up' and around midnight the poor machinist would be allowed to go home because there 'couldn't be much more oil in the lamp'. Employees had to bring their own thread for sewing and even bobbins and shuttle cases for the treadle machines. They were so exploited that at the weekend they would pawn the bobbin cases and be forced to seek an advance from the boss. They were always in debt to their 'Guv'nor'.

Did Nathan ever see his family again? No. Did they write to him? Yes. My cousin recalls letters from a sister in Russia, but these ceased in 1941 and it is possible Nathan's family died in the ravine at the Babi Yar massacre seventeen kilometres from Ignatovka. Did his mother and soldier father suffer penalties because he had deserted? I don't know. Was he happy in Britain? Was he glad he made a dash for it? I'll never know and so I can't tell you. How should I, or you, think of this young man? In today's world the words 'refugee' and 'asylum seeker' spring to mind. As a Jew, Nathan had none of the freedoms and rights we take for granted, and I applaud his courage in searching for something better, a refuge in England.

Nathan's sister and her husband in Russia, 1890s

Great-Grandfather Dov Green, c1890s

The Green family, my mother's maternal line, also came from the Russian Empire and were exceptionally poor. I'm told they made hessian sacks. We have a picture of a serious-looking man with wispy whiskers, wearing a square-ish black *kippa*, and he is acknowledged as the patriarch from the *alte heym*; not much else is remembered now (see Family Tree No. 5). There are several versions of their background. According to my father, his name was Dov. He married twice: Sybil Rose bore him five children; his second wife, always referred to as the 'Greener Bube', did not have children. His daughter Eva (my grandmother) first appears on a UK Census in 1891: she is twenty years old and born in Russia c1871.

Eva had an older sister, Elka. Her granddaughter Harriet, a sprightly ninety-year-old retiree in Florida, has worked industriously for years on the genealogy. Elka was born in 1864 in a town called Granov. This is confusing since Eva maintained that the family came from Kamenets-Podolsk. It doesn't much matter; Jewish communities have had a very long and appalling history throughout Ukraine and it is all too easy to understand why my great-grandparents chose to leave. The JewishGen website quotes the London *Jewish Chronicle* of 15 August 1886: 'The police at Kamenets-Podolsk have received instructions to expel from the town all the Jews who have settled there since 1857. In that year a law was passed forbidding Jews to reside or hold house and landed property within a distance of 50 versts (Russian unit of length, about a kilometre) from the frontier of Russia.'

Harriet's genealogy begins with a Berl Green from Kiev. The family probably immigrated to London in the 1880s. Dov (also recorded as David), my great-grandfather, became a grocer in British Street, Mile End; his daughter, my grandmother Eva, went to school. The census records that when she was twenty, she worked as a 'bankers' clerk'; for that job she would have needed good English and my mother always said she 'spoke beautifully'.

Grandfather Nathan Samuel

Grandmother Eva Green

So the Greens arrived in London earlier than Nathan and were established. Nathan became their lodger, and married Eva, probably at some time between 1891 and 1893. My mother, Sadie (Sarah), was born in 1894, the eldest of their nine surviving children; Nathan would have been thirty-two and Eva twenty-three. Throughout his life my grandfather was known as both Chwall and Samuel, which must have driven British bureaucrats crazy. My mother was also caught up in this confusion of names. In those times, workingmen in Britain all wore caps, so Nathan became a cap maker – a far cry from the Tsar's army. My grandparents set up home in Rothschild's Buildings, a huge tenement block (think Melbourne's Housing Commission flats) and their furniture was mostly orange boxes.

The tenements were known colloquially as 'the buildings', even until the early 1940s when the Luftwaffe targeted the East End and brought down many of these Victorian towers. Sadie told me how the children used to play in the courtyard, and from their third-floor flat Eva would send down sandwiches for them in a basket on a long rope. Yiddish culture was all-embracing and involved food, theatre, newspapers and, of course, the famous Jews' Free School. There were new clothes twice a year, for *Pesach* and *Rosh Hashanah* (Jewish New Year); the boys all received a pair of boots and the girls a new dress.

It was the beginning of the twentieth century. In the slums of the East End Nathan was making caps, probably in some ghastly sweatshop, as there were no protective unions in those times. The 'Bolshevik menace' was occupying the minds of many Londoners, and the anarchist movement was fomenting among the downtrodden. Social conditions were terrible. Health problems, compounded by the prevalence of coal fires and the resultant fogs, were taking their toll of the poor Jewish migrant families. Nathan's brother-in-law, Ithamar Feinstein, (married to Elka Green, my great-aunt) was keen to try his luck in the *goldene medine,* (golden land) of America. He wrote back urging Nathan to come too, which he does. By this time there were more children and times were bad. I find it hard to understand how my grandfather could just leave his family to the mercies of charity organisations and soup kitchens. My mother said it was the most humiliating time of her life, fronting up with a billy-can for free food. However, Nathan discovered that the streets of Philadelphia were not paved with gold and returned to London. Ithamar and Elka stayed in America and when Alan and I visited Ellis Island we found their names on the American Immigrant Wall of Honor.

Sadie said that Eva Green 'married beneath her', that she was 'a lady'. The unspoken implication was that Nathan, who was nine years older, was probably pretty rough-and-ready after serving in the Tsar's army. I can't add much because Eva died when I was four and Nathan and I couldn't speak the same language. I think the old cameo brooch I have in my jewellery box might have been hers.

As the eldest child, my mother became the family interpreter and took her responsibilities very seriously. When sickness struck the youngest children, she took them to the free hospital where the doctor said her parents must move the family away from the London fogs and get them into fresh air before the little ones became terminally ill. So Nathan and Eva left the East End and set up home at 32 Plantagenet Street, Cardiff, Wales. Nathan kept chickens and established a workshop where he made cloth caps. Eva, who was becoming blind, kept house, but increasingly needed help from her daughters.

Sadie bore the brunt of this, and I still feel resentful of Nathan. When she was twelve he removed her from school, which she adored, so she might help her mother with the younger children. Because she spoke English well (indeed she had a lovely voice with a slight Welsh accent), he took her to the market where he sold his caps so she could translate for him. She once told me that putting brown paper inside one's shoes helps to keep feet warm when standing in the cold and wet. But the education authorities caught up with Nathan. Although he maintained that Sadie was his daughter to do with as he pleased (!), he was forced to allow her back to school until the mandatory leaving age of fourteen. She remembered fainting from joy as she re-entered the playground.

Wood Street Girls Evening School
Cardiff Education Committee.
TECHNICAL EDUCATION SCHEME.
Preparatory Technical (Evening) Schools.
SINGLE SUBJECT CERTIFICATE.
This is to Certify
THAT Sarah Chwall.
has satisfactorily passed an examination conducted by the Education Committee in March, 1909. as follows:
Subject English.
Stage 2nd Class 2nd.
This Certificate is an acknowledgment of success in one subject, and counts towards the Course Certificate awarded to students who have been successful in all the subjects of a complete Course.
Signed Charles Elder Supt. of Technical Instruction.
Director of Education.

Sadie's English certificate from evening school, 1909

Sadie was proud of her few little school certificates, for needlework, domestic studies and English; she would have made a fine student given the chance. I've never 'unpicked' the documents before, and they are revealing. She is named Sarah Chwall, not Sadie Samuel; the awards are from Wood Street Girls' Evening School and dated

1909. My mother was fifteen years old and went to evening classes after what must have been a hard day's work. It's a pity that I am unable to tell her how proud of her I am.

L–R, back row: Aunt Rosie, my mother, Sadie; front row: Uncles Jimmie, Gus and Will, c1916

Sadie's three brothers, my uncles Will, Jimmy and Gus, all went off to World War I. I believe they exaggerated their ages in order to enlist. One of them lost an eye; another suffered poisoning from mustard gas. I wonder whether Nathan, remembering his army life in Russia, was anxious for his sons. Sadie and her sister Rosie look quite sombre in the studio portrait, probably taken before the boys left for the front.

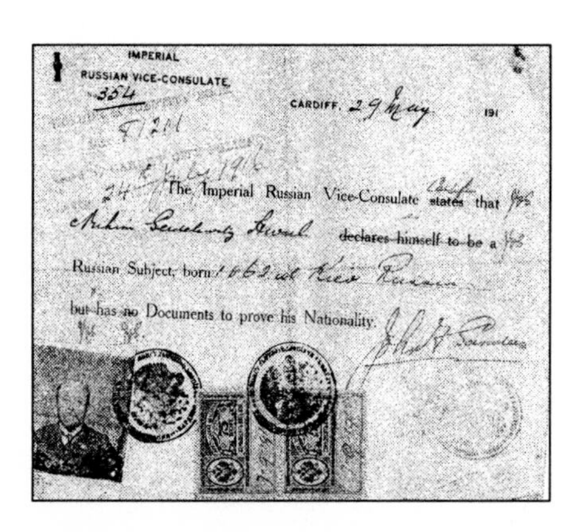

IMPERIAL
RUSSIAN VICE-CONSULATE.
354

CARDIFF, 29 May 191

The Imperial Russian Vice-Consulate states that
declares himself to be a
Russian Subject, born 1862 at Kiev Russia
but has no Documents to prove his Nationality.

Nationality document dated 1916 from Cardiff, Wales, for Grandfather Nathan Samuel (Kwul), who was born in Kiev

What else do I know about my grandfather Nathan Samuel (Chwall)? Not very much. His military pass refers to him as Nukhim Zevelev Khvul. In May 1916 the very grand-sounding Imperial Russian Vice-Consulate in Cardiff certified that 'Nukim Seidelowitz Kwul is a Russian subject born in 1862 in

Kiev but has no documents to prove his nationality'. I believe 'Seidelowitz' is a patronymic and that Nathan's father was named Seidel. As family histories go, it's on the short side, no further back than the mid-1800s. There are no famous rabbis, no scholars, and no entrepreneurs – just a family of soldiers and sack-makers. But Nathan left Russia, and bravely took his chances as a refugee from poverty, anti-Semitism and religious superstition. I owe him.

My paternal grandfather, Morris Gilbert, was born in 1870 in Brody, an important centre of Jewish life, 90 kilometres from Lemberg (now Lviv). His wife, Regina Schlesinger, was born in the village of Kozy near Bielitz 420 kilometres to the west. The region, known then as Galicia, was a province of the Austro-Hungarian Empire. The history is very complex: Germany and Russia were fighting for control of an area that today includes parts of Poland, Belarus, Lithuania and Ukraine. My father's parents looked to Austria for cultural input, unlike those Jews further east, such as Nathan and Eva, who identified more with Russia. Today, Lemberg (Lviv) is in Ukraine; Bielitz (Bielsko-Biala) is in Poland. These grandparents spoke Yiddish and German, but not Russian or Polish.

The pogroms of the nineteenth century must have affected them. There were murders in Odessa in 1821 followed by riots in 1859. Large-scale waves of anti-Semitism swept through south-western Imperial Russia from 1881 to 1884. Several family members immigrated to America or, like Berthe, moved to Vienna. As with my mother's ancestors, there were restrictions imposed upon Jewish communities, and freedom must have seemed an impossible dream. But Morris and Regina did dream, and their two granddaughters, Gina and I, were born free in London. It might have been very different. During the Holocaust, Lemberg's Jewish community – some 9,000 people, 80% of the total population – were sent to death in the concentration

Grandfather Morris Gilbert (Fox)

Grandmother Regina Schlesinger

camps of Bełżec and Majdanek. In Bielitz there were approximately 5,000 Jews in September 1939 when the Germans entered the town. Synagogues were burned down and sacred books were thrown on the fire. A ghetto was established in 1940 and liquidated in June 1942, at which time the remaining Jewish population, including our great-uncles, was deported to Auschwitz.

Morris was the only child of Chaim Zvi Gilbert and Socha Leah Leimseider (see Family Tree No. 3). His mother had two sisters; no one now can remember their names or histories. They would have been my great-great aunts. Each sister also had a son: one was Chaim, the other Isaac; and the three cousins grew up together. It was a traditional *shtetl* life but far from idyllic. Of course there are family anecdotes: outbreaks of cholera were not uncommon, and young Isaac, asleep in the grass one warm summer day, almost lost his life when health inspectors, armed with toxic 'sweets' came to do away with sickly looking children. My father, Solly, knew very little about his paternal grandfather, Chaim Zvi Gilbert, but there are many stories about *Zaida* (*Zeyde*) Leimseider. He was eighty-eight years old when he made the wedding dress for my grandmother Regina, ninety when he contemplated walking to London to see his grandson Morris, and 104 years old when he died in 1910.

Morris, Chaim and Isaac. I speculate what these three young men hoped the future would hold for them. Were they tempted by sophisticated Vienna? Did they find *shtetl* Judaism restrictive? Were they attracted to the ideas of the *Haskalah* (Enlightenment) movement? Did the bright lights and opportunities of America beckon? England offered sanctuary and was closer. Theodor Herzl, the father of modern Israel, famously said, 'If you will it, it is no dream' and I wonder why none of these boys joined the young idealists who rejected the misery that was Eastern Europe and set off to build a free society in Palestine. My father wrote that Morris attended an early Zionist Congress and heard Herzl speak. Gina tells me that a flag or banner used at that Congress was made by our grandfather and we should search for it among family memorabilia.

I don't recall the family having strong Zionist leanings; it seemed to me that their focus was all on England. But Solly wrote that he and his friends in 1920s London went to meetings of the Young Judeans and reminds me that his sister Sally tirelessly raised funds for an orphanage in Jerusalem. Of course, in my childhood home in the 1930s we had a Blue Box and saved pennies to buy trees in Palestine. It was to be eighty years before Morris and Regina's great-grandson Daniel would spend time in Israel; in 1980 I was able to take Solly and Sadie to see him milking cows on a kibbutz.

Morris became a master tailor, but like Nathan was drafted for military service, in his case into the army of the Emperor Franz Joseph I. If you think of frothy, chocolate-box operettas like *The Merry Widow,* you can imagine Morris making those elaborate uniforms with gold trimming and startling epaulettes for officers still quite keen on fencing duels. When I was a child, Solly made little coats for me in a pseudo-military style with fancy buttons and braid. How strange to see this link between me, a child of depression-era London, and the ornate, over-the-top extravagance of the Hapsburg Empire.

The middle-class family of my paternal grandmother, Regina Schlesinger, lived in a small country town and were at various times farm managers, innkeepers and grain merchants (see Family Tree No. 4). She was the daughter of Herman Schlesinger and Rosa Knoebel, who had four sons and four daughters: Simon, Marcus, Adolf, Bernhard, Julie, Netta, Berthe and Regina. All four boys, my great-uncles, perished in Auschwitz; Julie and Netta immigrated to America; Regina married Morris and came to London, and she was able to help in the rescue of Berthe and her family from Vienna in 1939.

My grandparents came from traditional communities in rural towns and villages; it was *shtetl* life. Now there is a flourishing interest in Jewish ancestry, and Eastern European countries have found a 'nice little earner' in Jews searching for the remnants of their families. It has been sobering for my cousin Gina and me to realise that we might well be the only direct Jewish descendants of a large European family and the imperative to remember becomes even stronger – a responsibility towards our own children and grandchildren. These ancestors of ours are also representative of a period in European history, a time of great change. The Jewish *Haskalah* gave opportunities to a people long disadvantaged by claustrophobia and poverty. *Fiddler on the Roof* glamorises their lives for the sake of some great musical numbers, but there's much more bite to be found in the stories of Sholem Aleichem and his contemporaries.

My father wrote that his parents were married, both religiously and civilly, in the Town Hall at Bielitz in either 1895 or 1896. There may even be records in the town archives. Morris must have been posted there and the Ulanan barracks are still standing. Evidently the military authorities were not pleased about the marriage, and Morris decided to leave. A much more delightful anecdote tells how Regina took exception to the fact that the wives of the officers, for whom my grandfather made such splendid uniforms, rather fancied him and she became jealous. They left for Frankfurt-am-Main, but Morris didn't have the right papers, so they journeyed on to London, where they arrived in 1896, the year before Queen Victoria's Diamond Jubilee.

The family grew: Sarah/Sally (Soorah Gitel) was born in 1897, followed by two boys who didn't survive; Annie (Chana Rivka) was born in 1901, and my father, Solomon Leon (Yissucher Leib), in 1903. In seven years there could not have been many months when Regina wasn't either pregnant or nursing, a common enough situation at a time when contraception was not easily available. I think Morris might have been somewhat wary about registering the births, for when my father needed a passport, there was no accurate record and a waiver was granted.

In 1907 Emperor Franz Joseph, about to celebrate his own Diamond Jubilee in 1908, announced an amnesty to all exiles. Morris was keen to return to Regina's family home in Galicia. My father was then about four years old. They travelled by way of Antwerp, where the local Jewish community made them welcome. Regina gave birth to another girl, Clara (Passel), and Morris considered settling in Belgium; however, after two years he decided to take the family back to Bielitz, where another daughter, Sophie (Shifra), was born. However, as so often happens when migrants change their mind, the grass was not greener in the East; the army recalled Morris and he had no wish for a military career. Once again, he packed up and headed back to London, instructing Regina to finalise their affairs and follow him. A daughter, Celia (Tzivia), was born in 1913 in London, and their last child, Harry, in 1915, but he died within a year of a 'wasting disease'. An undated portrait of my grandfather shows a handsome man holding some kind of award or degree. He is wearing a large floral buttonhole and looks very pleased. My father mentioned that Morris once taught at Danzig University, and maybe that's the connection.

Morris Gilbert (Fox), possibly at Danzig University, c1900

So, Nathan and Eva were battling on in Cardiff, Wales, whilst over in Ealing, West London, Morris and Regina were doing a little better. He had found a very up-market gentlemen's outfitters that specialised in robes for the clergy. Their business often came by mail, and they received requests from bishops and deacons for repeats of previous orders. The company had one of those improbable English names, something like Smith, Brown, Jones, Robinson and Fox Pty Ltd. However, although orders still arrived addressed to him, Mr Fox had passed away. A man of initiative, my grandfather declared, 'I'll be Mr Fox.' And so, without bothering to legalise this change, we became the Fox family. My father's name continued to vary between Gilbert and Fox, which made for problems when he later wanted to visit Australia, and his sisters, my aunts, did not always register their names consistently: sometimes Fox, sometimes Gilbert or Leimseider. Even the gravestone for my grandmother Regina records her as the widow of Morris Gilbert (Fox).

Back in Lemberg, Isaac also decides on immigration to London. Together the two cousins run a small tailoring workshop, and their children, including my father, join them once they leave school. Although it seems his father was named Israel Alexander, we all knew Isaac as 'Uncle Gilbert' and the family tree for these ancestors of mine is hopelessly confused with the names Leimseider, Gilbert and Fox sprinkled haphazardly throughout. When I was a child we used to visit Uncle Gilbert and his family in an East End tenement known as Dron Buildings. It was built in 1922 as cheap accommodation for the less fortunate; today's prices in the renovated, highly desirable Dron House would most likely astonish my late uncle. Chaim, the other little boy from the *shtetl*, became an upholsterer, came to London in 1918 to see his cousins but didn't much like the city. He returned to Galicia and died in a gas chamber.

Like my other grandfather, Morris did not become a citizen and, being Austrian, he was classed as an enemy alien during World War I, just as Nathan from Russia would be at the beginning of World War II. My family took its time to become British: Sadie and Solly were both – almost accidentally – born in London, but their East End Jewish upbringing held them firmly and nostalgically to their roots in Eastern Europe. Not until my birth in 1930 did a genuine little English girl appear on the family tree.

Solly was the only surviving boy and had five sisters. Morris was exceptionally protective of his son, and with memories of his own time in the army, had no wish to see the same future for his boy. My father was a clever student and wanted to go to secondary school to study art, but the curriculum included army cadet training, and my grandfather would have none of it. So Solly stayed in the top class at primary school year after year, until it was legal for him to leave and start a tailoring apprenticeship with his father. He did well and became an expert designer, highly respected in the trade; but like Sadie, was unable to do what he really wanted. He made the best of it and throughout his life was an avid reader and a compulsive writer. It's easy for me to criticise the two grandfathers who denied my parents an education – and often I do. But Solly was needed to earn money for the family and Sadie was required to help her mother around the house and translate in the market for her father. The times were hard.

Morris died of cancer in 1924 when he was fifty-four. My father wrote of him:

> Not a spectacular life – no vast enterprises left as a memorial – no great deeds of adventure that people will talk about – no world shattering inventions to bear his imprint. Just an ordinary man who loved and was loved by his family, but buffeted by circumstances that prevented him from doing what he wanted – just to make a living free from fear – free from that hatred that people had towards him because he wanted to be a Jew.

Nathan died 'from depression' in 1946 in Cardiff at eighty-six. My cousin Gerald told me he became religious only in later life. The little anecdotes are so intriguing: *Zeyde* (for that's how he was known to all the grandchildren) was fond of Gerald and must have told him many tall stories such as: 'Ve ate sandviches left over from the previous vor, crawling with vorms like in the film *Battleship Potemkin*; and, 'Ve marched und ve marched until ve saw ze Turks'. 'Yes, *Zeyde*, what happened then?' 'Ve turned und ve marched und ve marched until ve no longer could see ze Turks!' He spoke 'Yinglish' as well as Yiddish.

Every year he'd make a trip from Cardiff to London to visit his married children, staying about a week with each family. My mother went to pieces with anxiety when he was due to come to us. I recall his visits during World War II when, being an alien, he had to report to the local police station. He got on very well with the authorities and greatly admired them. He must have been in his religious phase by this time, for on Saturdays he went to the *shul* service with my father, drank a small tumbler of *bronfn* (brandy) before *Shabbes* lunch and then dozed by the fire for the afternoon. All he ever said regarding me was that I was a *sheyn meydl* (pretty girl). I seem to remember him making a fiercely strong *khreyn* (horseradish sauce).

Gerald says he only read the Yiddish newspaper *Di Tsayt* (*The*

Times) and was upset at reports about the behaviour of the British soldiers in Palestine in 1945 and 1946. All his life he was grateful to 'Englant' for giving him freedom in a country where the police were on his side. A final little tale about Nathan: Gerald asked why he'd left London for Cardiff, to which *Zeyde* replied (untruthfully) that he was employed by a tailor: 'Vell, Geralt, the tailor had a daughter he vanted I should marry. Oy, Geralt, you should have seen the daughter!'

My grandmothers died when I was a small child: Eva in 1934 and Regina in 1939. These young immigrant women at the turn of the twentieth century showed remarkable courage. Regina crossed Europe four times, twice without Morris and often with small children in tow. Her final journey was particularly difficult. Jewish communities along the way helped them, but Solly said the money ran out in Berlin, and he and his sister Annie were busking in the streets for *pfennig*. He tells the little anecdote as a humorous tale, but I think of Regina, destitute with four small children in a strange city.

I have a lot of time for Eva and regret not knowing her. In the one portrait we have, her expression seems sad, and I wonder whether she loved Nathan. She must have been clever: by 1891 she had acquired good English and qualified for a job in the commercial world, probably the first woman in my family to have achieved so much. Eva impressed her daughter, my mother, because she had good manners, strove for refinement in a hard world, and was, I suspect, denied many of the little pleasures that might have improved her life. I wonder about these two women as I now wonder about my mother. What qualities did they pass on to me?

It seems important to acknowledge my debt to these grandparents I hardly knew. Their worldly achievements were quite minimal, their material wealth very slight. Eastern Europe offered them nothing but discrimination, poverty and pogroms. Long before

Hitler and the Holocaust, Nathan and Eva and Morris and Regina made a bid for freedom. At the end of the nineteenth century, Jews from the East were leaving ignorance, superstition and centuries of oppression, for enlightenment, education and opportunity. The fortunate made it to America, the *goldene medine*; the brave and hopeful young idealists went to Palestine; my ancestors chose England. One hundred years later, here in Australia, I am grateful.

CHAPTER 5
MOSTLY ROMANTIC

And so we come to the great romance in my family: Sadie was in Cardiff and Solly was in Bow, near Stratford, just on the edge of London's East End. World War I had ended in 1918, the 'roaring twenties' were almost over, and the 1929 stock market crash, followed by the Great Depression, was just around the corner.

Grandmother Regina and family, c1927.
L–R, back row: Clara, Annie, Sophie, Solly; front row: Celia, Sally, Regina, Sadie

By 1924 my widowed paternal grandmother, Regina, was left with five daughters (aged eleven to twenty-seven) and a twenty-one-year-old son who was the man of the family. They were renting a large Victorian house next to Bow Road railway station in London's east. Sally, the eldest, and my father, Solly, had taken charge of the workshop on the top floor where they earned a meagre living as piece workers, making up garments for clothing manufacturers. Because they were inexperienced youngsters, they were often cheated of a fair price for their work.

I can well appreciate that my father's wish to marry in 1927 must have provoked great alarm and was probably viewed as desertion. Even more disturbing must have been his decision to buy a little terrace house in an outer suburb, away from the East End, the heart of Jewish London. (Many years later, Alan's and my leaving St Kilda for Box Hill North wasn't that different.) Solly was twenty-four years old, and I wonder now whether freedom, as well as love, was in his mind.

Sadie Millicent Samuel. In Hebrew she is Sarah Malka, but Sadie Millicent is so spot on for the times. My mother was born in London in 1894, spent her childhood in the East End and her teens and twenties in Cardiff, Wales. That says absolutely nothing about her personality, so I must do better by her. Searching for appropriate terms, I fasten on the words 'shy' and 'modest'. Sadie was nothing like the stereotypical Jewish mother. She was never confrontational, didn't shout or play the martyr and was the soul of politeness. If she was upset she never let on, which probably accounted for our lack of closeness. I got away with far too much, and she was reluctant to curb me, perhaps because I was

Sadie Samuel (Chwall), my mother, c1910

the one precious child she had produced, having miscarried twice. Her sister, Rosie, was forever praising her own 'four angels' and this must have hurt. Sadie was the eldest of nine. Helping the family was her priority until Solly just about blackmailed her into marriage by threatening to throw an engagement ring into the Thames if she refused yet again. For she did refuse him, repeatedly – not because she didn't love him, but because she had a duty streak that was hard to shake off.

Cardiff in the 1920s. Sadie is second from left wearing a black beret

Sadie, her sisters and friends, had good times growing up in Cardiff. Photographs show vivacious young girls, and I don't think they felt deprived, even though I know there was very little money. Rosie was the next sister in age, and the story is that with their mother's connivance, the pair of them would sneak out after *Shabbes* lunch on a Saturday whilst Nathan was asleep, and catch the London train in order to go to the theatre. After the performance, they'd travel on the milk train back to Cardiff and be home before their father got up in the morning. This was how she met Solly and his friends in a queue outside the Theatre Royal, Drury Lane, waiting for cheap seats in the 'gods'. It was a musical, *Rose Marie*, and they were sentimental over such shows all their lives. When they celebrated their diamond wedding anniversary, I took them back to Drury Lane to see a revival of *42nd Street* based on the 1933 musical film, another favourite from those early days..

Apparently the London lads started to chat up these Welsh girls. Solly impressed Sadie by holding open the doors when the crowd surged in; she was tiny and might have been crushed. She was about thirty-two and he twenty-three, a big age difference for those times. It was only eight years since the armistice in 1918, and a generation of young men had been lost in the 'war to end all wars'. I don't know if she'd had other offers. She was very attractive, but I'd guess had more or less resigned herself to her family obligations. Her mother, Eva, was becoming blind and her brothers were given preference, so who else was there? Solly persisted; he 'pressed his suit', as the old-fashioned phrase has it, and it must have been hard for Sadie. They met when she came up to London, and he proposed many times as they walked along the Thames Embankment. Sadie abhorred waste, and his threat to toss the little ring (which I treasure) into the water horrified her. She opted for freedom with a young man who wore a fancy waistcoat, a bowler hat and carried a cane with a silver top.

Two friends in the 1920s; Sadie is on the left

It was a long-distance courtship as Cardiff to London was at least a three-hour train journey. They exchanged letters I don't have and photographs, some of which have survived. I imagine he asked her to have studio portraits taken so he might show his mates, and these pictures are lovely. For his part Solly, who had a life-long passion

My father, Solly, in his early twenties. On the back of the picture he wrote: 'I look as if I possess the world'.

for gadgets of all kinds, would surely have had a Box Brownie camera and sent her amusing photographs. She must have already said 'yes' when he wrote on the back of one of these that 'I look as if I possess the world'.

The two families met and the marriage was approved. Eva's sister-in-law, Great-Aunt Annie Green, was Sadie's mentor for the wedding, and my mother told me she arrived in London with a basket of eggs from Nathan's chickens as a thank-you gift. They were married in Stepney at Philpot Street Synagogue on 1 January 1928. On the *ketubah* he's identified as Solly Lyon Fox and she as Sadie Millie Samuels. There are studio portraits of the bride, groom and their bridesmaids, who included two of his sisters and two of hers. I have no photographs to show me Eva, Nathan or the widowed Regina, who must also have been present. Hemlines were up in the 1920s. (In 1957 I too chose a short wedding dress.) I remember a large wooden storage box on the upstairs landing at our house, and Sadie shyly showing me her wedding shoes, tiny satin slippers with t-bars. The reception was held at Cottage Grove Assembly Rooms, Mile End. Solly wrote in his memoir that they went away 'for a couple of days' afterwards, but when they arrived late at night the hotel porter couldn't be roused, so they sat on the steps in their wedding finery until dawn.

Sadie and Solly's wedding in London, 1 January 1928

Sadie and Solly with bridesmaids. L–R: Clara Fox (Gilbert), Rachel Samuel, bridegroom and bride, Rosie Samuel, Sophie Fox (Leimseider)

The *London Times* weather forecast was for frost and snow and a temperature of zero. (Alan and I left our wedding on *La Cigale* in similar conditions.) My parents started their married life in a tiny two-up, two-down terrace house in a raw new suburb. There they lived for the next sixty years, and my childhood was spent at 36 Ashurst Drive, Gants Hill, Ilford, Essex.

Ilford, with its signature feature, Valentines Park, has a lot of history, right back to 1086, when it is mentioned in the Domesday Book. The local council appreciated the importance of a large area of open parkland for the relaxation and entertainment of citizens, and the purchase of Valentines Park was complete by the mid-1920s. As I try to understand more about my parents and their motives, I realise with increasing surprise that Alan and I acted in much the same way, and for similar reasons. One hundred and twenty-five acres of parkland compared with the slums of London's East End must have seemed like paradise to Solly, just as a cream brick-veneer house on a quarter-acre block next to a bushy little park with a creek in Box Hill North spelled freedom to Alan.

Sadie was spooked by the unfamiliar surroundings. The warmth and community spirit she had known in Cardiff and the East End were missing in Gants Hill, where developers were putting up rows of terrace houses so fast the local council was unable to keep pace with facilities such as pavements and street lighting. One dark night she imagined she'd seen a *golem*, a monster from Yiddish legend, but it turned out to be merely a cow from the nearby grazing area. They were, after all, living in 'the country'. Owning a house would have been something of a novelty for my parents, who had grown up in rented accommodation.

They only made a serious mistake once, and it involved buying furniture on hire purchase. They defaulted on repayments, unaware that interest was charged, and the bailiffs came to repossess the table and chairs. Thereafter, Sadie instituted a financial accounting system that never varied throughout their lives. There was a weekly ritual whereby Solly's wages (in their later years the pension) always in pounds, shillings and pence, was divided among a collection of little envelopes and old purses with a set amount, sometimes only a shilling, put aside for every anticipated expense such as the mortgage, the insurance, the *shul*, gas, electricity – every conceivable eventuality. Only when it was all apportioned would she take out housekeeping money. The system worked for them; they avoided time payment and the bailiffs never came again. There was neither debt nor waste, and it shames me to consider our profligate, 'throw-away' society. We teased her for keeping every brown paper bag from food purchases and each small piece of string. She didn't have a budget for herself, and for years preserved a tiny wardrobe of dresses she always protected with a pinafore, a 'pinny'.

Sadie's sense of duty was accompanied by an alarming work ethic. Her very modest home had to be pristine, not in order to show off, but because cleanliness was a virtue. This meant she laboured very hard to keep her little 1927 terrace house sparkling. Routine was all important, and it was difficult for Solly to persuade her to take time off from housework and enjoy a day trip to the seaside, Southend and neighbouring Leigh-on-Sea being favourites. In 1960 Sadie broke all her rules in order to hold her grandsons in far away Australia. They were to make the journey several more times, but that first trip to the end of the world was a breakthrough for my frugal little mother.

I don't think they ever quarrelled seriously. She loved and admired Solly. 'Isn't he clever,' she'd whisper to me. He adored her and still wrote poems to her when she was over ninety. Solly never saw Sadie as an old lady, deaf and crippled with arthritis; for him, she was always the Welsh lass catching the milk train back to Cardiff. His poem 'Paddington Station' is a beautiful tribute from a true romantic. Their idea of an outing was a visit to this busy London terminus, not actually to go anywhere, just to sit and remember. In his memoir he wrote of 'the same feeling of excitement when I have to go and meet her somewhere as there was when I would see her getting off the train on those early excursions'.

Sadie (the picture Solly brought with him to Melbourne)

I carried a cane then with a silver knob;
we thought it was smart, it was just the job
She carries a cane now on which to lean;
she's not quite so agile as at seventeen.

After she died at the age of ninety-seven, Solly visited Melbourne twice more, and each time he brought her picture in a silver frame. He slept with it under his pillow, together with the little red woollen mittens she wore to keep her hands warm.

In the 1930s there were three Jewish families living near us: the Gitelmans, the Sanders and the Fox family (no relation). Jack and

Sarah Sanders lived further up our street in a slightly smarter house, which my mother admired because it was semi-detached with a side entrance, whereas ours was part of a connected terrace row. Jack was a talented craftsman, a cabinetmaker. There was a daughter my age and sometimes I went up there to visit. But their highly polished mahogany and rosewood furniture was intimidating; it was more fun to play in the street and in those days very few cars interrupted a game of hopscotch or marbles. In 1936 a synagogue was established in Beehive Lane. Solly and Sadie were founding members – and Alan and I were married there.

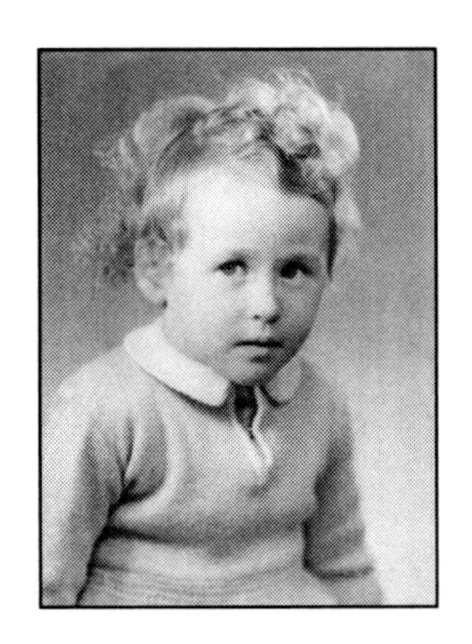

Ros, c1931

Tom Foster and Ros, c1932

During the loneliness of those early days, Sadie found a most unlikely lifeline in their next-door neighbour, Tom Foster, who had served with the British police in India. He was a fierce-looking Irishman with the most elaborate moustache, white with waxed pointy ends sharp enough to do damage; he smoked a pipe and played billiards. When Sadie found herself unable to cope with her new environment, Tom took over. First, he cut a gate in the fence that divided the two back gardens; then he took charge of her screaming baby so she might take a breather. He was a practical man and assured her that children would eat when they were hungry, sleep when they were tired and have bowel movements when appropriate. She should let nature take its course and go and lie down! Naturally,

I adored him. As I grew older I was allowed to tease out the tobacco for his pipe, and whenever I was in need of company I'd be next door. Solly and Tom became good mates too. My first bike was a gift from this dear friend.

When I was a child I saw Solly and Sadie in a good-cop, bad-cop light and thought of myself as Solly's girl, never Sadie's; he was fun, she was a spoilsport. How could I possibly have appreciated the trauma she'd experienced in leaving home, marrying into Solly's family (where she was disparaged), living in an outer London suburb far from a comforting Jewish community network, dealing with a fretful baby, alone all day with no one to talk to? As I got older I became an even more difficult child, playing off one parent against the other, resenting the way in which Sadie appeared to boss Solly around. Little did I realise how much he absolutely loved being nagged. It's like the old Jewish joke about who makes the decisions in the family – she calls the shots about household expenditure whilst he deals with the important questions, such as whether the government should declare war or raise taxes.

Sadie, Solly and I stopped living together when I was about twenty-three, though the relationship was still prickly when I was living away from home. I was non-conformist, didn't have Jewish friends and showed no sign of getting married – a disappointment all round, though they never said so. Later, Alan wisely did some fence mending on the deck of the *Stratheden* and Sadie and I became much closer. Once I was far away from my parents, our meetings, whether in London or Melbourne, became occasions for celebration. But my guilt never went away completely.

It's strange to be unpicking a relationship with one's parents after their deaths. The only way for me to manage this is to ignore the views of the aggressive atheists, to believe in mysteries and to hope that somehow Sadie and Solly know how much I would like to repair matters.

Solly's business card from the 1930s

During the thirties Solly had a number of jobs, but he also supplemented his meagre wages by taking in repairs and alterations for local customers. One of our two living rooms always served as a fitting room, and his skills with the Singer sewing machine have become part of my DNA too. I think of Alan and me making sheepskin slippers and smile at the similarity. But we had three little boys and Sadie and Solly were fixated solely on me. She worried constantly about eating, bowel habits, nail biting and not going outside with wet hair because pneumonia would assuredly be the result. Solly simply doted on me. Still only in his late twenties, he wanted to play games with his pretty little daughter. It was inevitable that I would adore him and resent her.

Each Saturday we'd go down to my grandmother's in Bow for *Shabbes* lunch. My poor mother must have just loathed it. My father's sisters, 'the girls', spoilt this little princess with her golden ringlets tied up with crisp bows, and I just wallowed in the adoration. Whilst I was being indulged in the dining room, Sadie was down in the basement kitchen washing up. The more fuss these frustrated, repressed girls made of me, the sterner my mother became.

Of course we didn't own a car, and bus fares were an expense that could be avoided on a reasonably dry evening, if Solly was prepared to carry me whilst he and Sadie walked the five or so miles from Stratford Broadway to Ilford. I remember the market stalls and the costermongers crying out their wares, like jellied eels and similar, strange *treyf* (not kosher) food, the flares and gas lamps, the liveliness of it all as I perched up on Solly's shoulders. The Blitz demolished much of the area, although my grandmother's house is still standing, with the railway tracks running behind the grimy brick wall at the back. Nowadays the East End is fashionable. The 2012 London Olympics at Stratford would have been unthinkable back in the thirties, when the area was considered something of a sordid slum – a warm community, but still a slum.

In the early days Solly rode a pushbike from Gants Hill to the workshop in Bow Road. His friend Mick Fox encouraged him to buy a motorbike but Sadie was horrified and made him return it. Sixty years later a display of Harley Davidson bikes on St Kilda foreshore in Melbourne made his eyes still gleam with longing. Regina could only afford to give him ten shillings a week, which wasn't enough to pay the mortgage and keep food on the table. It must have been a difficult decision for him to quit and seek a better-paid job, and probably 'the girls' blamed Sadie. The Great Depression was threatening the stability of the country and by the end of 1930, the year of my birth, there were 2.5 million unemployed, and National Hunger Marches took place in 1931, 1932 and 1934. By 1936 the government was following a policy of mass rearmament in the face of the rise of Nazi Germany. Oswald Mosley, the leader of the British fascist party, and his paramilitary Blackshirts had been inciting hatred and anti-Semitism, particularly in the East End. The Battle of Cable Street, at which they were prevented from marching, is an event remembered with great pride by the families of the many Jewish workers who took part.

However, London and the south were doing better than the north of England, and by 1938 there was sufficient improvement in our family's situation for us to have a modest holiday. It's memorable because already the talk was of war.

CHAPTER 6
THE THIRTIES

I reflect upon the 1930s from a child's point of view and can only guess how it must have been for Sadie and Solly. They had left the familiar communal warmth of the Jewish East End and were, in a way, pioneers, hoping to make a life among people they referred to as 'the English'.

During this decade Solly managed to find better jobs, but it was still necessary to have work coming in from local people. I remember the Singer sewing machine in its brown box, the long mirror on a stand where clients could view themselves, the dining-room table scored by thousands of little pin pricks from the spiked wheel he used for marking out the stiff brown paper patterns, pins stuck in the tufts of the carpet, two thimbles (his and hers), tape measures in inches, set squares and chalk, bobbins, a button box and style books with ladies in long, willowy costumes stepping out for tea at Fortnum's. My father was colour blind so Sadie was invaluable in selecting thread and, in many instances, helping him with the relatively unskilled jobs of basting, sewing on buttons or turning up hems. The front room, which had no furniture, was where customers were attended to, and the back room, with French windows leading onto the

36 Ashurst Drive, Ilford, Essex. The small upstairs windows are the 'box room'

garden, was where we had the dining-room table.

Upstairs were two bedrooms and a small 'box room' where I slept. At various times in the thirties, one or another of Sadie's unmarried sisters boarded with us and occupied the back bedroom, whilst my parents always had the one in the front overlooking Ashurst Drive. The furniture in their bedroom never changed in sixty years and two little ladder-backed chairs from that room are now in my home. There were primitive gas fires upstairs, but the house was heated with coal. It was a family joke that Sadie would be on her hands and knees cleaning out the cold ashes and re-laying a fresh fire, whilst I sat beside her with my nose in a book, oblivious to what was happening at my feet.

Here in Melbourne my washing-machine will hum away whilst I do something else, and it's a toss-up whether I will hang out the laundry or use the clothes dryer. For Sadie, the washing followed a much more complicated path, to which her rough hands bore testimony. First came the kitchen sink, complete with ribbed wooden washboard, bar soap and 'blue bag' to make things whiter. After many rinses the clothes would be taken outside and put through the mangle. If the weather was suitable they were then hung out with long wooden pegs on the clothesline, which was propped up high with a pole. All of this was merely the prelude. Our kitchen ceiling was equipped with racks operated by a system of ropes and pulleys, and all items had to spend a defined period up there before they were ironed. However, this wasn't the end of it, and no matter how urgently I wanted a clean blouse or dress, nothing was allowed back into a wardrobe or drawer until it had also spent time in the airing cupboard, which was located above the hot water tank in the back bedroom. As Sadie always said, 'You can catch pneumonia from damp clothes.'

I went to primary school with my best friend, Sonia, the daughter of Jack and Sarah Sanders up the road. Gearies Junior and Infants' Schools were established in 1929 so they were relatively new in 1935 when we started our education there. Year after year the little wooden chairs were set out in the playground and our school photos taken. When my baby teeth fell out there were reminders to 'keep your mouth closed', but sometimes I forgot. It must have been something of a turning point when Sadie stopped putting ribbon bows in my hair; perhaps I had just said 'no more'.

School photo of Ros from Gearies Junior School, c1938

I was a lonely child and turned to books with enthusiasm. The age at which one might join Gants Hill Municipal Library was seven, and on Friday 19 February 1937 I was waiting outside. The following year my birthday present from Sadie and Solly was *Alice in Wonderland*, the edition with the Harry Rountree illustrations; it is still a favourite book. In 1948 I was again at the library, waiting to take up my first job as a library assistant.

From Gants Hill we could get a bus or walk through Valentines Park to Ilford Broadway, from where we took another bus to Sadie's beloved East End. We'd go to 'the Lane' (Petticoat Lane) and she'd buy pickled herrings and cucumbers straight from the barrels, cream cheese made in the Polish manner, bagels and caraway-seed rye bread. Lunch might be a salt-beef sandwich from Bloom's in Old Montague Street. As the Ilford Jewish community grew and more people moved out of the East End, kosher butchers and grocery shops were established nearer our home. But this all took time, and for Sadie shopping trips to Aldgate and Whitechapel in the 1930s were magic.

Green Line coaches would take us to tourist attractions such as Hampton Court Palace or Kew Gardens. If we were going on an outing, the LNER (London North Eastern Railway) steam train went from Ilford Station to the coast, where Sadie enthused over the bracing sea air that was 'so good for you'. We never ate *treyf* fish and chips or pies; my mother always brought hard-boiled eggs and salty cracker biscuits for our lunch. After Solly died I did the trip by myself (it wasn't a steam train by then) and walked to Leigh-on-Sea. I wept for my parents who thought of the historic little fishing town as their own romantic hide-away.

Wedding of Sally Fox and David Shapiro, 1936. L–R: Sophie and Clara, and unknown bridesmaid; in front are Asher Korner and Ros

Wedding of Gus Samuel and Rosa Tannen, c1937. Ros is on the far left and the pageboy is Michael Samuel

There were births, deaths and marriages within the families during the 1930s. Solly's eldest sister, Sally, married David Shapiro in 1936; Sadie's brother Gus married Rosa Tannen in 1937. Hemlines had dropped by this time and the short, sleeveless Art Deco dresses and cloche hats in Sadie and Solly's 1928 wedding portrait are a far cry from the extravagant flounces and ribbons of these later occasions. I was a flower girl for Sally and a bridesmaid for Gus.

In Cardiff, mother's brother Jimmie (Hebrew name, Enoch; also known as Henry) and his wife, Rosie Gordon, had three children:

Netta, Bernard and Gerald. Netta immigrated to Israel in the 1970s and Bernard died many years ago. But my cousin Gerald, a mine of information about the family, lives in an idyllic part of the English countryside. He is a keen walker and writes to me of 'rambling', a sweetly old-fashioned term that conjures up an England long gone.

Will (Woolfie), Sadie's brother, married Ray Goodman. Their only child, Michael, immigrated to Israel with his wife, Audrey, and they settled in Haifa. Sadie's younger sister, Dinah, was romantically involved with Michael, a Jewish fireman, but ended up marrying non-Jewish Mr Peckett and going off to live in Luton, Bedfordshire. Before they parted, a daughter, my cousin Sandra, was born. Sadly, she died in Christchurch in 2012. Her husband, Alex, is a mountaineer, and when the weather is favourable he will place the memorial he has designed in her honour on top of a remote peak somewhere in New Zealand's South Island.

Rosie was the closest sister in age to my mother. She and her husband, Joe Osen, produced David, Maurice, Alan and Eve, the 'four angels'. To a solitary child like me their home seemed much livelier than mine. The three boys were passionate about sport. My aunt listened dutifully to the radio for the test cricket scores and the soccer results for Tottenham Hotspurs and relayed all this critical information when my cousins came home from school. I was very impressed and couldn't imagine my serious little mother doing the same.

It intrigues me that all the cousins in the Samuel family who happened to be only children – including me – left Britain and headed off to Israel, America, New Zealand and Australia. Were we all feeling so pressured?

Sadie's sisters, Dora and Rachel, married in the 1940s, as did Solly's sister, Sophie. My grandmothers both died in the thirties: Eva in 1934 and Regina in 1939. I was not allowed to attend either funeral, the first because I was too young and the second, probably to ward off the 'evil eye'; 'the girls' were a hopelessly superstitious lot. However, at the base of Regina's gravestone the stonemason has remembered me: 'Boobie from Rosaline'.

My aunts and uncles, descendants of the Chwalls (or Samuels), the Greens, the Gilberts (the Foxes) and the Schlesingers, were all first-generation children of immigrants who identified as English. They knew about the Great War, the Depression, the Spanish Civil War, the Abdication of Edward VIII, and the rise of fascism and communism, from news relayed through the 'wireless' and the newspapers in a language they, unlike their parents, understood.

There were other English Jews, families who had arrived after the barriers were removed in the seventeenth century. These were upper class, or aspired to be upper class, or pretended to be upper class. Often the rich and famous were from the so-called Jewish aristocracy, the Sephardi, or Spanish, Jews. My parents and their brothers and sisters would have had no contact at all with upper-class Jews and seemed to live in a kind of no man's land: not exactly British to their bootstraps and still loosely connected with the Eastern European lives their parents had left behind. It would be the next generation, mine and that of my cousins, that would assimilate more strongly, buy mock Tudor houses in the Home Counties, attend university, and even take their hard-won British passports and emigrate.

In Australia it was a different history. A handful of Jews arrived with the First Fleet as convicts in 1788. Jewish migrants, like Alan's family, came as free settlers, particularly as the colony developed and opportunities opened up in towns and on the goldfields. There was continuous Jewish migration to Australia from the beginning of the twentieth century, with families seeking relief from discrimination, or searching for a better economic future in a land with good opportunities, excellent weather and a reputation for egalitarianism. Many of today's prominent families began business enterprises in the 1920s and 1930s, and there are other famous names such as Sir John Monash and Sir Isaac Isaacs, but most Jews were lower- or middle-class traders and artisans. Many historians claim that had it not been for the revitalising influx of Holocaust 'reffos' in the 1940s and 1950s, the 'Anglos' would have disappeared altogether, and assimilated into general Australian society. The Anglo Jews were a close-knit community, and there was inevitable friction when the foreigners came. This culture-clash coloured the social period of Alan's childhood and was a focus for much of his writing.

Sadie, Solly and Ros in 1938 on our last holiday before the war

In 1938 Solly, Sadie and I had what was to be our last holiday before the war began. We travelled thirty miles by steam train to Southend and probably stayed in a boarding house, certainly not a hotel. I have no idea how much they knew about the situation in Europe, although of course the need to rescue Great-Aunt Berthe's family must have been occupying their minds.

When Chamberlain brought back his 'peace for our time' Munich Agreement in September 1938 I wonder whether anyone on either side of my family believed him. Uncle Gilbert had a son, Morry, who must have been one of the few members of the family to own a car. When war was declared on 1 September 1939, he took Sadie and me to Cardiff, where we spent about six months during the period known as the 'phoney war' when very little happened. It was Sadie's home city, where her father, Nathan, and brother Jimmie lived, and where billeting would be easier. The family thought south Wales would be safe because it was never attacked in World War I, but they were wrong; Cardiff docks and Swansea suffered heavy bombing later in the war. Gradually, families who had fled London returned, and Sadie and I came home at Easter 1940 just before the raids on London, the Blitz, began on 7 September.

In Sydney, Australia, Alan, a young street kid from Bondi, deemed to be in need of care and protection, was the first child admitted to the Isabella Lazarus Children's Home founded in 1939 primarily to accommodate Jewish refugee children from Europe.

CHAPTER 7
'I'LL SHOOT YOU FIRST'

Everyone has an individual special 'take' on World War II. It's difficult to avoid the set pieces, such as the Blitz, D-Day, and Stalingrad, and make the story personal. In 1940 Solly was thirty-six, Sadie forty-five, and I was ten years old.

It surprises me I was never frightened. I look at photos of terrified children in Europe, but my war was nothing at all like that. The children's memorial at Yad Vashem in Jerusalem is heartbreaking, and had my grandparents not left Eastern Europe, my picture might also be there. But this horror was not my experience. My war is not to be compared with running the gauntlet in a ghetto, hiding in a forest with partisans, or waving my family goodbye from a *Kindertransport* train. I didn't think that the enemy was after me personally, or my Jewish family; the threat was to our country, to England.

Sadie and Solly had hardly recovered from the earlier upheavals of the twentieth century when once again they were asked to be brave. Tom Foster-next-door has left me with a particularly riveting memory. Early on in the war he came over to our house for a serious talk. He told us he'd read about the concentration camps and was anxious on behalf of his Jewish neighbours. He said that if Hitler invaded England, as many expected, he would get out his ex-Indian army rifle. Rather than let us fall into German hands, he said, 'I'll shoot you first.' I was astonished.

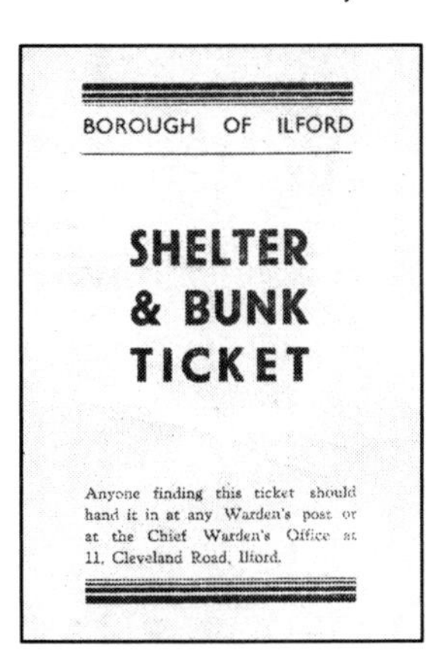
BOROUGH OF ILFORD

SHELTER & BUNK TICKET

Anyone finding this ticket should hand it in at any Warden's post or at the Chief Warden's Office at 11, Cleveland Road, Ilford.

Shelter ticket for Sadie and Solly, 1944

My childhood home was located in a particularly vulnerable area as a dual carriageway, Eastern Avenue (the A12), ran past the end of our street. This major arterial road led east to the coast, and any German invaders would most likely use this approach. Eastern Avenue was significant to me, not only because it had to be crossed to reach Valentines Park, but also because much later on in the war this was a route taken by Allied forces travelling to Tilbury in preparation for D-Day, the liberation of Europe. By then I was fourteen, and most interested in watching and waving to the endless stream of American troop carriers with the wildly attractive soldiers in their chocolate and beige coloured uniforms. My friends and I all wore bobby sox and saddle shoes (They were called penny loafers in America.) and I had an American coin fastened somewhere on the front of one. It seemed terribly unfair that the British Tommies wore such hideous felt-like uniforms when the Yanks, the Free French and the Poles were kitted out so smartly. It was no contest.

Once the bombing began, the German planes followed a flight path right over Eastern Avenue. Later on, the same route was taken by Lancaster bombers heading in the opposite direction – to Germany. We counted the number of our planes as they left for a raid and counted them again on their return to see if any had been shot down. Eastern Avenue joined other main roads at the Gants Hill roundabout, where under-passes facilitated pedestrian access to the underground station, the Tube. This extension of the Central Line was all set to open when war broke out, but the tunnels intended for the trains were converted to become an ammunition factory. In 1944, whilst I was again evacuated, Sadie and Solly took shelter from the rockets and slept on bunks or deck chairs on the station platforms.

Eastern Avenue was also the route I took when I rode my bike to Wanstead High School. Coming home I'd lay small bets with myself as to whether our home had been damaged during the day's air raids, and as I turned into Ashurst Drive I'd quickly shut and open my eyes before looking.

Sadie and I returned from our evacuation in Cardiff in time for the beginning of the Blitz. These were dark days, and as the bombing raids intensified it must have been an anxious time for my parents. Evidently it wasn't a problem for me. Like every other house, ours had blackout curtains, tape across the windows and gas masks always at the ready. We didn't have our own Anderson shelter, but joined the Joe Fox family in theirs. This dugout in their back garden, covered in earth and equipped with a wooden bench, was cold and damp. We went over the road at the sound of the air-raid sirens, and just sat there wrapped in blankets until the 'all clear', sometimes many hours later. We had biscuits and a thermos of tea to keep us going. The searchlights combed the sky for planes, and the ack-ack fire was reassuring, even though British cities were being destroyed and many lives lost. The iconic photograph of St Paul's Cathedral ringed by flames with the cross on top, defiantly protective, never fails to move me, not least because on that December night Solly took me into the street to see the red glow in the sky over the burning city. Eventually Sadie became fed up with having to sit in the shelter and decided we'd stay home in our beds. I wonder now if there was a contingency plan. Did Solly have any idea which part of the house was safest in the event of a direct hit? Did Sadie have emergency rations packed ready to go? Where did we hang our gas masks? I can't remember.

Solly was having problems finding a job and took a position with a manufacturer who made both army uniforms and civilian clothing. His pay was a mere five pounds a week and wartime regulations meant he was tied to this job for the duration. He received call-up papers in 1941 and 1943, but his employer would not sign a release, saying he couldn't operate the factory without him. Finally, in April 1943 Solly insisted on joining the army.

But my father's military career was short-lived because his health was deemed not good enough. He asked if he could work in the army clothing factory, but was refused because they were unable to provide kosher food, and he wouldn't eat *treyf*. He suggested that

Solly in uniform, 1943

he live outside the barracks and feed himself, but they said no. He also tried to join the special police force, but was half an inch too short. Finally, he was given an honourable discharge and became an air-raid warden. Back in civilian life, he eventually found work with a manufacturer who appreciated his talents, and from that time on his career began to flourish. It had been a difficult road from the workshop at the top of the house in Bow.

In the 1940s there were more changes in the two families. Regina's unexpected death in 1939 had devastated the now-orphaned 'girls', and *Pesach* 1940, a sombre affair, was celebrated at the home of my father's eldest sister, Sally. The four single sisters found running the workshop and the large house in Bow impossible, so Clara and Annie took jobs, whilst Sophie and Celia opened a little haberdashery shop in Maplin Street, Mile End, where there was accommodation for them all to continue living together. When they were bombed out they were forced to move once again. I must have been about ten when I spent a few days with them and 'wrote a book' on brown wrapping paper from the shop. To my besotted aunts this made me an instant genius.

The war had an impact on other family members too. Uncle Joe was drafted into the army and Sadie's brother Will helped support Rosie and the four children. Mother's youngest sister, Rachel, joined the Land Army. My cousin Bernard was in the army, and Solly's cousins, Morry and Harry Gilbert, were in uniform.

There were also celebrations. Sadie's sister Dora married Harry

Tutleman. The wedding was a modest affair; Nathan came up from Cardiff, and the one photograph I have seems to reflect the austerity of the times. My aunt and uncle were thoughtful people. Probably, and with justification, they regarded me as rather self-centred and wished to do a little consciousness raising. They gave me a birthday gift, a history book about the Chartists, a movement for social reform in nineteenth-century Britain. I'm still ashamed I didn't read it. On the other side of the world, in Sydney, in some second-hand bookshop, Alan, who didn't have loving aunts and uncles, found Robert Tressall's *The Ragged-Trousered Philanthropists*, (first published in 1914), a rather turgid novel about a group of socialist house painters. It was famous in its day and surely influenced Alan's politics, if not his writing style, which is much more humorous than that of the gloomy Tressall.

My cousin Gina, age four, in Valentines Park, c1957

Sadie's brother Gus and his wife, Rosa, had two children: my cousins Jennifer and Geoffrey. Solly's sister Sophie married Simon Rosenfeld and, most joyfully for the Fox family, produced another grandchild, a second little princess. My cousin Gina was born in 1951 and she and I often reflect upon the fact that we are the 'remnants', an appropriate word for a rag-trade family.

In my final year at primary school I did something particularly stupid. Whenever the air-raid siren sounded we all filed into the corridors, sat on the floor with our gas masks and 'iron rations' of cheese, biscuits and chocolate, and were allowed to read comics. One day I left the school without permission, shrapnel falling around me as I walked down the street. I picked up a piece that narrowly missed me. It was about eight inches long and still hot, and I carried it home to 'show and tell'. Sadie answered the door, took one look at the jagged metal and slapped me, the only time she ever did.

A new type of shelter was offered to the public: the Morrison, named after the Home Secretary, Herbert Morrison. It was a steel structure with mesh sides and replaced our dining-room table. These shelters were turned out so quickly there was no time to round off the sharp, pointed corners, which left bruises as we bumped into them. The three of us slept underneath the 'table' at night for several years and it was better than the cold dugout.

Pre-war fears about communism were put aside as we learned of the German assault on the Soviet Union. Clementine Churchill (Winston's wife) asked us to do what we could for 'our brave Russian allies', and my friends and I answered the call by making little brooches out of knitting wool and selling them door to door. Food shortages made life harder for Sadie, who stood for hours in queues to buy the tiny portions of butter or meat we were allocated, or the few precious eggs Solly needed because his ulcers required a careful diet. For many poor families, the special allowances for oranges or bananas gave children their first taste of these fresh fruits. Clothing coupons meant Solly was kept busy with local customers asking him to re-model their old coats and suits so the worn parts would no longer show.

Around 1941, I sat for something called the Eleven Plus Scholarship and must have done quite well because I was offered a place at the Ursuline Convent School in Ilford. I didn't want to attend an all-girls school and chose Wanstead County High School (now Wanstead High School) instead. The school badge features a black and white heron, a breed common to the Wanstead area, and we were identified by our black blazers and white shirts that echoed the colours of the bird. When my grandsons were in their Harry Potter phase, I scoffed at Gryffindor, Slytherin, Ravenclaw and Hufflepuff; *our* school houses were Romans, Saxons, Celts and Vikings, and I still have my red Viking badge. I was an enthusiastic student for seven years and had received a modest but useful education by the time I left in 1948. None of my school reports was particularly impressive: 'a nice girl, but worries too much', 'needs to try harder', 'if she works more diligently she might pass'.

Ros in Wanstead County High School uniform, c1946

In December 1945 I passed the School Certificate with credits in English, English Literature, Latin, French, Biology and Domestic Subjects, and a mere pass in a strange hybrid subject, Physics-with-Chemistry. However, Maths was compulsory and I'd failed. I was in a special class of talented students only because I was good at English, and I traded on this for years to compensate for my poor numeracy skills. When the results were posted on the gates of the school with my failure for all to see, I was heartbroken. Solly and Sadie had a difference of opinion about whether they would allow me to stay on, pick up the missing Maths and proceed further to take the more advanced Higher School Certificate. Sadie maintained that it 'wasn't necessary' for a girl but Solly said I should be given an opportunity.

During my secondary school years I grew less attached to Judaism and Jewish community life and more curious about the wider British society. My former best friend did not progress to high school but stayed at primary school until she reached the age at which she could leave and get a job. This ended the friendship because we simply didn't have anything in common. At secondary school there were perhaps a handful of other Jewish students, but we were not close. My non-Jewish school friends seemed a strange breed. I became aware of anti-Semitism and learned that it was important to stand up and be counted, even if I wasn't much of a believer. Solly sent me to *cheder* (what our religious classes were called) at the local synagogue, and I earned a prize for Hebrew, but it was infinitely more interesting to participate in school assembly and sing Christmas carols or rousing hymns such as 'Onward Christian Soldiers' – in English.

I made a new friend, Renée, whose background couldn't have been more different from mine. Her family lived in a tiny house with no bathroom, even though her dad was a plumber. They were not well off and her mother was particularly keen that her three daughters should all try their utmost to better themselves. Renée certainly did just that. She became a talented copywriter in what was, at that time, one of the largest advertising agencies in the world, and married its creative director. Eventually they settled down in an idyllic sixteenth-century mill house by a trout stream and taught over-indulged Americans how to catch fish. When her husband died, she moved to a thatched cottage, where ducks and swans glide past the bottom of her garden in a little rivulet straight out of Beatrix Potter. But back in the 1940s, in our black blazers and black-and-white striped ties, we were a long way from storybook villages in Wiltshire or Art Deco seaside suburbs in Melbourne.

Sometimes tuition took place in the school shelters, after the main building sustained some bomb damage. From the beginning of my time at Wanstead, a large section of the school was permanently evacuated to the country, but it wasn't until 1944 that I asked Sadie and Solly whether I might go away with a new group that was being sent to Ely, near Cambridge. I just fancied a change; it had nothing to do with fear. Ely was not that far from home, and off I went with my gas mask, to be lined up in a church hall where local citizens came and picked which one of us they wanted to billet. I lived with a policeman's family for a few weeks, and all I remember is his wife teaching me how to make an omelette from reconstituted dried eggs. But I became homesick and asked Sadie to come and take me away. On the way home she told me of a new type of attack, the flying bomb, nicknamed 'buzz-bomb' or 'doodlebug' and the predecessor of today's cruise missile.

As the war dragged on, weapons became more sophisticated. The V1 and the V2 rockets were developed by Germany as a last throw of the dice. This final phase was in many ways the worst, for whilst the British were stoic and brave through the Blitz, the mysterious missiles that arrived with little or no warning sent many a housewife into hospital with a complete breakdown of confidence. One memorable Friday, when Sadie had been busy preparing for *Shabbes*, a V1 droned overhead. Suddenly the motor cut out, signifying that the bomb was about to fall. I pushed my mother under the table shelter. The explosion shook houses in the next street; all our windows fell in, and the spotless little home was covered in debris. Was Sadie frightened? I don't think I was. At that age being at war seemed a normal state of affairs. I was nine when the conflict began and fifteen when it ended; it must have been completely different for Sadie and Solly.

My friends and I didn't discuss the war very much; it was just the background to our adolescent lives. I don't believe we even speculated about what we might do after the war. 'Teenagers' was not a common term then, but that's what we were. Perhaps we were self-centred or had just become inured to the way life was. Television had been invented but was on hold for the duration; however, the radio, gramophone records and the cinema ('the pictures') were all available to provide us with entertainment and information. Provincial and ethnic accents were not much used on the wireless, so in my head I can still hear the perfect King's English of the announcement: 'This is the BBC Home Service'. Radio brought us Churchillian rhetoric, Richard Dimbleby reporting from Belsen concentration camp and in 1946 the first *Letter from America* with Alastair Cooke. Vera Lynn was popular with the troops, but for me it was the start of the swing era, and the great names of the period, Armstrong, Fitzgerald, Dorsey, Miller and Shaw just swept us away. We heard them on the radio and rushed out to buy their records. My friends and I used our almost-empty front room to practice jive and jitterbug.

Films played an important role in maintaining morale, and we attended regularly at the Savoy Cinema, Gants Hill, where the queues stretched around the building for several hundred yards. If the air-raid siren went off whilst we were inside, a slide announcing this appeared on screen; a similar message informed us of the 'All Clear'. No one left the performance during raids; patrons just lit up another cigarette and stayed put. The lucky few who had some ration coupons to spare enjoyed sweets or chocolate. Through newsreels, an essential part of every program, we avidly charted the progress of the war, and whilst I was sitting in the cinema at Gants Hill, thousands of miles away in Sydney, Alan and his father were watching much the same footage on Australian Cinesound. (The title story in Alan's collection *A Thousand Nights at the Ritz* says it all.) There were many morale-boosting films made in Britain, with actors playing submarine commanders brusquely ordering 'Up periscope!', or spies infiltrating occupied Europe to assist the various resistance movements. In the beginning Solly and Sadie weren't willing to break the Sabbath by going to the pictures, but after a sustained period of air raids, Solly decided that for the sake of sanity we should join the queue at the Savoy. We saw *Fantasia*, which was so wonderful we stayed on to view it twice; continuous screening meant we could just sit there the entire afternoon.

I really wasn't very talented ('a nice girl, but immature') but I did enjoy school; it was an entry into a different world. Surprisingly, in 1948 I passed the Higher Schools Certificate of the University of London in English, French and German and might have applied for a university place, had I wished. But I'd already decided to become a librarian, and at that time a prior degree was not required. Twenty years later in Melbourne, Solly's indulgence in allowing me to stay on was to prove enormously important in getting me a job with the Victorian Education Department, a diploma as a librarian and a degree from an Australian university.

CHAPTER 8
WORKING GIRL

The war ended in 1945 but British society took a long time to recover; rationing and austerity measures continued for years. The Festival of Britain in 1951 was intended to boost morale, and the coronation of Queen Elizabeth II in June 1953 added greatly to the sense of renewal. The fifties are usually decried as dull, merely the prelude to the 'swinging sixties', Carnaby Street and the Beatles. For me it was a pivotal time: the beginning of my twenties, work, leaving home, marriage, emigration, children – quite a lot for one decade.

The last year I went on holiday with Sadie and Solly was 1947. It was a momentous event for them, but I didn't enjoy myself and the photographs show a resentful seventeen-year-old looking as miserable as sin. My parents had never travelled 'abroad' and had just survived a harrowing war, so a holiday at Lake Lucerne was arranged. I have a poignant memory of the train journey from France. Just across the border in Switzerland we stopped for breakfast at a station buffet, sitting down to a snow-white cloth, heavy cutlery, croissants, real butter, real jam, real cream and real coffee. It was all too much for Sadie after years of ration books and unbleached linen marked with the government's CC41 utility stamp; she

Ros on holiday in Devon, c1950

just dissolved into tears.

After Lucerne we had separate holidays. I visited various parts of England and Scotland, sometimes going by bicycle. There were holidays in Cornwall, where I braved a fishing boat off the coast at Fowey and made myself sick on non-kosher lobster. In a little seaside town in Devon called Beer, I won the ladies skittles championship, but it was unthinkable to take the prize of a live piglet home to Sadie. The Norfolk Broads was a real-life *Wind in the Willows* environment, but all these watery holidays are misleading, as I am afraid of the surf, can't swim very well and suffer seasickness. The little boats we bought years later were great fun for our sons, but I never went sailing. I must have disappointed Alan, for whom the ocean was a refuge, a playground and a place of magical beauty.

By the 1950s Sadie's sisters were all either married or independent and didn't need to board with us. I was no longer confined to the little box room and moved into the back bedroom where I could finally put up posters of actors, arrange my books and generally spread my wings.

Aunt Rachel (undated)

Rachel, the youngest of the Samuel girls, saw herself as my mentor and hoped I might follow in her professional footsteps; it was all rather flattering when I was eighteen or nineteen. She was darkly exotic, concerned with speaking beautifully but unfortunate in inheriting very poor eyesight. As the 'baby' of the family, she was given a better education than her elder sisters and aspired to be an intellectual. Ruchl, as we called her, was more or less raised by my mother, and Sadie told me that whenever she wanted to go out with her friends, she had to take the young child along too. Rachel called Sadie 'Sair', which might have been a leftover term from childhood, but it sounded very precious and irritated me.

Rachel worked on *The Daily Express* newspaper in Fleet Street, as a secretary not a journalist, had a crush on her boss and lived in a bed-sit in Hampstead. I have no idea how she became Mrs Beaver; there are secrets to which I am not privy. I don't think anyone in the family ever met Mr Beaver and Rachel always lived alone. It must have been in the 1960s when she immigrated to Durban to work for a magazine, but being unsympathetic to the anti-apartheid movement she returned to London in the 1970s. Unfortunately, we then had a complete falling-out. Rachel wanted to board with my parents once again, as she had in the 1930s, but I believed Sadie, already nearly eighty, was far too old and arthritic to be running around caring for her sister, whose sight was failing. From Melbourne I sent an audiotape saying so, and my father 'accidentally' played it when my aunt was visiting and was able to hear my views.

The result was very sad. British social services refused to find her sheltered accommodation back in desirable Hampstead, by that time a very exclusive area. Rachel was unhappily reduced to a miserable life in an outer-suburban welfare-type housing complex and eventually a nursing home for the blind. She died in 1999 at the age of ninety and was cremated. Needless to say, I didn't inherit her first edition Proust. My aunt was a very private person and toward the end, as far as I know, only two nephews were welcome to visit her. My cousin Maurice, who, to his great credit, assumed responsibility for so many of our older relatives, including my parents, showed me Rachel's little memorial in his beautiful garden.

In 1948 I started my first job as an assistant in the Gants Hill branch of the Ilford municipal library system. I earned nineteen shillings a week, paid monthly, and worked shifts. In the children's library I washed any grubby fingers and took the young borrowers into the little garden where we read stories. When I was moved into the adult section I did all the usual routine tasks: shelving books, lending books, covering books and maintaining the hand-written card catalogue. There were no CDs or DVDs or on-line databases in those days. Censorship was in operation too, so *Lady Chatterley's Lover* and the Kinsey reports on sexual behaviour were strictly for under the counter.

I was only eighteen and anxious to further my career. Courses in librarianship were very limited at that time. Studying by correspondence was the only option until, in the late 1940s, London University offered a one-year, full-time diploma. I applied, was accepted, and then disappointed to learn that the Ilford Borough Council would not grant me study leave because I was the newest member of the library staff and there were others with stronger claims than mine. Solly offered to pay for the course and support me, but I declined because the curriculum was untested, and no one really knew whether one year of preparation was sufficient for a career in librarianship. He was worried that my salary was so low I could never support myself on it, and insisted I acquire some skills that would be useful in the commercial world. Reluctantly I did a six-month intensive course in Gregg shorthand, typing and elementary bookkeeping. However, Solly was quite right, as these skills have been of enormous value in getting me the jobs I really wanted. It wasn't until 1967, in Australia, that I finally came full circle and returned to the world of libraries.

My first commercial job was in the financial heart of the City of London, with a Swedish timber company whose offices were located in a Dickensian building near Fenchurch Street rail terminus. I was the office junior, and it was my responsibility to light a coal fire when I arrived in the morning. The job and the people were very dull, so I searched for something more stimulating. It might have been Aunt Rachel who suggested applying to *The Evening Standard*, a sister newspaper to *The Daily Express*, and right in the heart of Fleet Street

– a mecca for journalists until Rupert Murdoch shifted everything to Wapping. It was a step in the right direction, and although I didn't have the qualifications to become a cadet journalist, I was given a position in the newspaper's picture library. It was quite primitive, fifty years before the twenty-four-hour news cycle, digital cameras, emails and mobile phones. Basically, it was a library of photographs. Mr Dunphy, our department head, believed in copperplate handwriting, so the manila folders holding the pictures had to be beautifully inscribed with the correct subject in the top left-hand corner. This was very labour intensive and my suggestion about typewritten labels was not accepted.

Even in our sedate library, there were moments. Brumas, the polar bear was born on 27 November 1949 and the British public were enthralled; photographers constantly monitored the little cub's progress, and our library was swamped with pictures from the press agencies. It was a genuinely happy event at a time when the country was still recovering from the war. We had a different kind of drama when the paper's hapless picture editor published a photograph of the *wrong* duchess in a divorce case. It wasn't the library's fault, but the poor editor was sacked on the spot, and the British aristocracy not amused. I longed to get on to the journalists' side of the paper, but there was no chance, so my chapel (union) membership remained with the printers.

I wasn't amused by very much either at the time. The job was boring; living in the suburbs had no appeal and I wanted a taste of freedom. In the 1950s nice Jewish girls didn't leave home unmarried, and in my family it was unheard of. Sadie and Solly were mortified at the idea. She said it would 'break his heart', and he said it would 'break her heart'. It was all quite stormy. I didn't connect with the Ilford Jewish community, wasn't attending Jewish social clubs or going to dances and wanted to experience an altogether wider world. A new job was high on my agenda.

My reading had included a very ordinary novel, *Savoy Grill at One!*, which was set in the world of advertising agencies. I was intrigued and determined to find myself work in what was evidently an exciting, fast-moving environment. A little further down Fleet Street into the Strand, opposite the Inns of Court, I found a position in a small advertising agency as the new junior assistant to a rather formidable female account executive ('account' being the term for client). Why formidable? In the 1950s there was no anti-discrimination legislation and many women in high positions adopted a tough pose to ward off competition. The job itself was, as they say, a learning curve but it was interesting, and I absorbed as much as I could about the advertising business, knowing that eventually I'd search for something better.

My school friend Renée and I decided to move to bed-sit accommodation in Hampstead. It was quite traumatic to step out into the world. Her mother was very encouraging and gave her some apples and tea towels, but Sadie and Solly were terribly upset, as was I. We ended up at 16 Daleham Gardens, on the fringes of Hampstead, not far from Swiss Cottage underground station. We lived on the top floor of a three-storey Edwardian house with sloping attic-style ceilings, in what must have been the original servants' quarters. Peter and Sylvia, the owners, were Holocaust refugees and lived on the ground floor with their small children. He was a composer and spent much of his time in the large front room, which was empty apart from a grand piano. To supplement their income they rented out the rest of the house.

Street sign, Daleham Gardens, Hampstead

16 Daleham Gardens, Hampstead. The top left-hand attic windows were ours

The other tenants were a fascinating group, particularly to two young women from very proper suburbs. One floor up lived Tom Stobart, the photographer of Edmund Hilary's Everest expedition. He had the bluest eyes (I imagined him scanning the Himalayas) and a portable record player that gave us all a taste of strange Sherpa music. Next door to Tom lived a Guyanese actor, Cy Grant, together with Dorith, his German girlfriend, later his wife. Cy, who was the first black actor to appear regularly on British television, was an attractive figure in grey London. We'd come down the stairs all ready to go to work in our smart outfits and high heels, and there would be Cy carrying a guitar and devastatingly handsome – so very different from boring, suburban Ilford.

Also in the attic rooms on the top floor lived a man who allegedly doped horses, Karen, the beautiful, tragic Dane and Gunther, the German-Jewish refugee. There was a repulsive communal bathroom at the end of the corridor. The man connected with horses only emerged at night. His sister used to contact him through the one telephone placed on the first-floor landing. It worked on an honesty system, with a cocoa tin into which we placed our money. When this man left he was replaced by another who, in times past, might have been called a pamphleteer. He wrote endless newssheets about the evils of South African apartheid and berated me for not wishing to help with the typing; he said I was lacking a social conscience. (Later on Alan and I occupied this bed-sit, from where would leave for Melbourne.)

Karen (not her real name) lived in the end room. She was hopelessly in love with a Jewish musician, who later became famous, but his family would never have allowed them to marry and, as a result, Karen suffered terrible migraines and depression. Our two rooms were at the other end of the corridor, and Gunther lived next door to us. One could set a clock by his movements: each day he'd return from work, switch on the BBC news and make boiled eggs for his supper. I believe he finally went on *aliyah* to Israel. The whole house had a kind of raffish aura about it and Peter and Sylvia's friends included many intellectual European refugees and émigrés, artists and actors, people like Peter Ustinov. Aunt Rachel, who lived nearby in Frognal, a better address in Hampstead proper, occasionally visited us but no one else in the family ever came.

Around 1951 or 1952, I left the small advertising agency in the Strand and moved further down the street to Waterloo Bridge, where a very large company, Mather and Crowther, had their offices. Once again, Solly's insistence on commercial skills was the key, the way in, and I joined the agency as secretary to James Stratton, the young executive in charge of the 'fruit accounts'. Mather and Crowther had a number of clients whose main business was fruit and its allied products: Jamaica Rum, Tunisian Dates, Outspan Oranges from South Africa, Jaffa Oranges from Israel and apples and pears from New Zealand. They were bundled together and James and I were responsible for them. These were heady days for me, running the office, working late, translating proposals into French for the Tunisians, organising visitors for the Coronation. It was every bit as exciting as *Savoy Grill at One!* had promised.

But it all came apart. I was before my time – the women's movement was yet to get underway. James had done very well, and the board of directors decided he might have an assistant. Officially, I was his secretary. James put my name forward but I was rejected because it was company policy to appoint women to senior positions only for specific clients such as Patons and Baldwins knitting wools and Tampax sanitary products. Instead, he was allocated a chinless wonder of a former public-school boy with no skills at all. I gave notice. As a farewell gift James gave me a book inscribed 'To Sunshine'.

It must have been easier in those days to find a job and switch careers, or perhaps it was just the brashness of youth. I decided to leave the advertising world and cast around for an interesting alternative. I was a devoted customer at Marks and Spencer and thought a career as a buyer would be prestigious and well paid.

I offered my services to the company as a trainee buyer and was politely told that recruitment was all done internally; if I cared to join their typing pool I would be given an interview. It would be a real comedown to join a typing pool and be shunted around from department to department, but I swallowed my pride and took the job. Three weeks later I was promoted to a real position as a junior buyer in the nightdress and pyjama department. At last I looked forward to a genuine career path.

Head office was in Baker Street, and the company was way ahead of its time in staff amenities and welfare. Buying departments were structured with buyers/designers at the top, merchandisers and distributors below. Someone like me would be under the wing of an experienced buyer. Further up the hierarchy were middle managers who took clusters of trainees and instructed us on how to deal with the manufacturers who produced the clothes and the stores where they were sold. I was taken to the Midlands where hard-nosed factory owners plied us with liquor so that we wouldn't notice irregularities in production, but our mentors showed us how to discreetly pour the whisky into nearby pot plants and keep our wits about us. The size of even a trial order was huge; quality control often meant counting the number of stitches per inch, and if the manufacturer was cheating and saving thread by increasing the stitch size, even trainees like me had the power to reject thousands of garments. It was also compulsory for us to spend several weeks each year behind the counters of stores so that we fully understood our responsibilities to the buying public who were, unequivocally, always right.

I've written so many reports in my various careers, but the very first was for M and S. It was a delightfully earnest piece about the good people of Manchester and their preferences regarding pyjamas with stripes, spots or floral patterns. The company employed a great many single girls like me who lived in bed-sits and spent their wages on clothes instead of food, so they made sure we had a good, cheap, hot lunch every day in the staff canteen. There was also a medical centre, and later on, when they heard I was immigrating to Australia, they insisted on regular sun lamp treatments so I wouldn't shame England by arriving pale faced in Melbourne. I enjoyed the work immensely. It was when nylon became popular, and I acquired any number of filmy nightdress samples that later on were to impress Alan greatly. Somewhere in the company archives must also be a picture of the pyjamas I designed – winter weight in bright red flannelette. I brought a set to Melbourne; they were useful when we went camping.

I was making good progress at M and S, but my personal life was really going nowhere. It was difficult to see a path. At the age of twenty-four I was becoming a major family problem. Relatives were anxious that I had not yet found a partner, and were doing all they could to stitch me up with a suitable *shidduch*. Almost anyone would do, as long as he was Jewish. They didn't want to see me go the same route as Sadie's sisters Rachel and Dinah; neither did they fancy a nervous spinster like Solly's sisters Annie, Clara and Celia. Then in 1955 the Australians came along.

CHAPTER 9
'MY COUNTRY, RIGHT OR WRONG'

Memory is random and this memoir is no straightforward chronology; I am prompted into unexpected detours. On television I watched the river pageant celebrating Queen Elizabeth's Diamond Jubilee. It was cold and wet on the Thames, and equally cold and wet in Melbourne. Of course, memories were aroused, allegiances reviewed, ideas about citizenship, patriotism and belonging considered.

As I watched the once-in-a-lifetime Jubilee pictures I was moved by the sight of a rather lonely little figure following the procession through St Paul's Cathedral. Prince Phillip was in hospital, so she navigated all those steps without a supportive arm, and my hips hurt in sympathy. As a grandmother I can empathise with her, but do I feel connected to the royals? Not really, apart from the pageantry that makes for great television. Charles and Camilla or William and Kate hardly register with me, and if we have another referendum on an Australian republic, I would vote in favour. How do I feel about Britain? That's another matter. It would be impossible for someone with my heritage not to feel as deeply attached to the country as my grandparents and parents did. Without the legislation passed by various British governments, I might have died in Eastern Europe.

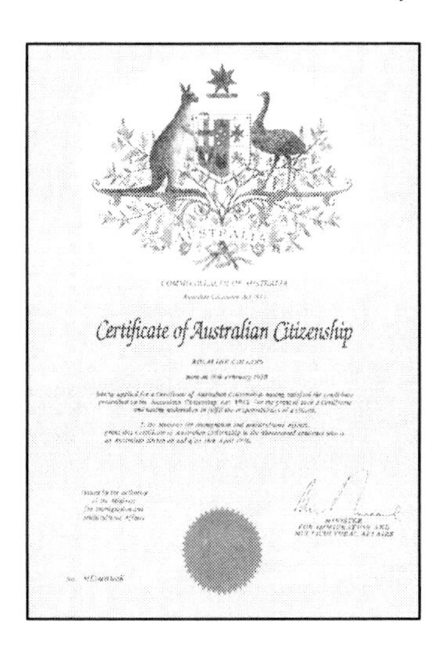

Certificate of Australian Citizenship

Ros's Australian Citizenship Certificate

Culturally, it's interesting to examine

my relationship to the history, geography and arts of the land. At one level I know full well that Sholem Aleichem should mean more to me than Jane Austen, but it isn't entirely so. I re-read George Eliot's *Middlemarch*, and whilst no one in my family actually lived in England in the 1830s, I can relate more easily to Dorothea than to Tevye's daughters in *Fiddler on the Roof*. And yet, and yet … Hodel, who goes off with Perchik the young Marxist, tugs at my heart, this young Jewish woman with ideals and curiosity. Isn't she more important to my background than the heroines of Austen, Eliot, or Dickens?

For over fifty years I've lived on an island continent where the weather can be extreme, the flora strange and the fauna sometimes daunting. My British cousins were unable to understand my amusement at a sign inviting villagers to 'an illustrated talk on badgers, with practical advice on badger watching'; I guess they may find the possums in my garden strange. I've been teased because I relish the occasional frost and drizzle that remind me of England, and the gentle landscapes I recall fill me with nostalgia. There's also my passport. Even though now it has an unfamiliar burgundy colour and a soft cover, it *is* a British passport. I keep renewing it, although I don't need to, since I'm also an Australian citizen and have a second one to guarantee my safety. In 1959, after the initial two years, my original passport was returned with a special permit pasted inside giving me the right to come and go. In 1996 I applied for Australian citizenship. At the ceremony held at St Kilda Town Hall, most of the new citizens were either Asian or from Eastern Europe, so mine was the easiest name for the mayor to read out. We took an oath, or elected to make an affirmation, and were given a small native plant in a pot as a symbol

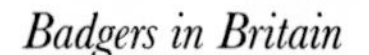
Badgers in Britain

Possum in my Melbourne garden

of our affiliation with this land.

Australian society has changed out of all recognition since the 1950s. Today, we are very multicultural. My tiler is of Indian and Portuguese extraction, the refrigeration mechanic is from Malta, my painters are Russian Jews, the greengrocer is Italian and the fishmonger is Greek. There is also Mabo. Eddie Mabo, a Torres Strait islander, initiated the legal challenge to the notion that Australia, as *terra nullius* (a land belonging to no one) might be taken over and owned by white colonists. I receive *News for Seniors*, a regular journal sent out from the Department of Human Services. The 2012 Senior Australian of the Year was Laurie Baymarrwangga, a ninety-five year old great-great-grandmother from the Crocodile Islands east of Darwin in the Northern Territory. It's a long way from the Thames Embankment.

Many of us live in several different worlds. For Jews, a bitter European heritage, the birth of political Zionism, the Balfour Declaration and the never-ending conflicts in the Middle East all make for great confusion, particularly among the young. When Alan wrote his trilogy *A Promised Land?* he set the earlier parts of the novel in the 1940s, and the question mark in the title was deliberate. He was looking back on his own youth. Many of his friends went on *aliyah* to build agricultural communities, *kibbutzim* and *moshavim* (communal farms). It's surprising he didn't go too because his life here was so difficult.

Years later in Box Hill, when we already had three small boys, a letter arrived inviting us as a family to join a new community of English-speaking, like-minded people somewhere in the Galilee. We were intrigued, but there was no money for either Alan or me to go and find out what Israel was all about, and without seeing for ourselves, we were not willing to make the move. Alan had two friends from the 1950s who worked hard to establish a kibbutz near Tel Aviv. Their adult children took time off after military service to travel the world, including a lengthy visit to Australia, the birthplace of their parents. After their trip they returned to make their lives on the kibbutz. I visited them much later, and asked how they had made the choice. They told me: 'We looked at many societies around the world and decided that creating an almond orchard on this land was the most satisfying work we could imagine doing.' They are secular Jews, not religious fundamentalists on some West Bank settlement. Might that have been Alan and me? The thought nags at me, and when I read Ari Shavit's *My Promised Land* (Spiegel & Grau, New York, 2013) the question became insistent. The 'intensity' of Israeli life, the 'truly free society' that is 'irreverent' and 'anarchic', the 'ongoing adventure' – in many ways, Shavit made me regret that we didn't embark on this odyssey.

The UN vote in 1947 did not seem a major issue for me back then; I was too pre-occupied with my own future. But it was a complex situation for the Jewish community when 'our' British sergeants were murdered by the Irgun, a Zionist paramilitary group. When the people from the Jaffa orange company came to London for the coronation in 1953, I turned down a job offer in Israel. (For that matter, I was offered jobs by all our fruit clients and might have gone to Tunisia, New Zealand, Jamaica or South Africa.) In 1956, when I was working for Marks and Spencer, it was suggested I move to their Israel offices. There have certainly been opportunities, and if Alan and I had gone on *aliyah*, we would probably have made a go of it.

The politics of the region leave me despairing, but it gives me great pleasure to know that in coffee shops throughout the country, people of diametrically opposed views can freely debate and argue. With all its faults, modern Israel is a democracy; women have equality, and freedom of speech is assured. And I am aware of the Law of Return, enacted by the Knesset on 5 July 1950, which states that every Jew has the right to come to this country as an *oleh* (immigrant).

The leaders of the Melbourne Jewish community periodically decide to test public opinion with surveys. I think it is all part of an identity crisis, common in the Diaspora, an inability to sort out our 'promised land'. The surveys pose questions about Judaism and religious observance, but then come the more complex enquiries, such as whether philanthropy should be directed to our own needs, or to those of Israel, or whether it's a good thing to fund our youth for consciousness-raising tours to Auschwitz and Jerusalem.

Because he was a writer, Alan was often asked about Judaism and creativity, and in the context of national identity his answer is revealing:

> Am I a Jewish fiction writer or a writer of Jewish fiction? They are, for me, one and indivisible – without my sense of Jewish history, I would not be a writer … I believe, too, that my writing … has its genesis in our Australian ethos; it would be most peculiar if it did not … It is the Australian–Jewish environment that takes priority and provides the parameters for my work.

Alan's Australian roots were always too deep for us to leave, and, unlike the reffos who were used to moving house, we could never have left the country where his ancestors made their homes back in the 1830s.

British, Jewish, Australian – I think the humour counts for a lot with me. Alan, my oh-so-Australian man, delighted in the very English wit of Gilbert and Sullivan, and as I caught up with the rest of the Jubilee pageant, the eccentricities of the British touched my heart. In the pouring rain, the fisherman-singers from Port Isaac in Cornwall sang of being convicts transported to South Australia, and the

London Philharmonic accompanied an absolutely drenched choir standing atop their barge, singing 'Land of Hope and Glory' with unbelievable fervour. Only in Britain!

Carl Schurz, a German-born revolutionary, American statesman and reformer, said, 'My country, right or wrong; if right, to be kept right; and if wrong, to be set right.' I feel rather like that about Australia. With my left-leaning political views I've marched with the teachers' unions and participated in protests against the Vietnam War. I'm old enough now to write to a journalist or phone a radio talkback host and argue. After a very long introductory period, I finally feel like a citizen. Unlike Britain, this is a young nation and still has to create national rituals and traditions. I can accept that it's barbecues, not Beefeaters, Celsius not Fahrenheit, footy not soccer; that the weather forecasts will refer to the Kimberley, Bass Strait, and the Pilbara. My memory of an impeccable BBC voice with news of the Hebrides, Fair Isles and Cromarty is really just a lovely touch of nostalgia. In fifty-odd years the balance of Australia's national affections has moved from Britain to America, and now looks toward China. I shall be buried next to Alan, beneath huge eucalyptus trees in a Jewish cemetery that is also a sea of rose bushes, probably the best place for a so-called English rose, an Australian Ten Pound Pom.

CHAPTER 10
ADVANCE AUSTRALIANS

Sometime in 1954 Tessa came to occupy a ground-floor room at 16 Daleham Gardens and we became friends. It was a revelation to meet a young woman from Melbourne, travelling the world alone with a rucksack. Renée and I would come downstairs all dressed up for work, and there'd be Tessa, casually setting off for a trip to France or Italy or Spain. It was inspiring! She knew quite a number of young Australian-Jewish ex-pats in London; most of them were post-graduates taking higher degrees and living at Hillel House, the Jewish residential accommodation at London University. We came to meet them too. But before we get to the 'Dear Reader, I married him' part, I want to backtrack to Alan in Sydney, Melbourne and Europe.

My writing is very different from Alan's. Reviewers used words like 'Dickensian', 'redemption', 'wry humour', 'wonderful dialogue', and so on about Alan, whilst I am just trawling through my memory, telling stories and putting together all the pieces that went to make my life, our lives, and that of the Collins family. The highly successful television program *Who do you think you are?* is aptly named, and our grandchildren may one day ask themselves that question. Other readers too may be curious about an Australian-Jewish family with no close connections to the European nightmare.

At the end of Alan's memoir, *Alva's Boy*, the reader is left with a teenager, just emerging from a traumatic childhood. At the end of *The Boys from Bondi* (an autobiographic novel) we have a young apprentice printer about to immigrate to Israel; in the following parts of the trilogy that comprise *A Promised Land?* (*Going Home* and *Joshua*) the central character leaves for Israel, and it turns out badly. It's confusing. In *real* life, Alan left the Isabella Lazarus Children's Home at fifteen and was indeed an apprentice printer. In those times, there was no after-care for youngsters like him, and he was fending for himself from 1943 until our marriage in 1957 – fourteen years of boarding houses, or sofas in the houses of friends.

Much later, in 1989, Alan and I attended a reunion of former Isabella Lazarus residents, and he gave a very emotional speech in which he said he was grateful to the Home, which had 'saved him from the gutter'. But I was angry about the way all authorities, not just Jewish ones, could abandon youngsters once they left an institution. Karenlee Thompson, a Queensland novelist who reviewed Alan's work, in thinking, as critics do, about the themes running through his writing, considered the concept of 'home' important. She's quite right. Home is critical because Alan simply never experienced one until we made our own. Alva, his mother, died at his birth and for the next few years Alan was in institutions designed for 'fallen' women and their children. When he was four, distant relatives, Harry and Cissie

Cohen, became unofficial foster parents until Sam Collins remarried and took his son to live with an abusive stepmother. In December 1939, when he was eleven, he was sent to the Isabella Lazarus Home where he remained until January 1944. It's all in the books.

His erratic schooling gave Alan a jumble of information, but words and reading were his passion. I have one small item, a quiz from the newsletter the children at the Home put together. It's quite revealing that in the midst of all the 'boys' own' questions about ships and hot-air balloons, Alan has posed a query about ghettos. Living with the reffos had an effect on him.

Alan didn't complete the printing apprenticeship and I think bullying and anti-Semitism played some part in his decision to quit. But the history of printing, the variety and beauty of typefaces, and the mechanics of compositing always fascinated him. In his short stories, his protagonist is often a young printer. He never told us much about these years, and what he said was usually laced with wry humour. He was so young, so naïve. Sometimes the boarding houses where he lived were in reality brothels, but the girls were kind. One day he found his bed in use when he came home early from work. He could tell bittersweet yarns about the meals, with pickled onions jammed so tightly in the jar that none of the residents could ever remove one. These were years when he experimented with all sorts of 'isms': Zionism, communism, socialism, but the real motivation for joining any of the associated groups was the attractiveness of the girls. Jacob Kaiser, Alan's alter ego in *The Boys from Bondi*, epitomises the total confusion of this period in his life. He was reading voraciously and educating himself in libraries and bookshops.

Harry Cohen, his only mentor, took a hand in his future and found him a live-in caretaker's job at the Young Men's Hebrew Association, the Y, which brought a whole new dimension into Alan's life. He made friends with young Jews, some of whom were at university, others already working. Many of these early friendships were for life. The Govendir family just took him into their home and hearts and must have seemed to him like a warm feather doona; they continue the same relationship with me. His academic friends, such as the Cass family, were also very kind, and our lives have continued to cross. There's a picture of Alan at their *Pesach seder*. Their son, Moss, and his wife, Shirley, gave the party in London where Alan and I met. Alec Cass was the registrar at St Vincent's Hospital who treated Alan's father, Sampson, when he was knocked over by a bus; Moss performed our son Toby's circumcision in 1962; he and Shirley came to our golden wedding anniversary garden party in 2007. They were the only guests who had been there at the beginning with us.

The job at the Y gave Alan an opportunity to publish his work, and I have a bound volume of their newsletters for the year 1948. One group of names appears regularly in the Junior Section, as the same people rotated between the positions of secretary, treasurer and editor. Alan was most often editor and contributed short articles, many in purple prose. I particularly treasure one, written from the heart, about the pleasures of browsing in second-hand bookshops:

> Now that my long-awaited annual holidays have at last arrived, I am free to follow what to me appeals as the most enjoyable of pastimes. I refer to that inoccuous, [sic] even lackadaisical occupation of 'browsing'.

As Alan grew older, he started attending free lectures at the university and found himself between two Australian-Jewish worlds: upwardly mobile intellectuals and more everyday friends who worked in shops, markets and in the trades. There were Anglos and reffos in both groups and friction between the established community and the newcomers with their strange accents and customs. This clash of cultures provided Alan with a rich source for his writing, and because there are few, if any, Australian-Jewish authors writing from his perspective, his books are important in this country's literary history.

There must have been many real and imagined romances, for he was always searching. One of these was very intense, at least for

Alan, and lasted several years. He called her Marianna in the short story that bears her name. I think she is also the model for Laura in the novel *A Promised Land?*

Three newspaper editors.
L–R: Lou Whitefield, Alan Collins and Maurice Adams, Sydney, c1950

The experience at the Y, and probably the influence of Harry Cohen, eventually landed Alan a job as editor of the Sydney edition of the *Australian Jewish News*, and he wrote a regular column 'Up and down Pitt Street'. A photograph from that period shows three newspapermen: Lou Whitefield from the *Hebrew Standard* and Maurice Adams from *Reuters* both look the part, but Alan seems far too young for the role of editor; he was, in many ways, too inexperienced, too brash and too abrasive. It appears he crossed swords with the owner of the paper over a piece he wanted to publish on alleged corruption in regard to kosher food prices. The publisher refused to offend Sydney's community leaders and Alan quit. In any case, he wanted to be in Melbourne where Marianna lived. Young Jewish people often did, and still do, move between the two cities looking for work, romance and friendship.

Alan left Sydney when he was twenty-five and never lived there again. It was the place of his birth, the misery of his childhood and the uncertainties of his youth. It was also where his ancestors had become Australians. Later, returning there was always exciting and emotional for him. On holidays our first visit was always to Bondi Beach, where we collected a handful of the 'sacred sands', after which we'd take a ferry from Circular Quay. This routine was mandatory; it was his history.

Alan arrived in Melbourne in 1953 or 1954 with no job prospects. He found lodgings in Vautier Street, Elwood, just around the corner from where I live now. When I walk the dog to the beach, we take that route, and I think of the young man so precariously balanced between acceptance and rejection, the outsider who so much wanted not to be, the smart aleck who was really a loner. I believe the short story 'A Guest at the Table' is from life: it's about a young man moving from Sydney to Melbourne, bringing with him a letter from one Jewish lady to her friend. It's an old, established ploy intended to ease the messenger's introduction to society and romance, and bypasses a perfectly efficient postal service.

Alan, Advertising Manager for Rockmans stores, c1955

The most pressing problem was paying for his board. With nothing much else in sight, he offered his non-existent skills as a gardener at some posh Brighton homes. It was the luckiest of days when he started working in Phil Rockman's garden. When Phil returned home from his South Melbourne office, he could see his new gardener was greener than the grass. 'You obviously don't know much about plants, so what *do* you know?' he enquired. When Alan said he could 'write a bit', Phil's interest was aroused. Rockmans stores needed an advertising manager, and Alan was to report first thing in the morning. It was the start of a very happy relationship. As Alan walked to work along the beach road beside the usually calm waters of Port Phillip Bay, maybe he thought about the wild surf of his beloved Bondi.

Brothers Phil and Norman Rockman were two Polish-Jewish entrepreneurs who were keen but homely in their approach to business. They established a chain of department stores that sold modestly priced women's fashions and household textiles. Most importantly, they offered a mail-order service to customers in rural areas. They targeted towns with large, government-funded, infrastructure projects, such as Eildon Weir, where many migrant families welcomed the access to good quality inexpensively priced merchandise. Alan hugely enjoyed the hustle and bustle of the fashion showroom. Organising photographers, models and samples, creating newspaper ads and mail-order catalogues – it was an exhilarating atmosphere. He was amused by Phil and Norman, who were old-fashioned traders with no patience for modern business methods, particularly the notion of time and motion studies. They would make exasperated comments like: 'Once we had a business and no systems; now we have systems but no business!'

Another Phil, the one who much later became my sponsor, was an old friend from Sydney and he had recently married Anna from Melbourne. Through them Alan was introduced to a very pleasant young girl whom I shall call Rose. An engagement was arranged, a slightly imperfect diamond ring was purchased at a heavily discounted price from some relative, and a party was organised. Rose hoped Alan would join the family business and work in her father's store, but he was horrified at the idea. As the time for the wedding drew near, Alan realised Rose and he had nothing in common and would most likely make each other very miserable. It must have taken enormous courage to explain all this to her father, but he was an understanding man and they agreed to call the whole thing off. Alan decided he needed to get away and have a break to sort himself out.

Television was still new and families only just beginning to acquire the huge consoles that were to dominate lounge rooms for years. Alan asked Phil and Norman Rockman whether he could take a year's leave without pay, travel to London and investigate whether this medium had any potential for advertising; it was the perfect excuse. The Rockmans agreed to keep his job open for twelve months, and in March 1956 Alan sold his little car, packed a rucksack and bought a return passage on the SS *Sydney* of the Italian Flotto Lauro Line. Travel had become cheaper, and many young Australians were making similar trips; it was the right time to go and see the world.

Alan's friend Simon, from Melbourne, had met and married Beryl from England and brought her to live in a tiny cottage in Elwood. With typical kindness, she offered to make a farewell party for Alan. She set about making dainty British savouries and cakes, only to be quite overwhelmed by unexpected numbers of people arriving with cartons of beer. It was quite a party. She found one visitor, Manfred, sleeping beneath her table the next morning, a pineapple decorated with glacé cherries resting on his chest.

Manfred deserves description. He came from Dinkelsbühl, Germany, as an eighteen-year-old refugee. After a stint in the Australian army and a period working on a farm, he opened a little florist shop in Acland Street, St Kilda. It became mandatory in the Jewish community to buy flowers from Manfred for all important occasions such as weddings and bar mitzvahs. Alan used to help with the deliveries. The two became friends and shared the same brand of politics. Neither of them had *yichus* (good family background) that would appeal to Jewish mothers seeking husbands for their daughters. In a per-

L–R: Manfred, Ros and Alan, somewhere in Victoria, winter, 1957

verse way they enjoyed their outsider status, going fishing on *Yom Kippur* with ham sandwiches for their lunch, joining the local branch of the Australian Labor Party and agitating for one cause or another. They played a mean game of Scrabble, and Manfred was something of an amateur painter. He was also a great dancer, despite his bulk. Many a Jewish matron is surely flushed with a certain *frisson* on recalling what it was like to dance the tango with Manfred.

He left Melbourne in 1959 for America, where he married and raised a family. But Manfred comes into our lives again and again, and most poignantly when Alan died. He was godfather to our first son, Daniel. Alan and he corresponded for over fifty years, condemning right-wing governments across the Pacific. In the early days he tried to market Australiana in New York, and Alan arranged for Aboriginal suppliers to send him boomerangs and kangaroo-skin wallets. He also tried to sell Australian opal to button manufacturers, and we would send parcels of potch, unpolished raw stone. However, these ventures were not very successful and Manfred became instead a serious collector of Judaica. As a tribute to his adopted country, he designed a museum piece, a *hanukkiah*, the nine-branched candelabra used at the festival of *Hanukkah*, and adapted miniature figurines of the Statue of Liberty for the candleholders. I was sad to put the notice in the *Australian Jewish News* when he died in New Jersey in 2012.

The voyage on the *Sydney* was magical for Alan and the captions in his photo album carry a sense of excitement. He devoured every new experience, seeing places he'd read about as a little street kid whilst hiding in the rock caves at Ben Buckler: Raffles Hotel in Singapore, Cairo, the pyramids and then the glory of Italy. Naples was home port for the ship and as soon as Alan stepped ashore and saw all those Vespas and Lambrettas, he knew he must have a motor scooter. The only way to finance the purchase was to cash in his return ticket in the expectation that he would find a good job in London and save up enough to pay for a passage home. Inflation in Italy was high at this time, so with a large paper bag full of *lira*, he went to the Innocenti factory in Milan. There was some perfunctory instruction, and then he rode away on *La Cigale*, a name he gave later to his new Lambretta. Florence, Rome, Venice and Verona – he loved it all. After the disasters of his youth, such beauty must have given him an enormous spiritual lift. From Italy, Alan set off through the south of France, Switzerland, then up to Calais and the English Channel. Camping along the way in his tiny one-man tent with the Southern Cross flag stitched to the fabric, he met many other young travellers. He had a little stove and a billy-can, and probably wouldn't have been happier in his entire life. In the photos I see many pretty girls who rode pillion and shared his tent.

La Cigale somewhere in France, 1956

The White Cliffs, Dover, the ride to London – almost journey's end, and then it would be down to serious work in the big city. But it didn't turn out that way. Alan rode down Piccadilly in shorts and boots looking for accommodation in very exclusive gentlemen's clubs, until a kindly *concierge* advised him to head off to Bloomsbury, near the university and the British Museum, a much more suitable place for students and impoverished colonials. Hillel House was welcoming and Alan found familiar faces among the Australians. It was nearly time for us to meet.

CHAPTER 11
AFTERNOON TEA

By summer 1956, Renée and I no longer lived at Daleham Gardens but shared a better flat nearby. I was doing very well at Marks and Spencer and learning how to become a buyer. As it happened, Alan moved into our old house in Daleham Gardens, taking the room vacated by the anti-apartheid campaigner. His happy touring holiday across Europe was over. He was in London to investigate television and advertising, but first it was necessary to earn money to live on and enough to save for his ticket home. Adventurous Tessa, the girl from Australia, still lived on the ground floor at No. 16, but it was time for her to return to Melbourne. She was friendly with a number of the students at Hillel House and Alan knew many of the same people.

Alan's London career was disastrous from start to finish. His first appointment, when he was still fairly optimistic, was with a company where the principals were ex-army types who insisted on being addressed as 'Major' or 'Colonel', but called Alan 'Collins'. He was deeply offended and said he wished to be addressed as either 'Alan' or 'Mr Collins'. He was, of course, sacked. Selfridges, the world-famous department store, was next. Alan told them Phil and Norman Rockman back in Melbourne wouldn't dream of putting raincoats up on the third floor; they'd have them on racks outside on the pavement where it was raining. He was smartly shown the door and told to take his ideas back to the colonies. One after another, all the interviews came to nothing. There was no money left and he found London hard and miserable. He wrote to his old friend Phil that he was deeply depressed. He thought about working his passage home on a merchant ship and was all ready to sign on until the purser told him he looked like a 'nice boy' and could share his cabin. By Christmas 1956, Alan was working with a West Indian crew lugging mailbags at Paddington Station.

He did have happier experiences. Because the Jewish community in Australasia was small and close-knit, through youth movements, Alan knew Gerrard Friedlander, a dentist from New Zealand who was also in London. He too had a Lambretta scooter and a 'Pommie' partner, Marti. Whilst the weather was still warm they went on outings to English tourist spots: Windsor, Oxford and Southend-on-Sea. Other old and some new friends kept Alan company, and quite a few girls were ready to ride on the back of *La Cigale* or go punting on the Thames.

Summer in England, 1956.
L–R: Alan and Gerrard

Tessa was preparing to leave London, and Moss and Shirley Cass decided to make a farewell party for her. Renée and I were invited. This is where Alan and I first met; on the staircase in the old house at Daleham Gardens. He was carrying a bag of drinks for the party and wearing the corduroy jacket he'd bought in Switzerland. I wore a soft black wool jersey dress with mink fur around the sleeves, cringe-worthy now, but in those days we weren't so aware. By the time the party was over my mind was set on marrying Alan.

It was moving into autumn when Alan began to drop around to our flat, often at meal times. He was starving and weighed only about seven stone (forty-five kilos). It wasn't long before we started going out together. One day he invited me to come to Daleham Gardens for afternoon tea. He explained the invitation carefully as he'd made several social blunders, confusing Australian 'tea' (meaning an evening meal) with English 'high tea' or 'afternoon tea'. Thinking about it fifty years on fills me with heartache for this young man who really had no idea about entertaining and no family experiences to call upon. There was a little coffee table and on it Alan had placed a tray with an embroidered tray cloth. There must have been tea and cakes, perhaps his favourite, lamingtons. All I remember is the old-fashioned tray cloth.

Perhaps it was that afternoon we decided I should move back to the old house and share his room, but by winter we were living there together and could watch the first snow over the Hampstead roofs from our attic window. We huddled under the thin blankets and planned imaginary trips on *La Cigale* to exotic places. We never discussed marriage, but did talk about children, and thought four would be a good number. In those days, contraception was quite limited. I lied my way into an appropriate surgery and was provided with a hideous rubber diaphragm known colloquially as a Dutch cap.

Despite the very bad winter weather, we went on a trip to the West Country, hoping to make it as far as Cornwall. It was so cold I wore pyjamas under my pants and a sheepskin-lined leather jacket from an army disposal store. We stayed at little hotels, registering as Mr and Mrs, but were a dead give-away at the breakfast table when I had to ask Alan if he took sugar in his coffee; it *was* the 1950s. We stopped at Wells and Bath, then pushed on to Lyme Regis on

From our attic window – snow on the roofs in Hampstead, 1956

the Dorset coast. The weather was terrible and we knew we would never get further given the icy roads. Before we turned back, Alan begged to visit the local fleapit of a cinema. There, in the bleakness of an English winter, we saw sunny Australia on the tiny screen and watched Chips Rafferty in *Smiley* – twice.

Ros and La Cigale in Bath, winter, 1956

Sometime during that period my father, Solly, came to see us at Daleham Gardens. This was the first visit either of my parents had ever made since I'd left home. He came with a request for me to accompany him to a job interview with a company called Brenner Sports. The Brenner family came from the same place in Eastern Europe as my grandfather, and there had been a close relationship until they fell out over a business matter. Solly already had a good job where he was highly regarded and respected. He contributed regularly to *The Tailor and Cutter* trade journal and often gave lectures on pattern cutting. Out of shyness, he had sometimes asked me to come along as a model so that he might demonstrate how to take accurate measurements on a real person. It seemed the Brenners now wanted to make him an offer he couldn't refuse: to leave his current position and become the chief designer for their clothing empire. This job interview was an invitation to a penthouse in Mayfair to meet the directors. Solly needed a bit of moral support and my mother, Sadie, was far too timid to go with him. So he turned to me.

Solly was a remarkable man, with a natural instinct for diplomacy. He arrived at our bed-sit and never blinked at one bed, two toothbrushes and the minimal comforts we had. (I try very hard to be similarly cool about some of the domestic and personal arrangements of my children and grandchildren, but from time to time I do slip into Jewish mother mode.) At the interview I waited in an ornate sitting room whilst the Brenners tried to win Solly over. On the way home he told me he'd refused a really great offer involving more money and prestige. I was astounded at what I considered a mistake. But my father's reasons were, like the man himself, *mentshlekh* (honourable): 'They wanted to buy me,' he said. 'They wanted to control everything that makes me "me"; they wouldn't have allowed me to sing whilst I was working, and I couldn't put up with that.'

And so Solly chose contentment over prestige and Alan and I in our Hampstead attic continued to dream of impractical adventures on *La Cigale*. The cable from Rockmans in Melbourne must have come in January 1957, and all such dreams evaporated as the realities of marriage and immigration took over centre stage.

The synagogue at Beehive Lane, Gants Hill, was an uninspiring building, and I need to refer to my *ketubah*, to verify the name of the rabbi. I remember he wouldn't allow us to hold hands, and whatever he said in his address to us made no impression. Now it's the done thing for Jewish brides to go to the *mikveh* (ritual bath), and quite a few of the old European wedding traditions are fashionable again. None of this affected Alan and me, firstly because there was so little time, and secondly, I would have objected. As we left the ceremony Alan threw his unfamiliar hat into the crowd.

At the reception, I danced with Solly, never once thinking how much hurt he and Sadie would suffer without Alan, me and the grandchildren who would be born. Then Alan and I left on *La Cigale* to spend our wedding night with Marti and Gerrard, who were kind enough to lend us a mattress on the floor of their flat since we had nowhere else to go – though I can't remember why. The *Stratheden* sailed from Tilbury on 6 March 1957 and called at Las Palmas, Cape Town, Durban and Fremantle and finally arrived at Station Pier, Melbourne, on 10 April 1957. It would be almost ten years before I'd make the journey back in the other direction.

CHAPTER 12
TOBY TOYS

In the early 1960s, Box Hill in Melbourne's north-east, was a mix of old homes and new developments. The sole evidence of an Asian community was the Chinese café in Whitehorse Road, where we would queue up with saucepans and billy-cans to take away what we thought of as quite exotic food. On special occasions, such as a birthday, we would sit down for a meal at a Laminex table, and the high point of the evening would be a cake or ice cream with a 'sparkler' candle on top. Currie Street had red brick war-service homes on one side, and raw, new cream brick veneer houses like ours on the other. We were at the end of the road and close by a little park with a creek running through, a completely natural environment where the children could play safely all day. The house was very inexpensive; just as well, since all we had was Alan's modest income, which made us eligible for a government-backed mortgage at around 4%. After Alan had agreed to the purchase, Phil Rockman, the developer and his employer, was kindness itself in providing a lawyer who told us, 'I'll sit this side of the desk and act on behalf of the vendor; then we'll change places and I'll be acting on your behalf.' It was all designed to save us money, and the conveyance fee was reduced from sixty pounds to 'let's say thirty'.

So, there we were. In 1962 Alan was thirty-four, I was thirty-two, Daniel was four, Peter was three and Toby, born on 26 March, was a baby. Sugar, our first corgi, was about three. We were a standard model family, nothing particularly flash, and only just getting by. One Sunday, not long after Toby's birth, I suffered extreme stomach-ache. Alan's casual attitude to illness was a family joke ('No blood, no pain'), but he called the surgery, took the three little boys out for a walk, and left the front door open for our chain-smoking doctor. It turned out to be appendicitis. When I came home from hospital we were reminded, yet again, how very alone we were. I was unable to lift anything heavy and it was necessary to ask friends and neighbours to put Toby in and out of his cot. And yet even then I didn't consciously wish for my mother to be nearby, bringing over cooked meals and minding the kids; I have always accepted – and in a way welcomed – the fact that it was just 'Al and me and the boys.'

These were difficult and physically demanding years for me. It wasn't enjoyable being at home with three children under five. The neighbours were pleasant enough, but we didn't have a great deal in common. They baked very sugary Australian cakes and biscuits which, to the disgust of our boys, I could not. They also read magazines that didn't interest me. The liveliest family in the street were the Italians who cultivated every inch of their garden and grew the most glorious fruit and vegetables. Alan's story 'Morning at Green Hills' is obviously adapted from this place, these people and that time.

Toby Toys

Sadie and Solly sent many parcels of clothes for the boys, though it was ludicrous for them to be wearing very English-style Ladybird outfits when their mates up the street were in Australian Chesty Bond singlets. My parents also sent toys, little metal cars and trains which quickly became bent and broken. This upset everyone and I appealed to Alan to make something that wouldn't break and would withstand rough treatment in the sandpit. In the tiny workshop under the house he set to and made the prototypes of what would eventually become Toby Toys. The tip truck came first, then the fire engine, the train, the scales and the traffic lights. They were made of solid wood with a minimum dab of non-toxic paint, and each one was a winner with the kids.

When Daniel started kindergarten, Alan made a set of the toys as a gift. The director was so delighted she asked him to set up a range of samples which she would then invite other kindergarten directors to come along to inspect with a view to buying. The show was a huge success, and in a short time we started to receive orders. Suddenly we had a little business to manage and I named it Toby Toys. Alan worked very hard, hurrying home from his day job, rushing through a meal and then spending the evening in the workshop. The space was limited and a mishap was inevitable. One night he took the top off a finger and came upstairs clutching a bloody hand wrapped in a sawdust-sprinkled handkerchief. Neighbours minded the boys whilst I took him to Box Hill Hospital. A surgeon carefully stitched down a flap of skin over the place where a nail would never again grow, and for many years the finger always ached in cold weather.

After this accident, and with the prospect of Toby Toys developing, it was obvious we'd have to enlarge the space. We had to remortgage, this time at a higher rate. Our quarter-acre block sloped down at the back, so we built a two-storey extension with a big workshop below and a new living room above it.

Alan in his workshop, 1960s

It was all rather exciting. Alan loved the creative challenge, as well as the actual manufacturing. My job was to load up the little Morris car with orders to deliver, a sample range, Toby and Sugar (Peter had joined Daniel at kindergarten). We were enormously popular with pre-schools all over the north-eastern suburbs, but the very sturdiness of the toys became a problem. They never needed replacing, apart from an annual maintenance job on the wooden wheels, which did get worn down. However, toy shops became aware of our products, and soon we were supplying stores not only in Victoria, but also in South Australia. A Melbourne daily newspaper did an article on Toby Toys, and Alan was quite overwhelmed to receive recognition for his designs from the Royal Melbourne Institute of Technology.

The cubby house with Dan at the window, Toby on the roof and Peter on the rope, c1969

Alan built the boys the most magnificent cubby house, that icon of Australian childhood dreams. It was the pride of the street and all the kids came to play. The cubby could be transformed into any place the boys needed for a game, and was equipped with ladders, ropes, a balconied roof – and absolutely no safety provisions. He also made billy-carts for them, and we had a sandpit in the back garden. The modern overly protective attitude towards children wasn't in evidence in those days; a broken arm or leg was not an end-of-the-world catastrophe, merely something encased in plaster on which all the kids would write messages.

Our friends from the 'other side' of town sometimes visited on summer days. After a drive up into the Dandenong Ranges, we were a convenient stopping place for afternoon tea on their way home. With some practice, I did master the art of making scones. I think our lifestyle was different from theirs – less aspirational and more idiosyncratic. It was expected that Alan would be, do or say something offbeat, and I suppose my role was to play the straight guy.

The extension to the house had given us a new lounge-dining area above the workshop, and the old lounge room became our bedroom. Our old bedroom became the playroom, where Alan painted one wall with blackboard paint and made each boy a brightly painted desk – it was a perfect room. Two small bedrooms became one dormitory with three beds in a row.

Furnishing was always a big problem, for we couldn't afford much. Alan had attended an evening class at the local technical school to learn a little about carpentry and cabinetwork, and over the years made the furniture I still dust and polish. These days the dresser shelves display a mix of china (pieces bought over the years by us) and wedding gifts to Sadie and Solly from 1927. I delight in the sense of continuity. The pine chests are here too, and I smile each day at the drawer knobs that don't align vertically. I stood beside them at the windows of our old bedroom in Box Hill, looking down at the moonlight over our back garden with its huge liquidambar tree, wondering just what was to become of me. However, it turned out that there wasn't too much time for wondering, because life was to change quite profoundly with the arrival of a fourth boy, whom I'll call Joel.

By 1965 Daniel and Peter were at the little state school around the corner, which left just Toby at home with me. One day I received a phone call from Marion, a social worker at Jewish Welfare. I had no knowledge of this organisation and wondered how they knew about us. Much later in life I came to appreciate the amazing networking of the Jewish community, and how rare it is nowadays for someone in need to fall through the cracks, as Alan did in Sydney in the 1930s. Marion was seeking a temporary home for a fifteen-year-old boy, a student at Box Hill Boys' Technical School. We were the nearest Jewish family. Joel had been fostered by a couple in Kew who were

Joel and Toby, c1971

going on an overseas trip and Jewish Welfare wanted us to care for him for the three months they would be away. She appreciated that I'd need to discuss this with my husband and would we let her know so she might bring Joel over after school to meet us. For Alan, who knew far too much about fostering and welfare services, it was a simple decision: Of course we'd take Joel.

Marion and Joel came over after school and the boys and I were introduced. It was an unforgettable meeting. Apart from looking as dishevelled and grubby as boys of his age often do, this young man was not at a happy stage of life. Alan was at work so it was left to me to explain to the little boys that Joel would be coming to stay with us. Their responses were charming. Daniel, with all the gravity of a six-year-old, offered to show Joel where the toilet was; Peter must have offered some similar tour of the house; however, it was Toby, aged three, who instantly fell in love, and the feeling was mutual.

Joel, who is now a grandfather, was part of a Holocaust tragedy. I asked him to tell me the history in his own words:

> My father was married and lived in Vilna, Lithuania, where the Nazis murdered his entire family: his wife and two young children, his parents, two brothers, their wives and their young families. He was subsequently captured and whilst being marched through a forest, on his way to concentration camp, not caring whether he lived or died, he just walked off the path and disappeared among the trees. Eventually, he reached a Russian-controlled area,

> where he enlisted in their army. At the end of the war he met and married my mother, an Auschwitz survivor, in a Munich Displaced Persons Camp. The family moved to Melbourne when I was a baby and eventually opened a small fruit shop in Northcote, later relocating to Balwyn. My father was to know more tragedy when my mother died as a result of ill treatment she had suffered in the camps. Dad found it difficult to cope with this calamity and suffered a breakdown. I struggled to keep the household afloat, but was rescued from this situation by Jewish Welfare, who placed me in the Frances Barkman Children's Home. However, theories about the protection of children were changing, and institutions were giving way to fostering, which was how I came to the attention of social worker Marion. I joined the Collins family at a very critical time in my life, and after a great deal of trauma. My father was eventually admitted to the Montefiore Home for the Aged and I had no other family in Australia.

'Leave your mind alone!' Alan used to say. It's just as well we knew nothing at all about teenage angst and simply got on with family life. I believe we made a pretty good job of it. Straight away, Alan enlisted Joel's help in making the toys. I think he knew instinctively that doing something useful would be good for the boy, and as they worked together their affection for each other grew. The small boys had no trouble at all accepting him, and for his part Joel relaxed and grew calmer, playing games and roughhousing with the kids; perhaps he was catching up on a missed childhood.

Not long after his arrival, Joel caught a bad cold. I had given him the playroom as a bedroom, thinking he would need privacy, but when he became unwell I gave him Daniel's bed in the 'dormitory' for his convalescence. On recovering he said he would prefer to be with the boys on a permanent basis, so we ended up with four beds in a row, rather like a hospital ward. Once a week I went in to change the sheets, but the rest of the time it was a 'no-go' area. It was their domain. For Joel these were the days of *Go Set* on TV, The Easy Beats and Billy Thorpe and the Aztecs. The little boys were getting their cultural education from him rather than from Alan and me.

There came a time when he seemed to cross the line from child to young adult. Cast in the role of 'she who must be obeyed' as I was, one day when I was annoyed with them all, he just got up from the floor where they were playing, stood beside me and said, 'We're wrong. Mum's right.' Joel was growing up.

The three months were coming to a close and Alan and I wondered whether Joel would want to return to Kew. One Friday evening at the *Shabbes* table (and 'table' it was because we didn't have chairs until later; in the interim Alan had made us some wooden stools), we asked him if he wanted to go or stay. He was quite clear: he wanted to stay. And that's the only time we ever discussed the matter. We advised Marion, who agreed with the new arrangement, explaining that she would still act in a supervisory role, as Joel was a minor. Quite seamlessly, Alan and I now had the four children we'd talked about years earlier in Hampstead.

Joel's father became even more ill as dementia took over, and he was moved to the asylum in Kew. Alan took the boy there to visit, but it was very unsettling for him, and Marion advised against it. This provoked a distressing situation for us when some of the Holocaust survivor friends called at our house to berate him for not being sufficiently attentive. Alan sent them away, and we saw no more of them until 1966 when Joel's father died. I was in London with the children at the time, but Alan arranged the funeral. In the pouring rain at Springvale he, Joel and the men from the Chevra Kadisha, the Jewish Burial Society, struggled with the wet clay soil, whilst the elderly friends huddled beneath umbrellas. When it was over, Joel asked Alan what he should do next. There was a meeting of the Box Hill rugby team scheduled for that evening and he had planned on being there. Alan advised him to go. Today we would probably call it 'moving forward'.

CHAPTER 13
LEON

My lineage from Eastern Europe is unknown before the mid-1800s. Grandfather Nathan Samuel from Ignatovka, who struggled so hard to reach London in the 1890s, and Grandmother Eva Green, from Kamenets-Podolsk, had many children. My father's family line ended prematurely as great-uncles died in concentration camps. Grandparents Morris Gilbert and Regina Schlesinger from Galicia have left only my cousin Gina and me and our children.

However, the Collins family (the Van Kollem ancestors) can be traced back at least to the 1600s in Holland, and the Davis/Cortissos family, Alan's maternal line, even further, to the Inquisition in Spain in the 1400s. Apart from the convict Samuel Davis, both families emigrated from London to Sydney as free settlers in the 1830s–1840s. But although Alan's genealogy is extensive (there are Collins, Davis, and Cortissos relatives throughout the world), the immediate family in Australia is small, and I must record all the main characters. Reading *Solly's Girl* will help in understanding *Alva's Boy* (see Family Trees Nos. 6,7,8 and 9).

Alan's father, Sampson (Sam) Collins, had a sister, Brunetta, and a brother, Mark. Brunetta did not marry; Mark married a non-Jewish woman and had a son and a daughter, first cousins whom Alan knew very slightly in his childhood.

Mark Davis and Rebecca Levy had six children: Alva, Alan's mother; two other girls, Beryl and Enid; and three sons, Cyril, Alan and Ben. Beryl and Enid appear in *Alva's Boy*. Had Sam allowed it, Beryl would have adopted the motherless Alan and raised him together with her own children, Peter, Gordon and Pam, all now deceased. I still keep in touch with Gordon's widow, Joan, and their children. Enid's daughter, Sandra, and her family also are in contact. I cannot pretend to fond feelings for Enid; Alan liked her because he fantasised that his mother might have looked similar, but I am more unforgiving of the aunt who rejected him, week after week, when he came knocking on the door of her Rose Bay apartment. Alan wrote that she would give him a hard-boiled egg wrapped in a serviette and a sixpence to 'go away'. It breaks my heart to read that chapter, but a lot of things about Alan's early life upset me. Alva's brother Ben married Martha (known as Pat) and they had two children, Joan and Paul. Joan Morgan is a delightful woman and we enjoy our meetings with her and her children. She told me that Ben and Martha were married in a Methodist church but later became Christian Scientists. Although she and her brother were also first cousins to Alan, she has no childhood memories of him. It seems that this little boy might as well not have existed as part of the Davis clan. So, all in all, this doesn't add up to a large traditional Jewish family; cousins are often second or third, and there are few life-cycle events such as bar mitzvahs or weddings to record.

Leon, c1970

And so I come to Leon, Alan's half-brother and the only other direct descendant of Sam Collins, who failed in the marriage stakes so spectacularly: four wives – one divorced him, two died on him and one deserted him. Leon died in March 2011. My son Toby and his son Eli represented us at the funeral. A few weeks later, I wrote the following piece for my family so they would know as much as I could remember about 'Uncle' Leon.

23 April 2011.

Leon died on 29 March, a month ago. He was born in 1934 and would have been seventy-seven years old in July. He was the son of Sampson Collins and Lillian, the appalling stepmother of *Alva's Boy*. Leon never forgot the manner in which she deserted him when he was about six years old. He told me she called him into her bedroom – she was sitting in front of the mirror – and announced she was leaving with his younger brother and the time payment man from the furniture company (probably this child's father) and would not be taking Leon. She would not be returning. Then she gave Leon sixpence and told him to go off to school. He never saw her again. Alan, aged twelve, was already in the Isabella Lazarus Home. Leon remembered Alan used to ride his bike from the Home in Hunter's Hill to Bondi to collect and look after him until Sam returned from work. The opening chapter of *The Boys from Bondi* is obviously based on this period.

When I spoke about it with Wan, Leon's widow, she saw symmetry in the deaths of the two brothers. Both died in March (Alan on 27, Leon on 29) and passed away in the early hours of the morning. She told me Leon was both husband and father to her (there was a very big age difference) and we agreed he was a kind and loving person. Wan was particularly proud of the fact that Leon never used bad language. It is a very consoling thought that Wan and Leon had over twenty years of happiness together and have a fine boy, Simon.

Toby and Eli described the funeral for us. It was a very modestly attended ceremony; no question of a *minyan*. There were no eulogies, no service of any denomination, and Toby said he was mentally comparing this with Alan's funeral. Leon had requested cremation and asked to be dressed in a suit wearing a *kippa* and *tallit* and holding a prayer book. He also wished Wan and Simon to scatter his ashes at Bondi, over the cliffs at Ben Buckler, the same place where Alan used to hide and read. Wan told me she did all these things but also kept back some of the ashes to place in an ornamental casket. Toby said the entire occasion gave him a great deal to think about on his way home. This brings me to the question of identity and Leon's unfulfilled desire to 'belong' somewhere.

Around 1940 when Leon's mother ran off with the furniture salesman, Sam was left, once again, with a small child to care for on his own. I think he probably worked in a munitions factory, or something similar, and the situation would have been difficult. Obviously, Sam couldn't cope, so he sent Leon to a religious community of potato farmers in rural New South Wales, where he was used virtually as slave labour until in his teens. Alan visited him there and used this experience in *Alva's Boy*, and in the short story 'The Blood of the Lamb'. Leon's education was quite minimal and his literacy skills were never good. I assume that once he was of school leaving age and able to work, he returned to Sydney. Alan's life was hard enough, but Leon didn't get much of a chance either. Mothers were lacking in both cases but Alan was, as he said, rescued by the Isabella Lazarus Home.

I first met Leon in the late 1950s or early 1960s, when he was in his twenties. He lived, on and off, with Sam in various rented houses in Sydney, worked as a taxi driver and eventually owned his own cab. Leon's job took him into areas such as Kings Cross, and he was familiar with the colourful underworld life, although never a part of it. At heart, Leon was rather conservative and very moral in his outlook. Alan's attitude toward him was always somewhat ambivalent. In reflecting on their respective childhoods it's easy to see why. In *Alva's Boy* the stepmother not only favours her own children over Alan, but also actively encourages them to join in the general abuse he suffers. Leon didn't remember this, but Alan was old enough to. Leon was a sentimental character and always spoke fondly of 'my brother', but this wasn't reciprocated, and Alan had conflicting feelings about the relationship. He had enormous difficulty in relating to this half-brother who was always associated with his terrible childhood.

Even more problematic was the psychological damage Leon had suffered from his mother's abandonment. In his youth there were nervous problems manifested in erratic language patterns, and conversations were sometimes difficult. Alan had a strong Jewish identity, firstly from Harry Cohen, later from the Home, and subsequently reinforced by friends and Jewish youth movements such as *Habonim*. Leon didn't share any of this, but wanted very much to be part of the community. Alan had a toehold in Jewish society, but Leon was coming from so far back it was simply too hard. It is surprising, and indeed wonderful, that both these damaged boys turned out so well and, in quite different ways, became such honourable men.

We went to Sydney for summer holidays in the late 1950s and in the 1960s. Before we had a caravan we stayed with Sam and Leon in whatever accommodation they happened to be renting at the time. Leon would also come and visit us in Box Hill, driving his old Mercedes in one day from Sydney to Melbourne with a damp sack of Sydney rock oysters in the boot. He was an exotic figure. He had an extraordinarily long nail on his 'pinkie' finger and wore a signet ring, probably Sam's. During this time he was in what I might call his Greek phase, and in a long-running relationship with a married Greek woman. Leon did actually rather look the part, and emphasised it. We were apprehensive that one day her male relatives would find out and attack Leon in defence of her honour.

By the 1980s Leon was already in his fifties and very lonely. On holiday in Thailand he met Wan and, despite the considerable difference in their ages, they became very attached to one another. They were married in a traditional Buddhist ceremony and settled in Pattaya, where their son Simon was born. Wan's family are farmers and were very supportive of the couple. Leon sold his taxi and effectively retired.

Leon and Wan's wedding in Thailand, 1988

However, he was homesick for Australia. In the 1990s they came to Melbourne and bought a house in Frankston. But the climate was too cold for them and they moved to Queensland, where they made a very happy home. We visited them there and were pleased to see how contented they were. Simon is now a young man with a bright future.

So, what more can I record? Leon never forgot birthdays and anniversaries, a symptom perhaps of craving connections, links and roots. He always referred to Alan as 'my brother', me as his 'sister-in-law' and the boys as his 'nephews', but Alan was much more reticent. It saddens me to think of Leon's wish to be cremated with some semblance of Jewish custom. His passing brings to an end a chapter of Collins family history that is particularly painful. There is no doubt in my mind that the sons of Sampson Collins got a very raw deal. But then so did Sam himself with those four failed marriages, twice left 'holding the baby', ending his days in a dowdy room above a pub and being run over by a bus. Alan and Leon had happy marriages and leave children and grandchildren who have much promise. I think we can be very proud of them.

CHAPTER 14
GOING BACK

Jewish grandparents, the stereotypical *Buba* and *Zeyde,* glowing with pride ('my grandson, the doctor') are comedy staples. My parents, Sadie and Solly, known to the grandchildren as Nana and Poppa, were far too modest and unassuming to be anything like that, but I know they were missing out. They had seen Daniel and Peter just once – in 1960, when the former was eighteen months old and his brother just a baby. They had never met Toby, who by 1966 was four years old. Mark, the son of my cousin Gina, was not yet born. These boys were the only descendants of Morris and Regina. On the other hand, in the Samuel family, Sadie's brothers and sisters had been quite productive, and the nephews 'down under' were hardly missed.

Jewish guilt kicked in, and no amount of blue airmail letters, grainy photographs or incoherent audio tapes could compensate for being able to show and tell what Alan and I had made. It had been nine years since I'd left London and it was time to visit the family.

In 1966 Alan was an advertising man in a grey suit during the day and a craftsman making Toby Toys in the evenings and on weekends. He was yet to publish any of his books, and since this became his way of telling me his history, I was unable fully to understand how he felt about my proposed trip to Britain. In retrospect I can appreciate his dread at the idea of my taking the children to London. It was barely a decade since he had been transformed from a very lost young man into a married father of three with a job, a mortgage, a dog, a not-bad-looking wife and, as a bonus, a foster son for whom he could ensure a better life than the one he had experienced in 1930s Sydney. Now, I was going away. I might not return. He could lose all of us and end up like his father Sam; adrift in some lonely place with no one to give a damn.

With Joel there to keep Alan company I thought our absence for five months would be easier for him to bear. We couldn't possibly raise the cost of air fares but even ship travel was expensive, and all we had to sell was our business, Toby Toys. I can never decide if we made a mistake, but I know Alan and I missed the toys, and were forever to wonder if we could have built up a good company. Toby Toys was so quirky, it would have suited us and made Alan very happy. In due course he became the proprietor of his own little advertising agency and loved it, but Toby Toys were his creations, his pride. The boys used to speak mockingly of other Jewish children who ended up IDB (In Daddy's Business), but really they would have loved to have done the same. When Collins Advertising agency closed after twenty successful years, they joked that a drawing board and a box of pencils was all their father was leaving them. Quite true – the ideas were all in his head.

That day at Port Melbourne Alan must have been in a bad state of anxiety seeing his hard-won family preparing to leave him. He gave the cabin steward, Lambros, some money to 'look after' us. Then he stole a turquoise china Chandris Line ashtray and went back home to start counting the days. In our fifty-one years of marriage he never managed to cope with my absence, even if it was only for a short period. It was the old pattern: the fear of desertion, of being abandoned. My return was always greeted with absolute ecstasy. In later years whenever I was travelling overseas for work, Alan was unable to deal with solitary meals, and our friends knew that he needed a dinner invitation for every day I was away.

Our voyage on the RHMS *Ellinis* was dreadful. Peter, aged seven, eyed off the railings and stairwells and immediately saw possibilities for climbing and exploring, and Toby would have followed him. I envisioned them falling overboard so booked them all into children's activity groups for the duration of the trip. It was not really fair to Daniel, who at eight was reliable and utterly trustworthy. We were all very seasick and the Greek chefs had no idea of appropriate food for Australian children; there was not a jar of Vegemite, peanut butter or 'hundreds and thousands' on board. Lambros brought us chips and urged us to go on deck and breathe fresh air.

Wellington was cold; Panama and Curaçao were interesting. My parents came to Southampton to meet us with fresh bananas which the boys had specifically requested. There are few photographs of the three months we spent living at Ashurst Drive with Solly and Sadie. The boys were enrolled at my old primary school for one term, and the grandparents crammed as many of the lost years as they were able into the short time we had. For my part, I wandered around reconnecting with London, but it wasn't the city I'd left in 1957. This was 'swinging London' with Carnaby Street, the Rolling Stones, Twiggy, the Beatles, Mary Quant, Pink Floyd, *The Avengers* and mini-skirts. Oh no, it certainly wasn't the same city! It was very conflicting; I'd hardly had enough time to acclimatise to Australia and now felt alien in my home town. My cousins, naturally, had all been growing up too, and there were people who were now apparently connected to me by marriage, as well as children who'd been born since I had left. Our lives had all diverged and I don't think there was much interest in me, my strange husband and my peculiar life in the 'colonies'. I'd made my bed and was welcome to lie in it – they had their own concerns. Fifty years on, it's different again and cousins have become friends instead of just relatives.

I pleaded to come back to Melbourne by air, but it couldn't be done. We had to face another journey by ship, this time on the SS *Australis* travelling via Piraeus, home port for the Chandris Line. The cost of tours to Athens was prohibitive and I decided to take the boys on public transport to see the Acropolis. It was a hot day and difficult to encourage the children to climb the uphill road to the famous site. In those days visitors were permitted to walk through the Parthenon to marvel at its beauty, and for me it was a high point of the journey. Toby, however, was not impressed and asked why he'd been brought to see something that was 'all broken' and why there was no adjoining ice-cream shop.

Fremantle hadn't changed much since I'd first sighted it in 1957. This was long before Alan Bond, the America's Cup and the restoration of the town. In Melbourne it was the greatest of welcomes. Alan and I walked around the warehouses in Port Melbourne, stopping frequently to hug and kiss. The little boys were 'home' but had I confirmed my place in the world? I don't think so – not quite yet.

We had been away from September to December and it was summertime in Australia. Alan couldn't wait for us all to have a *real* holiday, and we set off for Wilson's Promontory where he had hired an on-site caravan. Looking at the photographs, I can remember his happiness. He had his family intact; we were in one of the most beautiful places in Australia; we'd graduated to our first station wagon; he was camping and using all the gadgets he'd put together to make a little home from home. He was in heaven! It was instinctively smart of him to have arranged this holiday, a confirmation of where we all belonged. Pictures reveal so much: a thirty-six-year-old mother, three little boys, sand, surf boards, fishing rods, rock pools, thongs – quintessentially Australian and a world away from London. It was a good time. The year turned and Toby would be starting school. Life would be different.

Wilson's Promontory, 1967. L–R: Toby, Peter, Dan, Ros

Wilson's Promontory, 1967.
L–R: Peter, Dan, Toby

Wilson's Promontory, 1967.
Alan

CHAPTER 15
GREEN DOOR

'Green Door' was a popular song that sold millions back in the 1950s. I recently checked it out on the Internet and, with the tune firmly back in my head, spent time at the keyboard bopping along to its catchy beat. The lyrics are all about exclusion, but my green door led me to Jim Docherty, inspector in the Technical Division of the Victorian Education Department, and for me it was the way in to a whole new life.

After the magic of the holiday at Wilson's Promontory, it was time to get ready for the new school year. The boys complained at having to switch from thongs to black lace-ups, whilst Alan told them, only half jokingly, to be grateful for even having shoes because he had spent his childhood with just sandshoes. Toby was enrolled at the local primary school with his brothers: Dan now in Grade 4 and Peter in Grade 3. My friend Freda asked me to consider what work I would do now that Toby was off my hands. I was surprised, because I'd rather looked forward to some free time. But it was the beginning of the feminist movement in Australia, and any woman worth her salt looked for a job. I don't think many of the neighbouring families had working wives; they mostly kept house, baked cakes and made hot dinners with 'meat and three veg'. What they did was still work – there was just no salary. I decided I had better make an effort. All that came to mind was to approach the Victorian Education Department and offer my services.

It was a novelty to dress up for the city and catch the 'red rattler' train from Box Hill to Flinders Street: No little boys to watch out for and no small hands to hold crossing the roads. The Education

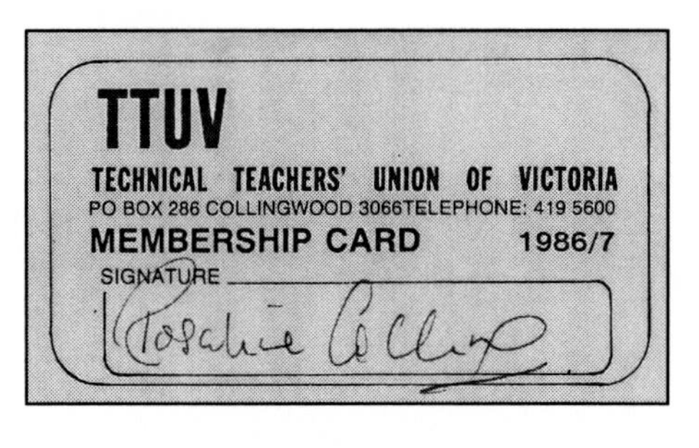

TTUV Membership Card

Department was a busy place and I did not have an appointment. However, an officious person in the High School Division found a moment to tell me that without a university degree I was not acceptable to them. If I cared to go through the green door to the Tech Division I would find they were not nearly so fussy. That was how I found Jim, who indirectly changed life for all of us.

He must have been in his forties, sitting alone eating a sandwich at his desk; maybe the Tech Division, always the poor relation, didn't run to a lunch room. Malcolm Fraser, soon to be Federal Minister for Education and Science, would have funding to establish Commonwealth libraries in secondary schools and Jim's job was to find staff. He asked me if I'd be willing to run a new library at an inner-suburban school. I said I felt unqualified to run anything, as my training in librarianship was so limited. Then he enquired about my family, and here the story really takes off – a modern fairy tale for the working woman. Jim's view went something like this: I should gradually restart my career as a librarian; given the ages of our children, I should only work part time during the middle part of the day – say from morning recess to afternoon recess – so I could be on hand to care for the boys before and after school; in view of my family responsibilities, I needed a job within five miles of home in order to cut down on travelling time; and, most importantly, he would help me acquire teaching qualifications.

He said he'd be in touch. Within a week I received a letter instructing me to report to Box Hill Girls' Technical School in Whitehorse Road. I find it a charming thought that two old warhorses, Prime Ministers Malcolm Fraser and Gough Whitlam, from opposite sides of the political divide, should have been so significant in my life. Whilst I did join a protest march against Fraser for something or other, and on one memorable occasion heard Whitlam speak when he was campaigning in Box Hill, I never knew either of these icons of Australian public life. Nevertheless, I feel immensely grateful to Malcolm and his libraries and to Gough, who abolished tertiary fees and gave me the chance for a university education.

I worked at the Whitehorse campus from 1967 to 1984, when I moved to Templestowe Technical School for a further three years – altogether twenty years in the Victorian Education Department Technical Division, whose teachers I grew to admire and respect. One job for such a long time is unusual today, and even back in the 1970s and 1980s friends asked why I wasn't bored. It was simple: though I stayed put, the institution kept changing around me. I didn't need to go elsewhere for stimulation. The girls' school I joined in 1967 became co-ed, then transformed into WhitehorseTechnical College, and finally became a TAFE (Technical and Further Education) College. Following the ground-breaking Kangan Report in 1974, secondary and TAFE components of the curriculum were gradually separating. It was very heady stuff, exciting and optimistic, with a sense of opportunity, inclusion and, above all, the notion that education was something anyone – even with modest means – might participate in at any time in life. Administrators were not blatantly counting bums on seats, overseas student enrolments or figuring out how high they could raise fees; teachers had a sense of vocation and were respected. These changes meant that staff like me who had been employed as secondary teachers had to consider where we best fitted in. I applied for promotion at Templestowe Technical School, where I stayed until 1987, at which time my life and work all became very Jewish.

However, back in 1967 the ‘hat and white gloves’ syndrome that still lingered meant I turned up at Box Hill Girls’ Tech fully kitted out for an interview. I didn’t realise that I’d already been posted there and that the principal, Miss Williams, had to take me whether she liked me or not. She merely pointed me in the direction of a portable classroom where the library was housed, and off I went to become a junior assistant teacher-librarian (unqualified) to Estelle, a charming woman who helped, encouraged and, ultimately, left me the library.

There were a number of traditional teachers, the kind students remember as fierce disciplinarians. I saw a different side to them when these ‘dragons’ came in early to make breakfast for children from poor homes, and sourced second-hand uniforms for those families who couldn’t afford new ones. No one ever knew about their kindnesses. But this old ‘tech’ ethos was fading away. New buildings were going up, including a new library. Estelle told me she felt her career was over, and I was upset when she retired. A bright young graduate teacher-librarian came for a while, but eventually I took over. These were still pre-computer times and our catalogue was on cards. It was a full-time job for someone to continually update it, and I’m probably not the only librarian who can still remember the distinctive sound of those little wooden drawers slamming shut. But the profession was changing. The college introduced a course to train library technicians, who served as support staff for librarians, who were now required to have a degree. The teacher-librarian was expected to be all things to all people: an expert in children’s literature, literacy teaching, reference work and business management. My staff hovered rather gently between a maternal attitude towards the little secondary-school girls and a desire to mix it with the ‘big boys’ – the up-and-coming TAFE colleges that were providing a new level of learning mid-way between the schools and universities.

Henry Bolte was premier of Victoria from 1955 to 1972. He managed to antagonise Victorian teachers, which resulted in a series of strikes. I was a staunch member of the Technical Teachers’ Association of Victoria (later the Technical Teachers’ Union) and offered our house for union meetings. Alan ironically labelled a cocoa tin 'Contributions to the Cause', and I remember proudly marching in protest at Bolte's rudeness to our profession. Conditions for women teachers were particularly discriminatory in regard to superannuation. I was relegated to something called the Married Women's Superannuation Fund, which was hardly worth the paper the legislation was written on. The union successfully lobbied for a fairer system, and a kindly maths teacher ensured I signed up for the real deal. This was to prove very important when I retired from the service.

Meanwhile, back at Whitehorse we had a new principal, Bill, who supported me in my search for qualifications. I owe him a great deal. During the 1960s and early 1970s I'd managed to complete the basic examinations of the Australian Library Association (ALA now ALIA). It had been a messy business, with correspondence courses and classes at the State Library, but I had a piece of paper and was able to move on to the next stage: certification as a technical school teacher at the Technical Teachers' College. However, rules were changing in both the Education Department and the ALA. If I wished to have any sort of career I'd need a degree. I applied for study leave and was accepted at Monash University. Solly's decision all those years ago to let me stay longer at school made all the difference. Jim in the Tech Division wrote supportive letters, as did Bill. The leave was very limited and meant I would have to attend lectures in the late afternoons and put in a lot of time at home. Like so many mature-age students at that period, I revelled in the sheer pleasure of learning.

I made an initial mistake enrolling for a first-year subject called Philosophy of Religion. We started off examining the question of god. The lecturer was most convincing when he proved there was *no* god, but the following week he was equally persuasive in proving there *was* a god. I couldn't cope with this and abandoned philosophy forever. On the other hand, English Literature was a joy, although not without its tricky moments. There was a certain disconnect between older students like me and those straight out of secondary school. Our tutor asked us to read a short poem by William Carlos Williams, four or five lines without punctuation about a red wheelbarrow in the rain. In our discussion of the work I said I wasn't very impressed, and there was an outcry from the young students who had found it full of deep meaning. The following week it was a passage from Jane Austen, which I loved and the kids derided as old-fashioned and irrelevant. Ah, the generation gap!

The other course I took was Classical Studies, a subject not even offered now, probably because it doesn't lead directly to recognisable employment. Departments have been closed down as universities reassess their priorities, and I am saddened by it all, just as I regret the disappearance of the Tech Division. What price the literature, art and sculpture of the ancient world? Stephen Sondheim's *A Funny Thing Happened on the Way to the Forum* enjoys rave notices, but we used to read the comedies Plautus wrote, and not many students have that opportunity any more.

Our English Drama class went to a midnight performance of the Yiddish classic *The Dybbuk*, interpreted by Peter Brook's multicultural theatre group that was touring Australia. It was an evening of terror as we sat on makeshift bare boards in an old theatre space somewhere in Fitzroy and allowed ourselves to be frightened out of our wits by this famous Hassidic drama of spiritual possession. Those years were magical times, and though I have forgotten much, I know that attending university in person altered me in a way online learning could never do. Of course I did well; I was brimming with enthusiasm. Although it was difficult to care for the family, concentrate on my job and then rush off to classes, I persisted. There were no computers and I typed everything on our small portable Olympia, using foolscap sheets, blue carbon paper and Tipp-ex white-out. I didn't want to be interrupted to cook or clean.

CHAPTER 16
THE AGE OF AQUARIUS

The 1960s and 1970s were eventful. The boys were all at school. Joel completed his secondary education and became an apprentice. Alan opened Collins Advertising and we embarked on our caravan phase. Australia signed up for the Vietnam War, Joel went to Nui Dat and Vung Tao. *Hair* was the musical of the day and it was the Age of Aquarius.

Our little circle of local friends grew. Most were overseas-born: from Russia, Poland, Palestine, Germany and England. A few started their Australian lives in Carlton, the first port of call for many Jewish immigrants. We made a very multicultural group, although that term was hardly used back then. Most of us were not strongly religious believers, but it was the Jewish heritage that brought us all together.

Educating the boys was a dilemma. We were never able to reconcile our strong support for state schools with the ethos of the private system (which in any case was far beyond our budget) and the desirability of a Jewish education. However, Mount Scopus College was committed to providing education to all, and if a family was able to prove financial hardship, then fees could be adjusted. Box Hill North was very light indeed on *yidishkayt* and we were also concerned about the limited facilities at the local state school. So Alan and I took our tax returns to the college and by 1968 the boys were duly equipped with blue school caps, blue and white *kippot* and pre-loved grey blazers with the motto 'Be strong and of good courage' in Hebrew on the pocket. But we were always ambivalent as to whether we'd made the right decision. We were certainly not the standard Scopus family and the boys never completely fitted in with the norms set by the college.

Boys ready for Mount Scopus College, c1968; L–R: Peter, Toby, Dan

It was a push-pull situation, with our values at home often in conflict with whatever the school was trying to instil. We lived in the wrong suburb, and it was difficult for the boys to maintain friendships with kids who lived in Caulfield. We were probably guilty of reverse snobbery, proud that we went on holidays in a caravan instead of swanning around at Surfers Paradise, Queensland, which was *the* place to go. We weren't very ambitious and Alan was happiest in his workshop. We were politically left wing and flexible about religion. Our close friends were all Jewish and many were involved in communal organisations – welfare, education, cultural, Israel-related. Alan and I were not big on committees, apart from our almost mandatory membership of the North Eastern Jewish War Memorial Centre, once it was established in 1972. Alan always volunteered to empty the Blue Boxes in which families collected money to buy trees in Israel.

Daniel had always been such an obedient student that when in Year 10 he told us he'd really had enough and please may he leave, the school personnel had difficulty identifying him. We went to collect his final documents and the principal of the day commented to his form teacher – within our hearing – that Daniel 'had no elbows'. Our boy was not pushy enough. Forget the elbows; Dan has heart and soul, far more important.

Peter, with the mind of a magpie, just switched off from things of no interest to him and only engaged with the computer course, at that time merely an optional lunch-time program. When he reached the end of Year 11, Alan and I were called to an interview at which the same principal told Peter he was 'a failure' and would not be permitted to go further. He could repeat the year or we could remove him. So we sent Peter to a state school, where they tailored a Year 12 course for him, including subjects in which he's retained a life-long interest. He went on to do a degree in computer science and enjoys a very satisfying career in information technology. Peter wins awards for innovation, is widely read and knowledgeable about all manner of things – hardly a failure.

Toby, the comic of the family, never took Scopus seriously and 'wagged' more religious classes than I ever knew about. His encounter with the careers counsellor is classic. Apparently she visited his class and asked for 'hands up' from those who intended to pursue medicine, law, dentistry or – last ditch call – pharmacy. There were always two hands not raised, as Toby wanted to be a pastry chef and his friend also wanted to be an apprentice – not exactly the Scopus image. He later did very well at William Angliss College, winning prizes for his patisserie and has become most enterprising. He and his wife, an artisan baker, have run their own business, and now he's a project manager in the food industry. He's always retained his sense of fun and never succumbed to the jargon and claptrap of the corporate world – a lot like Alan.

I think Scopus at that time simply wasn't the right place for the boys; maybe it's different now. I once took Dan with me on an excursion to an experimental school I had to visit for my teachers' college course. It was the complete antithesis of Scopus, with students free to do their own thing, whether this was learning Cantonese or crochet. Dan was so enamoured he refused to go to school the following day. I often wonder whether he and his brothers would have matured any more happily if we'd allowed them to fly, and not be so restricted by the ethos of Jewish schools of those times.

We also put a lot of thought into Joel's future. He'd shown interest in art and metalwork, and a vocational counsellor suggested a career in either jewellery manufacturing or as a dental technician. After a false start with jewellery, Joel was apprenticed to David, a Czech refugee dentist who had become a technician because his European training did not qualify him to practice in Australia. David and his wife had no children and treated Joel as a son. He received excellent mentoring and completed a model apprenticeship with high marks.

Alan and Joel had quite different approaches to life, and for Dan, Peter and Toby this was an opportunity to compare two male role models. One example: Our boys used public transport from Scopus to Box Hill North, which meant standing at the bus stop along with kids from the adjacent state school. They told us stories about anti-Semitic name-calling and asked for advice. Alan and I said, 'Ignore it,' but Joel said, 'You show me who the bullies are and I'll come and deal with them for you.' He did just that, and was an instant hero. Joel presented them with an alternative view on so many things, particularly sport and music.

Things were going well for Joel, but it was also the time of the Vietnam War and the birthday ballot. Between 1964 and December 1972, when the Whitlam Government suspended the scheme, 804,286 twenty-year-olds registered for national service; 63,735 national servicemen served in the army and 15,381 served in Vietnam. Joel's birthday came up in this lottery and he was required to register. Alan and I had marched behind MP Jim Cairns protesting against the war. We didn't want Joel to register and were more than willing to protect him from arrest, not only because we opposed the war but also because we felt he'd had enough tragedy in his life. However, Joel was optimistic and reported to the army. He knew he'd be exempt whilst still an apprentice and believed the war would be over by the time he was qualified. But in 1971, when he'd completed his studies, the authorities called him again.

Joel went off to Puckapunyal for basic training. A year later, prior to his being sent up to Kunungra to learn about jungle warfare, we all went to see *Hair* (what else?). After that he was sent to Nui Dat and Vung Tao with the Dental Corps. I remember a letter in which he told us he was working in an orphanage, 'a rifle in one hand and cotton wool in the other' and 'really had no idea what the hell it was all about'. I didn't ask him too much. I was just grateful he never seemed to have been affected by the toxic Agent Orange, although I don't know how certain one can be.

I find it a bit embarrassing to recall how pervasive the atmosphere of the 1970s was. The 'peaceniks' sang about 'harmony and understanding', how 'love will steer the stars' and, of all things, 'mystic crystal revelation'. We visited the artists' colony at Montsalvat and bought pottery badges to wear on leather thongs around our necks, but we didn't really get involved – cautiously trendy I guess. Aquarius! Aquarius! It wasn't us; caravans and the DIY challenges of camping were much more our style.

Our trip to Wilson's Prom at the end of 1966 had been so successful that Alan determined we should have a caravan of our own. It was

At Montsalvat, 1971. L–R: Peter, Solly, Toby, Dan, Ros

Wayfarer caravan, c1968

Watching dinner cook. L–R: Dan, Toby, Peter

York caravan, 1970s.

an economical way of giving the family a holiday, and there were all those wonderful gadgets he could devise to make camping fun. Year after year the five of us set off. Whilst their classmates at Mount Scopus were experiencing Jewish youth camps and a broader social life, Alan kept our boys close. Our first van, a Wayfarer, was a little oval-shaped wooden affair, and to my English family it probably looked like shanty-town accommodation. We soon graduated to a much more modern York caravan with a huge canvas annexe for the boys. The Hume Highway, or the beautiful coastal road to Sydney became familiar routes, and we travelled in the cool of the night, the boys sleeping in the back of the station wagon. Particular places became regular staging posts to which we assigned nicknames, such as 'Porridge Hill' in Orbost, where we would make breakfast at dawn by the roadside. We'd have a break at Merimbula, with a side trip to Bega where once we watched the country race meet, and of course backed Radiant Dan. Kiama was good for a bit of surfing, and then the climb up Bulli Pass and journey's end – Sydney. But caravanning is really a blokes' game. I shopped, cooked, washed and cleaned, and in between accompanied them all to the beach or wherever else they were going.

On holiday in the 1970s.
L–R: Peter, Alan, Dan and Toby

Although I was thoroughly involved with running the college library and university studies, Alan was not happy working in advertising agencies. He found the atmosphere often artificial or ridiculous. Only occasionally did he find it satisfying, such as when he designed a poster in the late 1960s for SKF ball-bearings. The concept was that the bearings had an exceptionally long life; 'SKF Ball-bearings keep on keeping on' was the slogan. Alan built a billy-cart and put the company logo on the side of the tray. Peter and Toby were instructed to ride it up and down our street whilst a photographer made a series of pictures and the bearings could be seen 'keeping on' with the good work, long after their commercial use was over. The poster was a huge success and was distributed around the world in various languages. Maybe it encouraged Alan to start thinking seriously about running his own agency.

Poster for the SKF campaign

Periodically we had studio portraits taken of the five of us to send to Sadie and Solly. In the 1969 series Dan looks a little strange: there had been an accident, an explosion and his eyebrows and hair had been badly singed. Joel had placed an aerosol can in the workshop rubbish box and Dan, trying to be helpful, had taken the box to the incinerator at the bottom of the backyard. The blast rocked the house and he was lucky to survive with only minor burns.

L–R: Alan, Peter, Ros, Dan; Toby is in front, 1969

I look at the Mount Scopus school photographs from 1970. Daniel's Grade 6 includes some fearsomely clever girls who, as expected by their ambitious families, became doctors and lawyers; Peter's Grade 5 shows a future Israeli diplomat; and in Toby's Grade 3, there's the cheeky little face of Jeff, his life-long good mate and rock-solid Blues footy club supporter. Most revealing are the knees of their teachers – mini-skirts all the way.

CHAPTER 17
GOLDEN SUMMERS

The Mornington Peninsula has attracted holiday-makers for many years. Rosebud, a small beach not far from Melbourne, was the spot for our first holiday that was not in Sydney, and where our earliest boat – a little red plastic inflatable with paddles – had been launched on the calm bay water at Safety Beach. In 1971 we started to explore the other peninsula, the Belarine, and found the area around Barwon Heads and Ocean Grove relatively unspoiled. We discovered a caravan park at Collendina, just behind sand dunes, leading to a beautiful stretch of surf. We bought a fibreglass dinghy and later a proper sailing boat. During the 1970s Daniel, Peter and Toby celebrated their bar mitzvahs and Sadie and Solly made their second and third visits to Australia.

L–R: Toby and Peter in plastic boat, Rosebud, c1965

Caravanning had advantages. We were allowed to park the van on our site and leave it there during the off season, so from January until Easter we could take long weekends or school term breaks and have all the benefits of the continuing summer. Sometimes unpredictable weather drove the boys inside the canvas annexe to escape rain. Courtesy of Joel, who rode his motorbike down, we had endless Creedence Clearwater Revival songs ('Good golly Miss Molly', 'I heard it through the grapevine', 'Proud Mary', etc) and of course

Toby ('Murph the surf'), Collendina, c1971

there were card games and Monopoly. There was no shortage of entertainment. We could still take a long trip at Christmas to Sydney and then prolong our beach time afterwards. It was idyllic for Alan and the boys and enjoyable for me too, but a holiday where the domestic chores still had to be done had its limitations, even though everyone helped. Sometimes, if I had assignments to prepare, I'd take my textbooks with me. There were often visitors. These were fun times for the family and perhaps it's not strange that I can so easily picture 'Murph the surf', as we called Toby, hauling an outsized board over the sand dunes, but have no clear recollection of any of the three bar mitzvahs that took place between 1971 and 1975.

Bar mitzvahs are usually celebrated in as lavish a style as the family can afford. Often it seems the arrangements go way over the top, but we were in no position to make a big splash. Solly and Sadie were enormously excited at the prospect of their eldest grandson reaching this important milestone and determined to be present. It was particularly significant for Solly, as he was going to share the ceremony with Daniel, completing his own bar mitzvah that had been interrupted by the bombing of London in World War I. Dan was the eldest great-grandson of Morris and Regina, and this gave added importance to the occasion. As the boys were all Mount

Scopus students, their preparation was the responsibility of the Hebrew Studies teachers. The North Eastern Jewish War Memorial Centre had not completed building the synagogue in 1971, so the ceremony took place in a house the congregation rented in Balwyn. We had a small catered dinner at home for our family and closest friends and that's about all I can remember. Dan tells me he has no memories of the occasion. When I asked Peter and Toby, they too couldn't recall much about their bar mitzvahs, which rather makes me wonder about the effect of all those earnest speeches. The *shul* was built in time for Peter's bar mitzvah the following year, but it was too expensive for Solly and Sadie to make the trip again so soon. This was a pity, for Peter was the only one of the three who could chant the Hebrew accurately and harmoniously, and there was universal acclaim for his performance. Once again, we had a small dinner at Currie Street. Toby's bar mitzvah was in March 1975, and Solly and Sadie made their third trip to Australia for the occasion. Toby is tone deaf and was a very reluctant Hebrew student, so Solly spent painful hours trying to help him learn his *parsha*. Once more, it was a home-based little dinner, and Sadie worked hard in the kitchen preparing kosher chickens for roasting.

It surprises me that we have no formal photographs of the family from any of these three celebrations, just casual pictures taken on our own camera, and certainly none of them posed in anticipation of silver frames. A bar mitzvah is such an important life-cycle event it seems odd this family has so few tangible or other memories. We could never have afforded a trip to Israel and a ceremony at the *Kotel* (Western Wall); nor did we hire a reception hall and deck it out in our team's footy colours (as a nod to the fact that we are also Australian); there were no pictures in the *Australian Jewish News* showing Daniel, Peter or Toby donating cheques to charities in honour of the occasion. There's no shame in being of modest means, but it's certainly strange that we appear to have treated these ceremonies in such a cavalier fashion. I don't know whether Alan had strong spiritual or religious thoughts about his sons symbolically passing from childhood and taking on responsibilities as Jewish adults; I don't believe I did. Jewish guilt is a terrible burden. I can find no photographs at all of Daniel's bar mitzvah (I suspect there are old-fashioned slides somewhere) but I feel duty bound to include some small record of at least two of our boys on their special day. I wonder if I should feel embarrassed that in our albums the bar mitzvah pictures of Peter and Toby are completely over-shadowed by photographs of boats, beaches and caravans.

Peter's bar mitzvah, 1972

Toby and Ros at Toby's bar mitzvah, 1975

I've often remarked that Alan always wanted to keep his boys close. It wasn't comparable to the attitudes of Holocaust survivors, who had every excuse for over-protectiveness of their children, but I can see it was related to his neglected childhood. Our geographical location, far from the centres of Melbourne Jewish life, gave the boys few opportunities to build a network of Jewish friends and left them, to some extent, in a social limbo. They were limited to the kids in our immediate neighbourhood, the children of our friends, and a handful of Scopus mates. I was sorry when Alan refused to drive Toby across town to attend *Habonim* meetings; he would have been a perfect candidate for the type of informal education Jewish youth groups such as *Habo* are designed to provide.

Joel returned from Vietnam very unsettled. As he'd got to know Solly and Sadie when they visited in 1971 (and for them he was another grandson), he decided to go to London and further his studies as a dental technician by working in first-class West End laboratories. Early in 1972 he set off. This was a milestone – our eldest had left home. He stayed with my parents and through them met other members of my family, made new friends and, like Alan before him, found an English girl to marry. So it was that Sadie and Solly stood under the *chuppa* (wedding canopy) with him in the same *shul* where Alan and I had been married, as my relatives celebrated yet another example of British-Australian *détente*. Joel and his wife made their home nearby in Ilford.

In Melbourne there were no relatives either to support us – or to interfere. Our friends were wonderful substitutes, and indeed we were always very blessed with the little group we knew for most of our lives. I look at photographs of many of them and their children visiting us down at Collendina, lunching in our caravan or striding over the sand dunes. I can smile at a picture of Olga, Tess and me, all in our forties looking happy and relaxed as we stroll along the beach.

L–R: Olga, Tess and Ros at Collendina, 1970s

Sadie and Solly too were able to experience camping when they came in 1975 for Toby's bar mitzvah. The caravan park had some rudimentary accommodation in little huts, and we booked one so we could all share the holiday. It was a revelation for my parents, who had never seen anything like it before. The photographs show that we gave them a good time and many adventures with which Solly could astound his timid sisters back in North London. There are charming pictures of my tiny mother watching in amazement as a shearer throws a fleece onto a board, and of Solly, tickled pink to see Toby cooking chops over a barbecue outside a caravan. Did they envy the freedom their grandsons were enjoying? Would they have been happier with conventional kids in the constipated community of Jewish London? Did they hesitate just a little about emigrating to join us? Were they critical of me for leaving England in the first place? By this time, Joel had brought his family back to live in Melbourne. I can imagine that when Sadie and Solly returned to London after this particular visit they might have been saddened that not even their foster grandson was going to be there.

In the 1970s we experienced the first loss in the family: Sugar, our corgi. We were heartbroken. The little puppy with the crooked front leg that joined us when Peter was born had been a devoted pet and a constant companion for the boys. She only ever made one major error: when we bought Peter a rabbit she worried it to death. On the whole she was a model dog. Soon after, on a farm near Collendina we saw a notice advertising puppies for sale, and that's how we acquired Taffy, our second corgi. Unlike Sugar, who shared bloodlines with the royal pets, he had no pedigree papers and was rather rough – not very classy. Somehow he didn't make a good impression.

Sugar and the boys lunching in the cubby house, c1970

In 1972 the Australian Labor Party under Gough Whitlam swept to power with the slogan 'It's time' (which indeed it was). It was the beginning of one of the country's most reformist governments, introducing universal health care and free university education, eliminating conscription and implementing legal aid programs. These were just a few of the refreshing changes to society. It was exciting, heady stuff, and when Whitlam gave a speech in Box Hill, Alan took us all along to participate in what he saw as important historical changes. Gough shook hands with Toby, who afterwards considered it treasonable to wash.

It was also a time of career changes within the family. By 1968 Alan had had enough of the mainstream advertising world with its dubious values and realised that his happiness lay in running his own business. He established a small advertising agency that eventually boasted an office in a studio he built in our backyard, next to his workshop and the laundry. This meant I could safely increase my time fraction at work because he'd be there to take care of the boys when they came home from school. I was no longer part time, I was on my way. Alan took his extra domestic responsibilities very seriously. He enrolled in a cookery class at Whitehorse Technical College and made great efforts in the kitchen. We owned a few recipe books with contributions from Jewish community groups. If Alan found himself in difficulties, he'd phone the person whose name was attached to the recipe and demand an explanation: 'How much exactly is a pinch of salt?', 'How soft is a soft dough?' He also did the shopping and the washing, so there was no reason in the world for me to join any of the flourishing feminist groups of the time.

It's hard to imagine what our lives might have been like had Alan remained an employee. Cynical about the way advertising agencies operated and contemptuous of their morality, he was determinedly individualistic in a world where the buzz words were 'team spirit' and ideas were 'run up the flagpole' to see if they would 'fly'. It was a big gamble, but I had become a permanent teacher, was working

Collins Advertising 'head office' in the garden at Currie Street

Alan at work at Collins Advertising, 1981

full time and able to bring home a slightly better wage. If all else failed, there was that income to fall back on. Collins Advertising opened in December 1968 and it became incorporated as Alros Pty. Ltd. in July 1976.

Alan initially set up shop in the lounge room. He went to the auctions run by the railways department and purchased a large wooden desk with a green leather top. Armed with a jar of sharpened pencils and an old typewriter, he waited for the clients he hoped would ring. At this time we were making one of our many attempts to quit smoking, and the program we were following recommended drinking a lot of water. On that first day of business the boys and I left him sitting apprehensively at the big desk with nothing specific to do except finish the contents of a large jug.

It was surprising, particularly to our accountant, that with only the most rudimentary business skills, Alan managed to run his own agency successfully, never once owing money or carrying bad debts. He was not the kind of man to make presentations in a board room; rather, he concentrated on modest companies that made fairly ordinary products such as pumps or window frames. He liked to stand with the dust-coated owner on the shop floor and talk the same language. All his clients were nearby in the eastern suburbs, and Alan had a friendly, engaging manner that appealed to these small manufacturers. (Toby has a very similar personality.) 'Head office' soon moved out of the lounge room into the little weatherboard studio in our back garden. Frank-next-door fixed up telephone connections, and Alan invested in a photocopier/fax machine and a second-hand swivel office chair. Very corporate! It wasn't far to pick up the boys from Mount Scopus if he could, which meant we never needed to feel guilty about raising 'latch key' children, as someone was always home. We were amused by the fact that Alan was able to work in his office wearing shorts and thongs in summer, or jeans and a windcheater in the winter, and no client ever knew. Whilst discussing advertising schedules on the phone, he might be keeping an eye on a load of washing or watching the clock in case it was time to light the oven for a casserole.

One of the strangest clients to visit Alan's studio was a respectable-looking woman from suburban Ringwood who ran a brothel from her home. A small ad for Collins Advertising in a local paper had caught her eye and she phoned for an appointment, without mentioning the nature of her business. She had a handbag bulging with notes and was prepared to pay cash, but Alan chickened out.

In the 1970s Alan did some promotional work for the painter Max Middleton, who lived in the Dandenongs. The artist offered him a dozen dilapidated Federation-era wooden chairs lying unwanted in the barn; their backs are ornamented with carved kangaroos, emus and Australian flora. Alan brought them home and restored eight of them to match the refectory-style dining-room table he had made. We didn't need the little stools any more. By this time he had made most of our furniture: a dresser, a desk for me, chests of drawers, coffee tables and numerous bookcases. We never did have a dressing table for the bedroom, somewhere to place brush, comb and ornamental hand mirror, just like Sadie did in Ilford.

The 1975-76 Christmas holidays were spent in Sydney; we then went on to Gosford where Leon was living. Alan had long wanted a boat, and at Sussex Inlet he bought a little fibreglass sailboat that we brought home strapped to the roof rack of the station wagon. We took it down to Collendina where the boys could sail in the calm water of the Barwon River. It was a very basic craft, and after a few years Alan decided to graduate to a Miracle-class dinghy with a wooden hull and a jib, so they could venture out onto Port Phillip Bay.

Peter sailing at Sussex Inlet, 1976

By the late 1970s the boys were all well into their teens. Dan wanted to do an apprenticeship in horticulture, and we thought we had found an ideal position for him. It fell through and we always speculated that it might have been an anti-Semitic response to his application, which listed a Jewish day school education. He chose to work at Telecom instead. Peter completed his secondary education at a state school and was accepted at the Royal Melbourne Institute of Technology to study for a degree in computer science. Toby had been working after school at a Swiss patisserie near home and was offered an apprenticeship. At fifteen he quit Mount Scopus and when we signed the papers, John Wanner, the owner, told us he would make Toby not only a good pastry chef, but also a 'good man.'

Our caravan holidays were coming to an end and our last family holiday would be a big overseas trip in 1977. Much later, in 1985 actually, when the National Gallery of Victoria mounted an exhibition 'Golden summers: Heidelberg and beyond' I thought about 1976 when our own golden summers ended.

CHAPTER 18
'WHAT'S IN A NAME?'

A new grandson has been born and though I was about to revisit the 1980s, I feel I need to consider him and how the family will change. I speculate about our relationship: How long are we likely to have to know each other? Will he remember me like my other grandsons? His name is Eli Alva. It was Shakespeare's Juliet who asked, 'What's in a name?' Her question neatly segues in my mind to the vexed question of 'What is a Jew?' But the even more difficult question is 'How much does this matter to me?' It seems this chapter is going to be about Jewish identity, that ubiquitous term covering everything from herring to *Halakha*.

L–R: Daniel, Toby, Peter, c1963. Photograph by Bob Goodbody

L–R: Joshua, Isaac, Eli, 2003. Photograph by Nigel Clements

Our sons and grandsons.
Clockwise from top left: Peter, Toby, Daniel, Eli, Eli Alva,
Isaac, Jashua. Photographs by Nigel Clements and Peter Collins

Much as the biblical characters of Ruth, Deborah or Esther are admired, and despite the best efforts of contemporary feminists, Judaism often comes across to me as very much a male preserve. I suspect there are those who would like to see it remain that way, with what appears to be lip-service paid to the ladies upstairs. In considering my family's Jewish identity, my focus tends to be on the men. Of course there were women, like my mysterious aunts Rachel and Dinah, who married out, and dear Aunt Dora, who was Orthodox and wore a *sheytl*. There were also my father's sisters, who regressed into Eastern European superstition, pinning little pieces of paper with Hebrew quotations around my cot to ward off the evil eye. In my own generation there are cousins, men and women, who are observant, and others who are anything but. So why do I think my ancestors (and Alan's) are at all important? 'Respec' (the 't' always got lost) was a word often used when I was a child. Our ancestors are entitled to respect. Most of them were not part of any recorded history, though Alan's family includes some colourful characters. I sense a debt. I believe we owe them recognition, and in time-honoured tradition I'll take a look at the past and try to tease out who I think we are 'Jewishly', and how we got here.

Morris Gilbert, my paternal grandfather, died before my parents married. Solly wrote that he was an observant Jew, probably traditional rather than extreme in his views. Although the family was Orthodox in its religious observance, the environment in Lemberg (Lvov, Lviv) where he spent his childhood and youth was progressive and intellectually stimulating. The army posted him to Bielitz-Biala, 400 kilometres to the west where the family of my grandmother Regina lived. I imagine that some members of my family were influenced by the enlightened opinions of the *Haskalah* movement, and no one seems to have succumbed to superstition and religious fundamentalism.

My other grandfather, Nathan Samuel (Chwall), the soldier's son, was himself in the Russian army, scarcely a place for Jewish religious practices. When I knew him he was already in his later years and more observant. Somehow I can't picture him being a *frum* Jew; more likely a rough-and-ready soldier type; after all, he crossed the Pale of Settlement and risked his life by going AWOL. So, two men from nineteenth-century Ukraine, both firmly Jewish in their allegiance, but neither of them blind to the possibilities of the secular world. Their granddaughter sits here in Melbourne, Australia, and wonders what she has inherited from them.

Alan's family were members of the Anglo-Jewish lower middle-class Sydney community. His books do not suggest an observant background; there is no famed *Lubavitcher Rebbe* or scholar from Vilna in the lineage. Arriving from London as they did in the 1830s, the Collins and Davis families were 'dinky-di' Aussies by the time the reffos came. Their religious practices no doubt reflected English traditions, complete with top hats. It's not surprising there was friction between the two groups – just as Alan has portrayed it in his writing.

When I first met Alan's father, Sampson Collins, in the 1950s I found it hard to see him as a Jew as he sat eating prawns and drinking Toohey's ale on the beach at Rushcutters' Bay. He'd worked as a commercial traveller, first in men's costume jewellery and then in hotel ware, and used to keep a carpet snake on the back seat of his car to protect his samples. We only met a few times, but Alan nailed him in *Alva's Boy*, and in the very disturbing poem 'Ballad of Sid'.

Andy Collins (a cousin in the UK, many times removed) has made an exhaustive study of the Collins lineage (see Family Trees Nos. 6 and 7). The descendants of Aron Coenraad van Kolum-Sofer, born 1665 at Muiden, in Holland, include his granddaughter Feijle (Sophia), who married Samuel Marks in London in 1793. Priscilla

Marks, daughter of Sophia and Samuel, married a Woolfe Collins in 1813. Their son, Mark Collins, married Lydia Colliss in 1843. Three of their children – William (Woolf), Samuel Mark (Sidney) and Annie – came to Australia. In 1879 William married Kate (Catherine) Isaacs. Born in quick succession were Frances Brunetta in 1880, Mark in 1881 and Sampson (my father-in-law) in 1882. The Kollum (or van Kolum) family probably originally came from Spain, like the Davis family, Alan's maternal line. They were printers in Amsterdam, hence the additional Hebrew name *Sofer* (scribe), which connects rather neatly with Alan's work and mine. In London the Collins family became hatters in Covent Garden. We would tease Alan about having apoplexy when the kids were naughty, but Lewis Carroll was quite right: hatters really did become 'mad' (apoplectic) and used to die of fits from the chemicals used in the trade.

When I married Alan it was a union of northern and southern hemispheres. It was also a connection between eastern and western Jews, Alan's Sephardi ancestors from Spain via Holland, and my Ashkenazi heritage out of Eastern Europe and Russia. England had provided a refuge for both groups, but only Alan's forebears had pushed on to the antipodes, and in at least one instance the journey had not been a voluntary one. Alan's family tree includes a young convict, Samuel Davis, who was transported for his participation in a robbery. He was seventeen and came from the slums of South London (think of Dickens). Samuel was a member of a gang of thieves who stole the ritual silver from Duke's Place Synagogue. He arrived in Sydney on the *Georgiana* in 1831 to begin his seven-year sentence. After a period in the Hyde Park Barracks, Sydney, he was assigned to a grain merchant, received his ticket of leave in 1836 and a certificate of freedom in 1838. Samuel settled in Goulburn, a country town in New South Wales, and founded the Australian Stores there. However, he never quite reformed and was nicknamed 'Thieving Davis'; in 1844 he was charged with having false weights in his possession. Our young convict is something of a prize: notwithstanding his thievery, he represents a 'fair dinkum' link to Australia's past and confirms a Jewish presence from the beginning of colonisation.

Many years later in the 1990s, Alan and I, as members of a newly established Masorti congregation, which had very little in the way of ritual silver, decided to make a small gesture of expiation for Samuel's misdeeds. We donated a set of *rimonim*, the crowns and silver bells that decorate the wooden rollers of the *Torah* scrolls.

My father was modest about his relationship with his God; he just quietly went off to *shul*, came home, kissed Sadie and me, made *Kiddush* (sanctification of the Sabbath) and that was pretty much it. Every day he'd recite morning prayers, but it was so discreetly done I was hardly aware of it until he visited us in Australia. When I was a child, there were things we couldn't do on *Shabbes* and *Yom Tov*, such as go to the pictures (involving money) or use scissors (involving work). There were no large family dinners; it was Sadie, Solly and me, just we three. The one big occasion was *Pesach*, when Solly conducted the *seder* for the whole of his extended family, but it was at his sisters' house, not ours. After I left England he put his heart into acting in a grandfatherly role to my cousin Gina's son, Mark, a surrogate for his own grandchildren in far away Australia.

I look at Solly's *siddur*, something I haven't done since I packed it up to bring home after he died. It's *The Authorised Daily Prayer Book of the United Hebrew Congregations of the British Empire*, with a new translation by the Rev. S Singer, the ninth edition published in 1912. Solly probably had it since he was bar mitzvah age. The binding is much worn and my father has neatly repaired it with a replacement spine taken from Letts Motorists' Diary. The tiny stitches must have tested

Solly's siddur

Sadie and Solly's challah plate

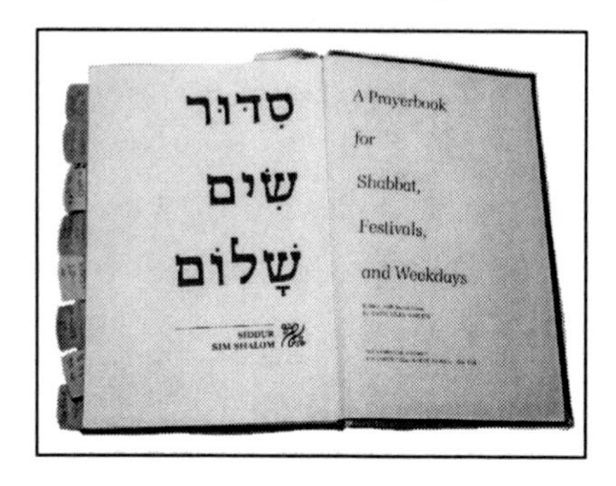

Alan's siddur

his thimble as he sewed through two layers of black leather. Many of the pages have been mended with brown sticky tape, and wine from the *Kiddush* cup has been spilt over them from the Sabbath evening service.

For so many years he and Sadie would 'make *Shabbes*' all by themselves on a Friday night. The *challah* would be on an orange-rimmed lustre plate they must have received as a wedding gift in 1927. The edges are scored from his bread knife. We treat it more gently now, and the slices are cut on a board before they reach 'Poppa's plate'. In the frontispiece of his book are the Hebrew *yortsayt* dates – the anniversaries of their deaths – for his parents, Morris and Regina, and tucked in between the pages is a small booklet *A Guide for the Living* outlining the customs for mourners. Solly's *siddur* affects me deeply. As his daughter, I can place my hand on the worn leather and know that I'm sharing a moment with him. As a librarian, I can treasure a book that was used every day for over eighty years, not an impersonal computer tablet that's here today and gone tomorrow. I wonder what will happen to the book when I die.

And then there's Alan's *siddur*, a very different publication. *A*

Prayerbook for Shabbat, Festivals, and Weekdays edited by Rabbi Jules Harlow and published in 1985 by the Rabbinical Assembly, New York. It is commonly referred to as *Siddur Sim Shalom* and has a Library of Congress Catalogue Card Number and an ISBN – a long way from Solly's Singer edition. I could digress here into a compare-and-contrast exercise between the two prayer books, wandering off into unfamiliar liturgical territory, but I think not. What is more important to me is the way in which Alan's book, like Solly's, tells so much about its owner. *Siddur Sim Shalom* is festooned with those small coloured stick-on marker flags used on business documents. Alan has written on each flag instructions regarding the service: which page comes next, the name of the prayer and where to find the important parts. There will not be another *siddur* in the world so decorated and so reflective of its owner's searching spirit. On the rare occasions I turn up at Kehilat Nitzan and take the book from its blue velvet bag, there are knowing smiles from the old-timers who remember Alan. I wonder what I should do with *Siddur Sim Shalom*.

Part of every liturgy is the matter of sin. In our family it came up when Daniel, who must have been in grade 4 at the state school, brought home a little card with a picture of a man wearing a crown of thorns. The visiting religious instruction teacher had explained to the children that they were all 'full of sin' and Dan wanted to know what that meant. (I'm reminded of Alan's short story 'The Blood of the Lamb'.) This wasn't the first time we'd had to front up to our very own 'Jewish question.' Toby had asked why the Box Hill shopping centre was decked out with Christmas decorations, but had nothing relating to *Hanukkah*.

There was also the matter of anti-Semitism. On a caravan holiday we made a pit-stop at Wagga Wagga, or maybe Gundegai. Because it was very hot, Alan took Dan and Peter to the municipal pool for a swim whilst Toby and I stayed in the van. They returned quite soon, very shaken up, because for no apparent reason the local kids had shouted anti-Semitic remarks at quiet, grey-eyed, blond Daniel. Alan was horrified to think that all those little boys in identical Speedos were not exactly equal in an Australian country town swimming pool. We talked about it with Martin and Freda, who had always been our mentors on Jewish matters. They had no doubts that we should investigate a Jewish education for the boys, and in those days the only option was Mount Scopus College.

With the boys at a Jewish school, we had a lot more religion in our lives. Martin and Freda were the souls of kindness and we went to them for *seder* for many years. Martin also built a *sukkah* every *Sukkot* and invited us to join them for a meal in the little booth to celebrate the festival. Because we didn't have much extended family in Australia, and probably because my parents didn't make big occasions out of the various festivals, Alan and I tended not to overdo the observances; nonetheless, it's perhaps significant that he built the boys a cubby house, but never made a *sukkah*. He had encountered a hotchpotch of religious experiences with Harry and Cissie Cohen, at the children's home, and in *Habonim*. His affinity with our Jewish heritage was always much stronger than mine, and probably part of his need to belong. On the other hand, I have never had any doubt that I *do* belong and therefore (perversely?) don't need to do anything about it. As a Cohen he was entitled to the honour of being the first to read from the *Torah* at services. This gave him enormous pleasure, although with typical self-deprecation, he refused to perform the traditional priestly blessings over the congregation. Nevertheless, the idea of being someone of value, after a childhood in which he was known only as 'poor Alva's boy', must have given him much joy.

By 1965 the Jewish community in Doncaster was large enough for a viable congregation. Services were held in a house in Balwyn, whilst funds were being raised to build a permanent synagogue. Alan played his part as a committee member, organising newsletters and advertising. The North Eastern Jewish War Memorial Centre

(NEJWMC) opened in 1972, and somewhere there's an honour board with our names on it. I volunteered to help establish a small library, but my involvement was really minimal. I've always been impressed at the seamless way committees are formed and meetings held at various homes in Melbourne, and for that matter in most diaspora Jewish communities. I didn't grow up in a family where these things happened, as Sadie and Solly never hosted gatherings of any groups. I felt out of my depth. When it was my turn to have the *shul* committee meeting at our house, I panicked, cooking up an elaborate supper when all that was expected was the standard tea, coffee and biscuits. The tasks at which our family did rather better involved doing or making things, like notice boards and posters. We were good at *shlepping* and Alan had excellent ideas for publicity, but neither of us had the entrepreneurial spirit necessary to be successful movers and shakers in the community. Even later, when Alan became so involved with Kehilat Nitzan, it was still 'words and wood': he wrote newsletters and made wooden stands for the *Sifrei Torah*, but had no interest in the business side of things. As for me, everything changed when I took over a Jewish library, had passionate causes to fight for and became a lot more *chutzpadik* (audacious).

Jewish learning has always been an important part of Jewish identity. Alan decided to take the plunge and enrol for a Bachelor of Arts course in Jewish Studies. Dan, at the time in Israel on a kibbutz, was somewhere up on the Golan Heights when we told him of his father's decision. He immediately asked to be enrolled too, as he had become very homesick However, Alan dropped out of his degree studies quite spectacularly, though Dan did finish his course. The late Rabbi Lubofsky was teaching the Jewish history class and Alan was not doing well, primarily because he was unable to compose an academic essay with footnotes and references. His attention was drawn to whatever was unusual or off-beat – in other words, a good story. When the rabbi tried to deal as briefly as possible with Sabbatai Zvi, the false messiah, Alan was so intrigued he quit his studies in order to write a radio play about this bizarre character. His desire for Jewish education remained unfulfilled until much later when he discovered the Melton Jewish Adult Education program, in which he was a devoted student for many years.

Shul faded right out of the picture when we left Box Hill. Our boys had been long gone from home and none of us had an allegiance to any congregation until Kehilat Nitzan was established. Alan was not comfortable at Liberal services, finding them too formal, and he was utterly opposed to the separation of men and women in Orthodox synagogues. As for me, I didn't want to go anywhere at all. In 1999 we attended an inaugural meeting at the home of John and Beverly Rosenberg and met Barry Starr, a Masorti rabbi from Boston on sabbatical in Australia. 'The Masorti Movement is committed to a pluralistic, egalitarian, and democratic vision of Zionism. Masorti represents a 'third' way. Not secular Judaism. Not ultra-Orthodoxy. But a Jewish life that integrates secular beliefs. *Halakha* with inclusion and egalitarianism. Tradition that recognises the realities of today's world.' (Source: https://masorti.org/index.php)

Barry offered to help us establish a congregation and Alan and I became founding members. It was exactly the sort of inclusive community Alan had always wanted. (This is probably the right moment for me to change *Shabbes* (Yiddish) to *Shabbat* (Hebrew) as it marks a shift in our family's religious leanings, and also more accurately reflects the environment in which I was soon to work.) From the beginning, Alan attended every *Shabbat* service, something he'd never done before. When Ehud Bandel became our first full-time rabbi in 2006, the friendship that developed between them surprised me. Intellectually and philosophically they didn't speak the same language, but something about the humanity of the Israeli former paratrooper impressed Alan.

Alan's poem 'My Sabbath' relates to his love of sailing and his views about religious fundamentalism:

> On Saturday I wear my shirt with nautical flags on it.
> In my street other Jews are wearing their signals too.
> Their signals speak to me in sable semaphore
> Of how my Sabbath shuns synagogue for sea.

His ideal agenda was Friday night dinner with the family, a Kehilat Nitzan synagogue service on Saturday morning, and then sailing on 'Sat'd'y arvo'. This mixed bag of Jewish observance and Australian recreational customs has surely given our children the message he and I would have always wanted for them. I would wave him goodbye with 'Have a nice pray!', 'Have a nice sail!' I was content to garden or read. I don't think this dilutes Jewish identity one bit and is more like a tribute to life. *L'chaim!*

And what of me? I had found the NEJWMC pretty irrelevant. I was far too busy enjoying university and running a TAFE college library. There was no discernible void in my spiritual life. My very own Jewish question only surfaced once I took over Makor Jewish Community Library. It was about heritage and continuity and had little to do with religious observance. As for Kehilat Nitzan, I cannot but think of it as Alan's place, rather than mine; when I attend a service now, I often weep. The congregation is exceptionally warm and welcoming, but for me there is still much pain. In the early 1990s I was officially given a bat mitzvah in order that I might be granted an *aliyah* and invited to stand at the *bima*. *'Bina bat Issachar Leib v'Sarah Malka'* ('Bina, daughter of Issachar Leib and Sarah Malka') are the names by which I am called to the *Torah.* Whilst I don't know how Issachar Leib translates as Solomon Leon, for my father, I can almost see how the very Victorian Sadie Millicent emerges from Sarah Malka. As for Bina (which means understanding) I'm mystified as to how it relates to Rosaline. My bat mitzvah, symbolic though it was, did not move my family to make me a party or any kind of celebration. I think this indicates our generally casual attitude towards religious observances.

With such an extraordinarily complex father heading off to *shul*, and a mother who waved him goodbye with the instruction to 'have a nice pray', it wouldn't be surprising that our children noted anomalies. Alan would come home from the service, grab a sandwich and be all ready for sailing on Port Phillip, a complete metamorphosis. The boys chose non-involvement in religious matters and would only take part if it was absolutely unavoidable. It might have been easier for them with a more heavy-duty father, setting out his views in an unambiguous manner, but Alan couldn't do that; and I wouldn't. Inevitably, this led us into deep water. He found it hard not to have his children with him in *shul*. The absence of his three grandsons was also very distressing, and it's sad to remember him taking other small children – any small children – up to the *bima* with him when he was called to read from the *Torah*. The period of the High Holy Days was particularly painful, for Alan's mother died at his birth on *Yom Kippur* 1928. Kehilat Nitzan appreciated him greatly, and on one occasion he was honoured as *Chatan Torah* (symbolic bridegroom of the *Torah* at the festival of *Simchat Torah*). The congregation escorted him into the hall holding a *tallit* above his head like a wedding canopy, and I was the only member of the family there to watch. It was similarly hard when, after an enormous struggle with Hebrew, he fronted up to reprise his bar mitzvah by reading his *parsha*. Ehud spent hours trying to help him learn, and in the end he and Alan sang together, one very quietly and the other very loudly. I don't think all the boys were there on that occasion either.

I am writing these sentences on *Yom Kippur*, a day on which I should be fasting and praying for forgiveness. But I don't fast, and repentance is something I deal with as soon as I realise I have made a mistake. I never feel the need to confront all my sins on this one day of the year. I can't make promises to any deity. It would be hypocritical for me to go to *shul*. And yet I belong in Kehilat Nitzan too. The rabbi does not wag a finger in admonition at people like me; he understands there are many ways to be a Jew. I always attend on Alan's *yortsayt*, the anniversary of his death. Last year was particularly memorable – and egalitarian – as five members of the family were all called up to the *bima* together (men, women and the new little grandson) to hear Alan honoured by the congregation of which he was so fond. I usually go to *shul* for *Rosh Hashanah* – a hopeful service, I think. My imagination runs riot listening to the sound of the ram's horn; I picture ancient tribes communicating across the desert, a call for people to come and listen. On one occasion I enjoyed watching a young woman in a purple skirt and pink boots blow the *shofar* magnificently (she's a professional musician). Her two small daughters joined her at the *bima*, played with the fringes of her *tallit* and were allowed to have a go too; it may have shocked the very pious but it made great sense to me.

I seem to be damning myself out of hand. I can't pretend to religious feelings I've never had. To my observant friends it may be disgraceful that I'm not in *shul* reciting the mourner's *Kaddish*, yet each morning I greet and honour my dead – Sadie, Solly and Alan – in English. One *Yom Kippur* when I was about fourteen I ate some chocolate and waited for the sky to fall. As a young man, Alan too shook his fist at the deity and went fishing with Manfred on this solemn day. But Alan knew more about the ground rules, probably because of the time he'd spent in the Isabella Lazarus Children's Home. Paradoxically I, who had come from an Orthodox Jewish family, had made a point of *not* knowing. *Cheder* classes soon faded from my memory and, unlike Alan, I was never a member of any Jewish youth organisation. And yet Jewish identity is not a problem for me. I think of it as a genetic inheritance, rather like blue eyes or red hair and not something to agonise over. A phrase from the *Rosh*

Hashanah service comes to mind:

> We believe that He abides in mystery.
> Therefore we need not solve life's every problem.

And I don't try. Spiritual is not me. I think of Judaism as one long continuous question and answer debate, never to be resolved and fascinating for those of us who love a good argument. Words. Solly was a compulsive writer: poems, short stories, humorous retellings of Bible tales, memoirs. Alan was a journalist, a copywriter, a published author. 'Solly's girl' is a librarian. *Jews and words* (Yale University Press, 2012) 'a speculative, raw, and occasionally playful attempt' on the 'relationship of Jews with words' is written by Amos Oz and Fania Oz-Salzberger, 'secular Jewish Israelis'. Their book resonates with me, as does their thesis that words 'compose the chain connecting Abraham with the Jews of every subsequent generation'.

I attended the *brit* of my newest grandson. Eli Alva is the son of Peter and Rebecca, and not to be confused with the grown-up Eli Aaron, the second son of Toby and Rhonda. The circumcision was performed by a black-garbed doctor of Chabad persuasion, who scared the living daylights out of me. Thankfully Adam, our twenty-first century rabbi from Kehilat Nitzan, was there to recite the prayers and guide us with compassion. Remembering the *brit* leads me to reflect on my relationship with all my grandsons and my role as matriarch of this small family. The glue that holds us together is *Shabbat* dinner every Friday night. It is only a perfunctory nod in a religious direction, yet each of us knows this is an important punctuation point in the week, a moment when we reconnect. It's always a proper dinner, never take-away fish and chips or pizza. I battle to be heard over the conversation as I bless the candles and watch small Eli's eyes light up. Traditionally, the mother of the family covers her hair with a lace scarf and hides her eyes behind her hands, but I don't do that because I want to see my family and lace scarves are not me. This ritual meal has been a fixture throughout my married life. Now I take over Alan's chair, and his presiding photograph is ceremoniously placed on the mantelpiece by Isaac. We don't have silver candlesticks of our own, and the Art Deco ones Sadie and Solly used are so worn from my mother's polishing I've put them away in favour of small bronze enamel Israeli ones. Rhonda, Toby's wife, is usually at work, but she will have sent the *challah* she baked, and Eli and Isaac will cut and salt it. Toby, the total rationalist, will bless the wine; Daniel will recite the *brakha* in respectable Hebrew, with interpolations from Peter in a mockery of Yiddish accents. Then we can get down to the serious business of the weekend – football matches.

We celebrate *Pesach* and *Hanukkah* because the drama is attractive, but more importantly, there are opportunities to enlarge on themes such as freedom and heritage. I discuss these and other festivals with the children in terms that seem relevant to me, and if I'm going to a Kehilat Nitzan service always invite any of the family to accompany me. The High Holy Days are a difficult period. I'm particularly sensitive to those conversations where housewives talk about the number of guests they will entertain and sympathise with families who decide to leave town for the duration. 'Flexible family festivals' is how I would describe my current approach. It seems unrealistic to insist that we observe these occasions on precisely the correct day if most of us are at work, not at worship. I nominate the nearest suitable night and try to impart a little knowledge.

How will Jewish identity survive in this little family? The history of Australian Jews prior to the influx of Holocaust refugees is certainly still under-represented – a fact that always upset Alan. The common argument is that the Jewish community was dying on its feet prior to the coming of the reffos. So what of the rather Anglicised Collins family? What about all those boys, descended in part from Alan, the 'Boy from Bondi' and me, his Ten Pound Pom? I fear fundamentalism of all flavours and am not attracted by Eastern European *shtetl* culture or Brooklyn messiahs. The Anglo Jewish life of the last century has also passed its use-by date and I wonder how Jewish life here will evolve.

There's nothing like births, deaths and marriages to make one reflect. Births: the new grandson and I need to build a relationship. Deaths: old friends are passing on and our visits to Alan's grave in the Jewish Memorial Rose Garden at Springvale last longer as we leave sea-shell markers (not pebbles, which seem inappropriate for a sailor), not only for him, but also on the graves of others we have known. Toby, who always drives us there, probably has no idea how deeply I appreciate his thoughtfulness. *Zachor!* – remember. I wonder whether this tradition will continue. Who will go and who will remind them. Marriages: as I look at the darkening garden I can see the huge painted white horseshoe (from a draught horse, at least), that Solly nailed above the door of their tiny kitchen in 1927 as a symbol of good luck, and I like to think an expression of his love for Sadie. I brought it here when they died and Alan fixed it to a limb of our Japanese maple where I see it each day as I write.

When Alan and I bought our house in Elwood, there was a similar gesture from Solly. We have a little black Bakelite box, covered on the outside with adhesive labels on which he has written loving messages to the family so far away: G-d bless, *mazel* [luck], *gezunt* [good health], *glick* [happiness]'. Inside the box are the following symbols: a piece of coal (we should be warm); a penny coin (we should always have enough); a Sabbath candle (to remind us of our duty); a twist of grease-proof paper containing salt, another with a piece of bread and a Tate and Lyle packet of sugar – all the essentials. At the time we probably thought it was a lovely sentimental gesture; now it seems unbelievably significant: outside the window the white horseshoe; inside, sitting on my desk next to the computer, the small box of wishes. Between the two symbols thousands of miles, thousands of thoughts, threads of our history.

Marriages, partnerships, relationships, unions and friendships; Jewish, half-Jewish, and non-Jewish – the possibilities are endless. Whatever my children and grandchildren do in life, I wish them to know love such as this. The Jewish identity issue has occupied the minds of many, and debate will no doubt continue. I probably think of myself as a humanist secular Jew with a strong connection to my heritage. But 'heritage' is such a loaded word and the mind wanders off: heritage furniture, heritage clothes, heritage tomatoes and roses. So what exactly is a Jewish heritage – particularly in the contemporary Diaspora? Identity – something like the blue card I carried during the war? Who is a Jew?

The white horseshoe from Sadie and Solly's kitchen door

The Bakelite box of good wishes

It's probably easier for young Jews who have those strong guidelines that come with an unambiguous upbringing, but Alan and I never gave such clear signals to our children, perhaps because we ourselves were quite confused. On one occasion in my teens I deliberately tried to provoke Solly with stupid queries about the meaning of life. He was an amazingly tolerant man and just told me, mildly and correctly, to look in *Ecclesiastes*: 'there is a time for everything, for all things under the sun'. So what of our grandsons? I hope they will all turn out to be curious, questioning and sensitive people. I hope they will not ignore such a rich heritage. Last year Joshua and Eli went to Israel on the Birthright Program and returned with much to think about. I don't believe they will ever appreciate the herrings, but I'll be glad if they think of the history.

CHAPTER 19
FIVE TICKETS TO DACHAU

By 1977 I had reached the ten-year mark with the Victorian Education Department and was eligible for long-service leave. Collins Advertising was rolling along nicely; Toby was an apprentice *pâtissier*, Peter a student and Dan working for Telecom. Alan and I probably realised this would be our last holiday all together and were determined to make it memorable. The budget was tight but the plans were ambitious: We would go to Israel first, then on to see Sadie and Solly in London; after that, the big adventure – Eurail-ing around Europe.

Martin and Freda, ever reliable as mentors on matters Jewish, gave us a list of not-to-be-missed places in Israel, and in December 1977 we flew via Rome to Tel Aviv. We didn't have the right clothing for a cold, wet Jerusalem winter, so there was no alternative but to buy Israeli army dubons, those padded weather-proof jackets, and boots. Jerusalem, and everything we saw in Israel, made a great impression on all of us. I've made several visits since then and always find it thrilling to be in a country where no one can fling an anti-Semitic remark at me; where there are Jewish crims, prostitutes and cops; where at the Yad Vashem memorial I can see for myself how Hitler tried to destroy me and my people; and where at the Israel Museum in Jerusalem, or at *Beit Hatfutsot*, the Museum of the Jewish People in Tel Aviv, I can see how many of his predecessors also had a go at us and failed. I hope we remain indestructible. Everything came together for me in the Knesset, where I admired Marc Chagall's tapestries. The artist has interwoven motifs from his childhood home in Vitebsk, Hebrew myths and legends and Holocaust themes: our history hangs here in this Israeli parliament building and I marvelled, not merely at the beauty of the work, but also at the fact that this place exists as its home.

From Israel we went to London to see Sadie and Solly, and then it was the adventure of Europe. Alan and I considered it an obligation to take the boys to Dachau. This involved travelling from Venice to Salzburg, from where we could take a train to Munich, the nearest city to the site of the concentration camp. After laid-back Italy, it unnerved us to be in Austria with its Nazi-era associations, and we felt deeply suspicious about the unpleasant owner of the small hotel where we stayed. He was just about the right age … We were not happy there. When it was time for us to take the day trip to Munich, we both felt disturbed. Even signs, something innocuous like *Diese Plattform für Deutschland* (This platform for Germany), in our minds had overtones of *Arbeit macht frei* (Work makes you free – the wording on the gates of Auschwitz). At Munich station there were no directions for Dachau. We had to go to a special ticket office, where a clerk produced a badly duplicated sheet from under the counter. We were to take the train and then a local bus to the entrance of the camp. When it was Alan's turn to buy the bus tickets he asked in a firm voice for 'Five tickets to Dachau Concentration Camp – return!' Years later he wrote a poem about it, including the lines:

> Can Oz children of Oz children of Oz children
> Really understand the Holocaust?

It was a bitterly cold day and snow had fallen, so the camp seemed almost serene under its soft, white blanket. We saw the ovens where the dead were burned. It was right that we had made the visit.

Back in London we had a little more time with Sadie and Solly; none of us knew when, or if, we'd meet again; she was eighty-three and he was seventy-four.

Ros at Monash University, c 1978

Our last boat, a Miracle class with a wooden hull and a jib, c1979

In 1978 I was already into the third year of my degree and doing very well, earning mostly Distinctions, and even a High Distinction here and there. I was quite carried away at the thought of being a scholar, and my clothes started to look a bit more serious – less of the Indian gear with beads, and more English county. I even harboured thoughts of going on to do an MA. We were all getting over flared pants, and Al had given up on his beard by the time of his fiftieth birthday, for which Toby made a magnificent *Schwarzwälder Kirschtorte* (Black Forest cake).

Pesach celebrations were no longer with Martin and Freda; we made *seders* in our own home. Our house was more or less finished and furnished and we took a series of photographs that would be useful for 'show and tell' if we visited England. It was a time when Australian native gardens were all the rage, and so our front lawn disappeared and an imitation bush setting replaced it – all leaves and twigs as a ground cover and nowhere to put a picnic rug. The 1978-1979 holiday period is marked in our photograph album as 'Last summer at Frankston', which sounds wistful. This must have been the time when Martin and Freda sold the big old holiday house by the beach, with all its Art Deco furniture. Even the pictures of our boat have a nostalgic tinge – 'sailing off into the sunset'.

Dan going to Israel, February 1979

In February 1979 Daniel, then twenty, took leave without pay from Telecom and went off on a year's program to Israel. Along with other young people he worked in agriculture on a kibbutz, learned basic Hebrew and got to tour Israel with the group. Peter, nineteen, was still studying at RMIT and Toby, seventeen, was apprenticed.

In December 1979, two years after our last family holiday, Alan and I decided to travel overseas on our own. In London we could meet Daniel, who would have completed his year in Israel, and Sadie and Solly would have time with at least three of us. Peter had his driver's licence and Alan bought him a very solid second-hand car, a Cortina. He and Toby were to stay at home over the summer and planned a little trip along the coast near Lakes Entrance. In hindsight, we should have ensured that Peter had much more driving experience before attempting a long journey on country roads. There was a head-on collision on a bend in the road, a death and two boys in hospital.

Alan and I had arrived in London and it was our first evening at my parents' house in Ilford. Alan and I were both tired, didn't bother to unpack and went to bed early. In the middle of the night there was a phone call downstairs in the dining room. I was only able to hear one side of the conversation. It was Joel from Melbourne and from the tone of Alan's responses it was obvious something was terribly wrong. When Alan cried out, 'Both of them!' I believed two of our boys were dead.

I have carried this memory for over thirty years and it never fades or softens. It was only a matter of seconds before I was told Peter and Toby were alive but, like my sons, I too have scars. There is a manila folder with photographs of the wrecked Cortina, but I cannot open it.

My parents, and particularly cousins Maurice and Geoffrey, were immensely supportive in getting the three of us, Daniel, Alan and me, back to Heathrow and onto a flight home. Joel had told us that Toby had only minor injuries but Peter was in a serious condition in Bairnsdale Hospital. There was no way we could communicate with Melbourne once we took off so for the next twenty-four hours we didn't know if Peter would recover consciousness or, if he did, whether he had suffered brain damage. I was distraught during the flight; each time I woke and cried, they gave me copious drinks of whisky to induce sleep.

Joel and his wife met us at Melbourne Airport, bringing Toby with them to show us he was alive. He wore a bandage around his head but was otherwise unhurt. We raced home to Box Hill, changed our winter clothes and drove straight to Bairnsdale, where Peter was drifting in and out of consciousness. There was talk of taking him by air ambulance to a Melbourne city hospital but, eventually, he was transferred by road to the Austin Hospital in Heidelberg. He had injuries to his mouth and leg but no lasting head injuries. I don't know how much of the accident he remembers and will never ask.

We visited the hospital each day. I also spent much time in bed, traumatised and weeping. Friends came to see us but I refused to be consoled. I was overwhelmed. There was one occasion when Peter asked whether he should talk to Martin, the most religious of our friends, as he wanted to discuss matters of life and death. I don't believe they had that conversation, but I wish Solly had been there. After several weeks, Peter came home with a leg in plaster and was on crutches for some time whilst Joel organised extensive dental work to repair his damaged mouth.

The inquest determined it to have been a straightforward accident. No one was speeding, no one had been drinking; it was a dangerous curve in the road and a more experienced driver might have been able to avoid a crash.

In time, Peter returned to university. He eventually bought a small car, which he neglected (deliberately I think) until it became unusable. After it went to the scrap heap he decided not to drive anymore, and to this day he uses public transport, taxis and gets lifts from friends. The only other time he got behind the wheel was when he and I took Alan to hospital for the last time.

Daniel had been the first of the three to gain a licence, but his road skills were terrible; he's also a non-driver. Maybe the accident left its mark on him too. Toby is a very competent driver, as is his wife, Rhonda. They are the only two people with whom I feel comfortable as a passenger. I did not like driving with Alan, who had poor coordination; I always clung fiercely to the safety belt.

I got my licence when we had small children and it was a necessity. I've never enjoyed driving, and on long trips was always relieved to reach the destination. Now the car is merely a convenience to get me to local shops and appointments. It gives me great freedom and much-needed assistance, but no pleasure. When the weather is warm and time is not an issue, I quite like public transport – watching the scenery and looking at the other travellers – and there's something exciting and anticipatory about boarding a tram or train.

CHAPTER 20

[A] ROSE IS A ROSE IS A ROSE IS A ROSE*

In 1980 Alan was fifty-two; I was fifty; Daniel, twenty-two; Peter, twenty-one and Toby, eighteen. From January to March Peter convalesced and went back to university to complete his degree. In April Daniel returned to Israel. Toby was half way through his apprenticeship. I was still working at Box Hill TAFE and studying at Monash University. We had new dogs, Ben, then Bessie. Toby got his driving licence and Alan and I graduated to smaller cars, because we were finished with caravans. Turn, turn – it was a time of transition. We were no longer a unit – Alan, Ros and the boys; we had become a family of individuals. Daniel, Peter and Toby all left home together. Alan and I dealt with this life-changing event beautifully, and we did everything absolutely right. On the evening we helped them move, we all had dinner at a small Chinese restaurant where a woman went from table to table selling individually wrapped roses from a basket. The boys presented me with one and I kept it for years until it fell to pieces.

When Daniel returned to Telecom after his year-long leave of absence, his colleagues wanted to hear about life on an Israeli kibbutz. They were enthralled with his descriptions and asked why he'd chosen to return to a boring job in Melbourne. Dan weighed it all up and decided to make *aliyah*, to go back to Israel with the idea of staying. I was distressed that any member of this small family should be so far away, but put a brave face on it. We had a farewell barbecue and I baked a big apple pie. Dan donned an Akubra slouch-hat, shouldered a backpack and left for a kibbutz not far from Tel Aviv. His letters

* After Gertrude Stein.

Toby's award-winning patisserie at William Angliss College, 1980

Ros graduating Bachelor of Arts, Monash University, 1980

Toby holding Bessie

home sounded happy enough; he was milking cows, driving tractors and learning the language.

Meanwhile, Toby, Peter and I were doing well in our respective studies. At William Angliss College Toby was winning awards. The tray of *petits fours* and the magnificent *croquembouche* we photographed at Open Day look mouth-watering. My graduation ceremony took place in May 1980, and just being part of that parade of successful students was an overwhelmingly happy experience. I continued with fourth-year studies, wondering whether I had the intellect to make a serious contribution to the world's knowledge of English literature. (Four years later, the university wrote to say I might proceed to full candidature for an MA, but by that time I was too busy fixing up the library at Templestowe Technical School. Soon after, I joined the Jewish community's network, which left no time for any ground-breaking new study of the Victorian novelists.)

After corgis Sugar and Taffy, we decided to have Border collies. Ben came to us, though sadly for just a short while. He escaped from Toby during a walk and was run over. We were heartbroken. There was nothing for it but to get another dog, and I can remember Toby standing at the door with beautiful Bess in his arms. She had a magnificent personality and we were lucky she lived long enough for our return to Elwood, where she could experience walking along the sea front.

By August 1980 Daniel had been away from home for six months and I wanted to see him. For all we knew, he might choose to remain in Israel and make it his promised land. Sadie, at eighty-six, and Solly, at seventy-seven, had never been to Israel. During their lifetimes the country had taken on a mythic quality. They knew about the Balfour Declaration, mandates and broken promises, and putting pennies in little Blue Boxes to fund trees for the old/new land. We thought that with their eldest grandson living on a kibbutz it would be a wonderful experience if they could actually see Israel for themselves. I would come from Melbourne; they'd come from London and we'd meet Daniel in Jerusalem.

Sadie and Solly were able to see how Herzl's dreams and those of their own parents had come true. One hundred years earlier, in Eastern Europe, their families had been subjected to murderous pogroms and denied the fundamental rights we take for granted. Some of the *chalutzim* (pioneers) of the First Aliyah in the 1880s must have come from the same towns where my grandparents lived. I wonder how Solly and Sadie felt as they waited at the hotel in Jerusalem for their daughter's plane from Australia, for their grandson's bus from the kibbutz. But my parents were also British, and this, their first and only visit to Israel, must have stirred up many thoughts. The young idealists hadn't come to plant the Union Jack in another colonial corner of the British Empire; they had come to rebuild a home. For Sadie and Solly, to see their grandson milking cows on a kibbutz

Sadie and Solly in Jaffa, Israel, 1980

must have been a very moving experience; to walk in streets among other Jews knowing they were there by right, not through the courtesy of another nation's government, must have left a huge impression.

For Daniel, his time there was an experiment. Would he stay or would he return to Melbourne? His kibbutz had been established in the 1920s and the atmosphere was middle-aged. Dan thought it would be more stimulating in a younger environment and decided to move to a different one in the north, not far from Syria. The holiday itself was most successful, but after my parents had returned to England, I found it very difficult to say goodbye to my son. Perhaps I was still in shock from the car accident that might have killed Peter and Toby. On my last day in Israel Dan and I went together to the central station in Tel Aviv, where he took a bus to the Golan and I took another to the airport. I was deeply upset. But Daniel didn't stay after all. The young people in his new home were a close-knit group who'd been together for years, and he felt out of place. His letters became less and less enthusiastic, and he came back to study in Melbourne.

I still didn't know much about Alan's early life, his ancestry and his family. Whenever Alan and I went Sydney, we'd do some research; I wonder now how he felt about opening this can of worms. However, it was exciting to find the records for 'our' convict, young Samuel

Davis. Although the certificate from the Hyde Park Barracks lists him as Protestant, he wasn't.

On one occasion Alan took me to Rookwood Cemetery to see if we could find the graves of his parents, Sampson and Alva. It was a surprise to see the name Collins on so many Jewish headstones and I took photographs. We located the places for Sam and Alva, but there was no gravestone for either of them. When Sam died in 1962 we were in no position to buy a memorial, and Alan probably just didn't want to. But why was there nothing for Alva? The Davis family had announced her funeral in the *Sydney Morning Herald*. Why had they not marked her grave? Why did Sam do nothing to record the passing of his third wife? So many mysteries. However, in 2012 the Jewish Cemetery Trust in New South Wales advised me that philanthropists have donated money to buy small stainless steel plaques for otherwise unmarked graves, including those of Sam and Alva, and they were kind enough to send me photographs. It is one of those acts of charity that make one proud of, and grateful for, the Jewish community services. If I visit Sydney again, I'll take flowers for these long-ago parents of the man I married. There's no one else to do it.

Grave marker for Sampson Collins in Rookwood Cemetery, Sydney
Grave marker for Alva Collins in Rookwood Cemetery, Sydney

Toby completed his apprenticeship and he and Peter made a short trip to Europe where they rode motor scooters along the Riviera, tried hash cookies in Amsterdam and visited Sadie and Solly in London. Our youngest son was becoming independent. After a number of local jobs, Toby decided to take his chances in London. We knew he wouldn't stay away permanently, and I can't recall being as upset as we were when Daniel contemplated life in Israel. Long-service leave in those days was measured in five-year blocks and by 1982 I'd clocked up another five years and was entitled to time off. I decided to take just a couple of weeks and add them to the September term break. I would make a short visit to see Toby and check up on Sadie and Solly, now eighty-eight and seventy-nine. I was aware of their advancing years and looked for every opportunity to go to London, although there was always the problem of leaving Alan, who still fretted constantly and had to be 'minded' by our friends.

By this time my parents had been married for fifty-four years. Apart from our evacuation to Cardiff at the beginning of the war, they had never lived anywhere other than in the little terrace house to which Solly had brought his bride in 1928. It was their haven. Sadie scrubbed, polished and swept with compulsive dedication, until arthritis compelled her to seek help. Solly was a house husband long before the term became commonplace. He shared all the housework and shopping, and took early retirement in order to care for Sadie. There was a minute shed in the back garden where my father amused himself making miniature models of their own furniture. It distresses me to think how much he would have welcomed his son-in-law and his grandsons to share his hobbies. When the stairs in their tiny two-up, two-down home became too difficult for Sadie, they installed a chair lift. But nothing could mask the fact that I simply wasn't there; my husband wasn't there and the grandsons were never there for long. Over many years, Sadie's nephew, my cousin Maurice, showed enormous kindness and empathy for all the 'oldies', particularly those like my parents, whose only children had emigrated. I owe him a great debt. My parents never once complained to us, which made it much worse than if they had. It was a no-win situation for me and always had been. If we had stayed in London, Alan would have withered away without the sun; like the ocean, it had extraordinary spiritual meaning for him and cleansed away his hideous childhood. I wanted freedom from the real and imaginary constraints of family and community. In 1957 we had both looked for a fresh start in life.

My visits to Sadie and Solly left me with time on my hands in London. Researching Alan's family history was just the right task for a librarian, and over the years I came home with surprising information. I discovered a seventeenth-century portrait, learned that the family had been hatters in Covent Garden and, best of all, saw the very house close by in Seven Dials where the Collins family had lived in the 1830s. The area, as illustrated by Hogarth and described by Dickens, was one of the utmost filth and squalor and I needed old maps of London to locate Lumber Court (since renamed Tower Court). It's a tiny laneway behind Shaftesbury Avenue, home to so many famous theatres, and now some of the most expensive real estate in the world. Far from being a slum, I found No. 22 had a bright blue painted door, a security grille and geraniums in urns – an elegant address in a desirable area.

Samuel Davis (1813–1892), convict

Painting of Don José Cortissos, 1656–1742

Mark Davis, c1920s

Rebecca Levy, c1930s

Alva Phoebe Davis, c1927

Davis and Collins are such Anglo names it's not surprising the archivist at the British Board of Deputies scoffed when I asked for help. 'Not Jewish, Irish,' he sniffed, even though I had photographs of the Hebrew headstones from Rookwood Cemetery. I discovered the line of the Cortissos family (see Family Tree No. 8), which was very exciting for everyone. Sarah Cortissos, daughter of Elias the coalman and (the gloriously named) Rachel de Raphael Barzilay Capua of Italy, married the far less exotic sounding Isaac Davis from London in 1849. They immigrated to Sydney and, I guess in a nod to Sarah's father, named a son Coleman. Another son, Mark, and his wife, Rebecca Levy, were Alan's grandparents. The line leads back to Barcelona, the Inquisition in the 1400s and Emanuel José Cortissos, Marquis de Villa, a grandee of Spain. Don José Cortissos (1656-1742), fifth in direct descent from Emanuel, was a contractor who went to London seeking payment for services he had rendered to the British and Portuguese armies. He was unsuccessful and died in poverty leaving 'my portrait done in oils' and 'a gold ring' to be melted down and divided among his children. I found the portrait in the Spanish and Portuguese Synagogue. He is wearing the court dress of the reign of Queen Anne with a petition concerning his claim in his hands. In c1780 the grandson of Don José recorded the dramatic history of Emanuel and his sons in a document written in Spanish and beginning:

> There was this man who had three sons, and because of the troubles [the Inquisition] he gave his sons Spanish as well as Hebrew names …

There is a poignant aspect to this story. Emanuel José Cortissos, Marquis de Villa, was connected, maybe 'in service' to the Duke of Alba. In Spanish 'b' and 'v' are pronounced similarly, hence Alba/ Alva. Five hundred years on from the Inquisition, and thousands of miles away from Barcelona, Spain, in Sydney, New South Wales, Mark Davis and Rebecca Levy name their daughter Alva – the only Alva on the family tree – and she dies giving birth to Alan on *Yom Kippur*, 1928.

Peter graduated from RMIT in May 1982 and found a teaching position at the Footscray Institute of Technology. The travelling, however, was arduous and he moved into a flat closer to public transport. Daniel was enrolled in a course in Jewish Studies and living at home. Toby had got himself a job in a very up-market restaurant in Piccadilly, and after an initial few weeks living with Sadie and Solly, found a share-house in North London. Winter must have been depressing for him, so when spring arrived he left for Israel with vague ideas of a working holiday on a kibbutz. He should have known better than to economise by sleeping on the beach, for in Eilat he was robbed and suffered a bad case of sunburn. He was so disgusted by the whole business, that as soon as he had managed to retrieve his passport and his return air ticket from the authorities, he headed back to London. He phoned me from Heathrow to say he was 'coming home immediately'.

I'd been using Toby's room as a study, but when I promised to get it ready he said not to bother as he planned to move in with Peter. With children it's so often the very small things that can stay with

Peter graduating Bachelor of Science (Computer Science) at the Royal Melbourne Institute of Technology, 1982

you: a thoughtless comment, an unexpected compliment, or a surprising reaction. Peter often surprises, and on this occasion he was adamant that if Toby wished to live with him, then Daniel was not going to be left out. He would find them a flat with three bedrooms. And so it was that I found myself holding a red rose in a Chinese café. Alan and I deposited the boys in their new home and drove back to Box Hill where Bessie was waiting for us. We were on our own.

CHAPTER 21
DIGITAL

In 1980 Alan's story 'The Balconies' won second prize in *The Sun-Herald* Short Story Competition in Sydney. The judges included Kit Denton and Thomas Keneally, who said they found the writing poignant. Alan had always written stories, many of them humorous, and took a selection of his work to show Judah Waten, the Australian-Jewish author. Judah was encouraging and generous enough to write a foreword to *Troubles: 21 Short Stories*, which Alan self-published in 1983. The first story, 'The Trouble with Felix', was a reworking of 'The Balconies'; the collection was highly commended in the Alan Marshall Award. At fifty-two Alan was finally thinking seriously about writing.

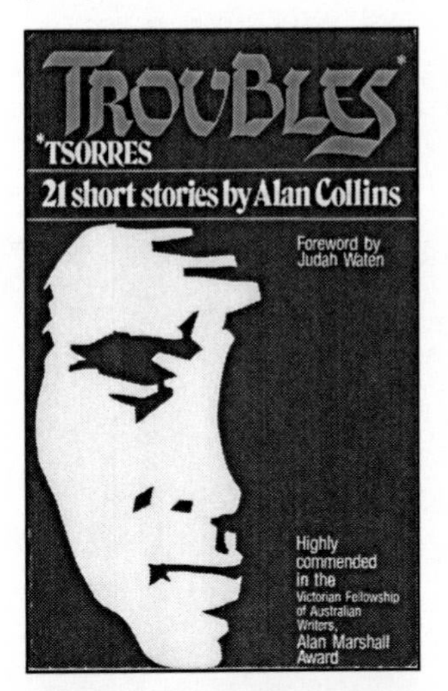

Alan sailing, c1985

We were heading towards middle-age and the boys were men. Alan, always yearning for the ocean, resumed an old friendship with the artist Jack Koskie, who had a yacht. He joined the crew (whom we rudely called 'Dad's Navy') and spent gloriously happy days on Port Phillip Bay.

By 1984 Sadie and Solly were ninety and eighty-one and still just managing to maintain their little house. Cobbling together term holidays and a couple of

Sadie's Japonais china; a wedding gift in 1928

Solly's 1927 wind-up gramophone; Joshua searching for the 'remote', c1995

Sadie (88) and Solly (79) in the bedroom at Ashurst Drive

weeks' leave, I made a quick visit in April and May. Even though I refused to face their mortality, my parents must have had it on their minds, for each time I returned to Melbourne I carried some treasure they had pressed upon me. They had very little of monetary value and the parcels Solly lovingly packed for me to carry on board the plane contained the china they'd received as wedding gifts in 1928: a dainty coffee set from Czechoslovakia, another highly ornamental set in the *Japonais* style, all gilt and kimonos, a blue lustre breakfast setting for two (very romantic) and a full English afternoon tea service. They never used any of the pieces, and I don't either – just dust and admire. These were the extent of their assets; no share portfolio, no solid silver ornaments, no jewellery. What must they have felt sending me home with the china? Did the empty cabinet remind them of loss? As Sadie became quite frail, cooking became too difficult, and 'meals on wheels' from the Jewish welfare society began to appear. She took this very hard, for the kitchen was her fiefdom. With considerable bitterness she then tried to give me her old enamel-lined saucepans and casserole dishes, saying, 'I'll never use them again.'

After their deaths I had to finalise the estate (what a grand title for such a little home!) I shipped the rosewood gramophone and two small oak ladder-back chairs to Melbourne. It would have amazed Solly to know that dealers would love to get their hands on his treasured 1927 vintage wind-up Paragon phonograph, and that when Joshua, his eldest great-grandson, was five, he refused to believe there was no remote control for it. I have Sadie's engagement ring – the one Solly threatened to throw in the river Thames if she refused him – but her wedding band was stolen when we were burgled. My mother always regretted that the big brass samovar from my grandparents' home was taken by another of her sisters, as she was the one who had always polished it.

At home in Melbourne, medical matters began to surface round about this time. At first the issues were not critical, but Alan was regularly in hospital for a number of procedures. Physically he wasn't as fit as he liked to fancy he was. A childhood of neglect had not done much to build strong bones. Cutting off the top of his finger when he was making Toby Toys in the 1960s was an unfortunate accident, but later damaging his spine trying to lift a caravan into position was much more serious. In 1984 there was a foot problem: a calcified spur in his heel put him in hospital for a few days; an elbow was next, and then began a series of orthopaedic procedures followed by open heart surgery and, finally, cancer.

The boys' flat was too expensive, and they moved into a smaller one adjoining Joel's dental laboratory. Much more exciting in the family's real estate history was that after twenty-five years Alan and I had at last paid out the mortgage on our 1959 vintage cream brick-veneer house in Box Hill North. We were getting restless and thinking about changing suburbs, careers and lifestyles. Elwood by the beach was where we'd started out, close to the raffish atmosphere of St Kilda, and just that little bit outside the Jewish community of Caulfield, so we would be assured privacy. We felt very adventurous buying a second property in 1984. A tiny, run-down 1920s red-brick cottage seemed promising as a place we might renovate and eventually retire to, but for the time being we rented it out.

There was no opportunity for promotion at Box Hill TAFE, but a senior teacher vacancy was open at the secondary level, at Templestowe Technical School. In a rash moment the library had been established as a joint school-community facility. It didn't work out well and it was time to disentangle the complicated arrangement whereby two lots of staff worked under separate awards and conditions, and library services appropriate for local citizens were confused with those suited to school students. The position had been posted for a couple of years, but all applicants had been rejected by the existing staff as being too difficult to work with. I was deemed acceptable, so in 1984 I left Box Hill.

Ed was the principal, and he had a degree in computer science. As part of the reconstructed library he envisaged a computerised catalogue, and I was to make it all happen. We installed a primitive program on cumbersome equipment and, using quantities of large-sized perforated paper, printed off reams of resources' lists. I wrote articles for professional journals, and the exhilaration of those early explorations into library automation still touches me as I read my own words. My efforts to move into the digital world were often funny: There was the scruffy Year 10 student, an embryonic computer genius, whom I asked to write programs; he was very patronising and smelled terrible, but we became friends; there was the software engineer who gently explained that 0k didn't mean 'ok' but referred to zero kilobytes. As a result of the articles about our innovations, we found ourselves hosting visits for teachers from other schools. Ed and I would stay back at the end of the school day to give demonstrations, and it was exciting to be at the beginning of something so new. One unexpected visitor was Pearl from the State Zionist Council of Victoria, who also had library issues on her mind.

I was earning a higher salary as a Senior Teacher at Templestowe

Tech and in December 1985 could afford another flying visit to London to see my parents. Some of the older members of my family had already died, and there were more children I'd never met; Sadie and Solly seemed to be fixtures in a changing world. I didn't think about their age and pushed the idea of them actually dying to the back of my mind. On these solo trips it was my cousin Maurice who would get up at 4.00 am to meet the early flight into Heathrow, phoning my parents from his car to tell them I'd arrived safely. *En route* I would buy some flowers for Sadie. There would be a big plate of fried fish, her speciality, waiting for me, a lumpy bed with darned sheets and on the dining-room walls framed photographs of Alan and our boys.

These visits confused me and I hardly knew how to conduct myself. Our communication skills were never that good, so once the 'how are you all?' questions had been asked, conversation was not easy. I was the 'fly in-fly out' daughter who rushed around buying things for them: domestic items, a new dress for Sadie, a gadget for Solly; but really, to use Alan's colourful language, I wasn't worth 'a penn'th of possum poop'. The goodbyes were dreadful. They came to Heathrow and we pretended everything was just fine as we had tea and sandwiches on airport trays, until off I went through a door marked Departures. I didn't cry until I was on the plane, and I suppose they wept on the way back to Ilford.

Back in Melbourne, the digital age was a little late coming to our household, but it arrived most seriously in 1986. The publication and positive reception of *Troubles* had prised open the door to Alan's memories, and he wanted to continue the story that had first appeared as 'The Balconies' and then became 'The Trouble with Felix'. The University of Queensland Press was interested and encouraged him to write a novel. Their letter of December 1985 ('very promising', 'hope you will decide to go ahead') came at just the right time in Alan's life. It all seemed pretty easy and straightforward, particularly when UQP followed up with an enquiry in May 1986 wondering whether he was 'just about to send off the completed manuscript'.

By the end of 1986 he had a contract and an advance royalty for *The Boys from Bondi.* There was just one problem: the manuscript wasn't completed, but the editor was talking about publishing deadlines. Alan was a terrible typist so the solution was a computer. What had once been our bedroom (then the boys' playroom, then Peter's room) was now transformed into a writer's room. A small Amstrad computer and printer were installed, but the principles of word processing were beyond Alan's understanding. We came to an agreement: I would put the computer on before I left for work each morning; he would promise faithfully to 'save' as he wrote, and I would print it all off for him in the evening. It worked, but there were some bad moments along the way. I would find Alan searching the floor for work that had mysteriously 'fallen' from the screen; he still put a hand out to make a carriage return, as on a typewriter, and he sometimes forgot to 'save' so hours of work were lost.

However, the manuscript was delivered on time, and *The Boys from Bondi* was well received. It was sold to the US (re-titled *Jacob's Ladder* because American readers couldn't be expected to know where Bondi was) and an option for film rights was negotiated. It was long before email, so the US proofs came in a large envelope. We were dismayed to see the yellow stickers marking the changes and to find that most of the colourful Australian language had disappeared: lifts became elevators, pavements became sidewalks, and strides became pants. We thought it hilarious that the prim American publishers were shocked by the following exchange between Jacob, the young apprentice printer, and Peg, the trainee nurse, who are sitting on the Bondi tram:

Jacob's Ladder,
US edition of The Boys from Bondi

> She rummaged in her handbag. I told her I was paying the fares. 'Don't get upset, Jack,' she said, 'I'm only looking for a fag.'

Fay Zwicky, poet, critic and (although she doesn't much like the term) an 'Australian literary treasure', launched the book in August 1987. In her speech she said: 'This book is a kind of Australian psalm to life ... there's humour, sensitivity and wisdom here.' She astounded Alan by referring to metaphors and symbols in his work, picking up on his emotional need for the sun and the sea, recollecting 'the boy with the hungry eyes' whom she'd first met when both were teenagers. It was Fay who told him to 'leave your mind alone' and just write.

Now, when we try so hard to hang on to our jobs, early retirement is a dreaded phrase, but it was an attractive choice in the 1980s. At fifty-five I had the option of taking my superannuation and quitting the Victorian Education Department, which I chose to do at the end of the school year. Alan and I were thinking of renovating the little cottage we'd bought in Elwood and moving into it. The University of Queensland Press were asking for a sequel to *The Boys from Bondi.*

In late 1986 Pearl at the State Zionist Council of Victoria placed a job advertisement in the *Australian Jewish News* for a librarian. It was a part-time position to run a Jewish library. Alan urged me to apply, but I wasn't keen. When the notice appeared a second time I agreed to give it a go and phoned for an appointment. Beth Weizmann on St Kilda Road was a building named in honour of Chaim Weizmann, the first President of Israel, and home *(beth)* to many Jewish organisations. Unlike most Melbourne Jews, I had never been there and knew very little about this hub of activity that played such an important part in community life. Tucked away at the back on the third floor was Makor Library (*Makor* is Hebrew for 'source'). I was interviewed by Pearl and two other people and agreed to take the job on two conditions: I asked for the same salary that I earned at Templestowe Tech and requested a computer to help me run the library. The Council were desperate for someone to take over Makor. They agreed on salary but took fright over the computer issue, saying they were willing to lease a machine but did not feel comfortable buying one outright. It's amusing now to recall the huge piece of equipment they got for me; it was the first computer ever acquired at Beth Weizmann, and people from all the other offices used to visit the library to see how it worked.

My long career with the Education Department was coming to an end and we agreed to celebrate with a holiday. Alan had missed out on many overseas trips and we decided to go away together in December 1986 to see Sadie and Solly and visit Israel again. In Israel we visited mystical Safed and watched the archaeologists digging away at Caesarea; we saw the wonders of the Dead and Red seas and stood between Israel and Jordan at Aqaba. We weren't very knowledgeable about the nuances of Israeli politics or social divisions and were taken aback in Mea Shearim, the ultra-Orthodox quarter of Jerusalem. My pants suit was an affront to the residents; black-garbed men with beards and side curls crossed the street rather than walk too close to me. I got disapproving looks as I browsed through a bookshop selling religious texts.

Ros outside bookshop in Mea Shearim, Jerusalem, 1986

CHAPTER 22
THE COMMUNITY

I retired from the Victorian Public Service at the end of 1986 and on 10 February 1987 became part of the Jewish 'public service', a fascinating mix of communal, philanthropic, political, welfare and cultural organisations that supports people of all ages, persuasions and backgrounds. I knew practically nothing about any of them and was quite out of my depth. Twenty years of working for the government, where everything was linked to an Act of Parliament, a department regulation or a definition published in the *Education Gazette* had not prepared me at all for entry into what was, effectively, a large, vibrant and sometimes very volatile family network. It was to be the best job I ever had, professionally stimulating and deeply satisfying at a personal level.

I was finally learning about the community of which I'd nominally been a part since 1957, but which I had more or less kept at arm's length for thirty years – sometimes from inclination (I wasn't a joiner), sometimes because geography (Box Hill instead of Caulfield) made it difficult for me to connect. Many of my colleagues at Beth Weizmann had grown up in Melbourne and thus shared memories of Jewish youth movements or, in adult life, of working for service organisations. Quite a few were either Holocaust survivors themselves, or the children of survivors, and for a librarian it was useful to have on hand translators for half a dozen European languages. There were also old-timers whose families had settled in Carlton, as well as Israelis who were in Australia for a short period, studying or representing organisations such as the Hebrew University of Jerusalem. This Jewish environment was a world away from my experience. I knew about attending departmental meetings, writing minutes, presenting reports, compiling statistics, running a budget, acquiring stock, organising staff; in short, I could run a library that had a clearly defined identity, was funded by government, staffed by qualified people on a recognised salary scale and supported by a vigorous union; Makor was nothing like that.

At this point we were a staff of three: myself, Ros Harari and Leonie Fleiszig. Gradually it became clear to me that the library would have to be fought for, that it was no time for timidity but for rolling up the sleeves and showing a bit of *chutzpah*. I had no designated budget and we depended on philanthropy. There were critical times, and often it was a 'swings and roundabouts' situation. Gloomy headlines in the *Australian Jewish News* announced our imminent demise: 'Makor Library now faces closure' (November 1991), followed by 'Makor to stay open' (December 1991). On one desperate occasion I called my tiny staff to come out 'on strike.' It wasn't a full-blown protest – no banners – but we did manage to get the community's support by working four days a week, claiming only three days' pay and making sure this was reported in the press. I was quite proud when the editor wrote that he 'knew a good campaign when he saw one'. Marketing Makor was also a challenge: librarians in government schools and colleges are seldom called upon to 'sell' their services, but in this job I searched hard for public-relations opportunities, wrote letters and articles, applied for grants and made approaches to philanthropists.

There were a couple of options as to how the jumbled collection I'd taken on might be developed. Many of the items had been donated by Jewish youth movements and were of an educational nature, so we could build this up and incorporate similar material that might be useful for teachers in Jewish day schools. Alternatively, Makor could have a much wider agenda and become a genuine cultural hub, serving Jews and non-Jews throughout Australia. I wanted to create a community library and must have sounded convincing, because the staff came along with me and made it happen. Many years later when I retired they gave me a silver tray inscribed for my 'wonderful dedication, vision and tenacity'. It's not a bad assessment. I *was* dedicated and my family often ran second in the race for my attention; I *did* have a vision and the National Council of Jewish Women was kind enough to make me Woman Achiever of the Year, 1999. Tenacity is just a more polite way of saying that I drove everyone crazy with my persistence. My dream of a national library has come true. With funding from an enlightened government and the inspired philanthropy of the Lamm family, the Lamm Jewish Library of Australia has been founded, and it would be false modesty to say I'm not immensely proud of having had the dream.

The old Beth Weizmann on St Kilda Road was rather gloomy in the evening, unless there was a function in the hall. One dark and stormy winter's night I was on duty when heavy uneven footsteps could be heard coming towards the library; it was creepy and unnerving. I wondered if the security officer on front-desk duty two floors below would hear me if I screamed. A man with a club foot, puffed out from the exertion of the stairs, came into Makor as I considered how much damage I could inflict with a date stamp. He turned out to be a lovely Irish-Catholic bloke with a problem. His children had been reading some dreadful report by a Canadian, Fred A Leuchter, and were trying to convince him that there had been no gas ovens, no extermination camps and no Holocaust. This patron wanted material to show his family how very wrong they were. It's still one of my most satisfying memories, to know that I gave books to this man, made a connection for him with the Anti-Defamation League and arranged a visit to the Holocaust Museum.

Makor Library sent resources all over Australia and I don't think anyone ever defaulted on returning them. Many non-Jewish enquirers were shy and diffident, and we knew then how very important it was, and is, to connect as widely as possible with the community at large. One day I took a call from the Northern Territory, from somewhere out in the bush. In the broadest Ocker accent the caller asked, 'Are youse the Jewish libr'y?' After we'd established credentials there was a bit of a flurry ('cos me spuds is boilin' over'). It turned out that this man had been 'doin' a bit of readin' up on me fam'ly' and 'reckoned' they came from Spain and were 'of the Jewish persuasion'. Would I be able to tell him if there were ever any Jews in Spain? Of course we sent him books about Sephardi Jews and the Spanish Inquisition.

Once, an unpleasant young woman came in with a bag of Yiddish books. An elderly relative had died; no one in the family read Yiddish and the books were going to the tip if we didn't want them. It was one of those light-bulb moments when you know you must make the correct decision. Apart from Sholem Aleichem and Isaac Bashevis Singer, at that time I probably could not have named another Yiddish writer. I was unable to read or write Yiddish; it wasn't my mother tongue and my parents only used it when they didn't want me to understand what they were talking about. The books were old, in poor condition. But someone had brought them in a suitcase from Europe where they'd been printed, and thought it important to preserve a precious heritage in this strange new land. There was absolutely no way they were going to the tip, and the staff and I vowed that we'd never allow this to happen, even if we had to store boxes of old books in warehouses. I am again reminded of Amos Oz and Fania Oz-Salzberger who wrote, 'Centuries passed, they migrated, they moved, they ran, they trudged, and they carried the books on their backs.'

Shortly after I took up the job at Makor, the Annual Conference of the State Zionist Council of Victoria was held at Beth Weizmann and I was invited to speak. I'd already attended several of their regular monthly meetings where I'd been hard-pressed to explain what the library did and why I considered it a valuable asset to the community. I produced overhead projections on which I'd drawn a network of

Jewish libraries linked in with national institutions covering the entire country, and spoke about an Australia-wide, computer-based system. The audience thought I was talking nonsense.

An international World Zionist Congress was scheduled for Jerusalem in December 1987, and I was invited to attend with the Australian delegation. This was the first of several overseas trips I made whilst I was Makor's director. I'd visited Israel twice before: in 1977 with Alan and the boys, and again with Alan in 1986. But a holiday is one thing; listening to speeches, attending lectures and trying to understand a complicated political situation are something else. However my clearest memories have nothing to do with the congress; the personal runs deeper than the political. I was booked through Athens on a flight that left Melbourne later than the other delegates. Security was very tight and the passengers transferring to a flight for Tel Aviv were required to walk out onto the tarmac and identify luggage piled up on a flat-bed truck. It had been an exhausting journey from Australia and when it turned out that my luggage wasn't there, I just dissolved into tears. I had to board the El Al (Israel Air Lines) plane only too aware that my 'trackie daks' were not suitable gear for the opening ceremony and dinner scheduled for the following evening. There's a lovely Yiddish word, *heymish*, which means homely and cosy. The Israeli cabin crew were just like that in dealing with my distress. 'Have a nice cup of tea and a piece of cake; it will make you feel better.' 'What about a bagel and cream cheese?' 'Don't you *worry*, I guarantee El Al will find your luggage and bring it to your hotel.' They were 'Jewish-mothering' me. Sure enough (though I attended the dinner in borrowed clothes), two nights later my suitcase was brought to my hotel room door, having taken a side trip to Rome.

It wasn't all business. At night I walked through the Old City of Jerusalem with some of the delegates from New Zealand. It was *Hanukkah* and *hanukkiot* were on display everywhere. Outside many of the lovely old stone buildings were little wall alcoves with flickering candles in glass bowls and we marvelled at the beauty of it all. But it was also the beginning of the first Intifada.

Sadie and Solly celebrated their diamond wedding anniversary (sixty years) on 1 January 1988 and I was there. Alan and I had decided to buy trees in an Israeli forest in their honour and the Jewish National Fund, whose office was also in Beth Weizmann, gave us an inscribed poster – old-fashioned, just like my parents – with romanticised illustrations of pioneers tilling the land and planting crops. An application to Buckingham Palace had been all I needed to ensure a congratulatory card from the Queen. Sadie's face was a study when a Royal Mail van stopped outside her house and a courier delivered the envelope (no stamp required). 'How does she *know*? Who reminds her of all these dates?' asked my tiny mother. Solly and I just smiled. There were bouquets and cards all over the little house and Sadie was utterly overcome.

Sadie and Solly's diamond wedding anniversary, 1988

Sadie and Solly's diamond wedding anniversary afternoon tea at Jewish Care, Gants Hill, 1988. Photo courtesy the Jewish Chronicle

The Jewish welfare services in Gants Hill were kind enough to make a small afternoon tea celebration and photographers from both the local press and the *Jewish Chronicle* came. As it was the time of *Hanukkah*, I took the old brass *hanukkiah* along and Sadie and Solly lit the candles. Solly – like Alan, always the joker – wore his very special bowler hat that had so impressed Sadie. It was one of the few anniversaries their daughter was able to share with them.

I had also wanted to surprise them. At the Theatre Royal, Drury Lane, where they'd first met in the queue to see the musical, *Rose Marie* (followed, naturally, by *The Desert Song* and *Showboat*) the current offering was *42nd Street*, adapted from the 1933 musical film. I had bought three of the best seats in the front stalls and when we arrived, I told the usher why the theatre held special memories for my parents. In a short while he returned, made a little bow to Sadie and said the theatre manager would be honoured if we'd take afternoon tea with him in the Royal Box. It really was the icing on the cake, or rather on the Marie biscuits, which are, apparently, standard fare for the royals.

Whenever I was to be in London, I looked for opportunities to meet other Jewish librarians. I used this occasion to contact a number of organisations. Balfour House is the British equivalent to Beth Weizmann, but I found the library set-up there rather different from what we were trying to establish in Melbourne. Their focus was solely on educational materials, and the concept of a community library seemed foreign. And yet, I was convinced that we had the potential to offer much more than just a resource for teachers. I saw Makor as a hive of activity and a cultural centre that really reflected its potential as an Australian-Jewish national library offering a wide range of services to all communities.

By 1989 Sadie and Solly were ninety-five and eighty-six. Despite the installation of the chair-lift, maintaining the little terrace house had become very hard. Solly was doing the brunt of the heavy housework, and 'meals on wheels' were being delivered regularly. 'Making *Pesach*', which involved changing over all the everyday crockery, cutlery and saucepans for special sets to be used only for the eight days of the festival, had long since become too difficult for them. Each year they booked into a kosher guest house where the two *seder* nights were celebrated and they were able to enjoy friendly company. It was not the same as being with a daughter and her family, but they never complained.

My more recent fleeting visits had made me aware of the dilapidated condition of the house. There were broken floor boards, dangerously old gas hot-water heaters, and threadbare carpets. It was a time when retirement villages were becoming fashionable and at Gants Hill, the local area they'd known all their married lives, flats in a very smart complex called Limewood Court were being offered for sale. Officially, Sadie was too frail to be considered an acceptable resident, but I think my cousin Maurice eased the way for Solly to buy them an apartment. To finance the purchase, their home at 36 Ashurst Drive would have to be sold but my parents would still be short of the full purchase price, so Maurice made them an interest-free loan to be repaid only when both Sadie and Solly had passed away and I was winding up their affairs. *Mentsh* is a Yiddish word and means an upright, honourable person. Maurice was such a man. How painful it must have been for them to quit the little house and sort through sixty-one years of memories, discarding everything that wouldn't fit into a one-bedroom flat. It was just another one of the many occasions when I should have been there and wasn't.

Limewood was all imitation Laura Ashley and chintz. There were three storeys and Solly chose an apartment in the middle tier. Sadie never got over swapping her little house, which stood squarely on its own piece of ground, for a flat sandwiched between one above and one below. It was June 1989 when they moved in and when I went to see them in December that year, it was heartbreaking. The move had pretty much exhausted them and they had no idea how to make a new home. The familiar dining room furniture was there and the rosewood wind-up gramophone; the bedroom furniture too was from the old house. But the kitchen! A tiny alcove galley where Solly could heat up 'meals on wheels' seemed a preposterous contrast to my mother's old-fashioned little empire with its temperamental gas heater and real porcelain 'butler's' sink. I walked in with my bunch of flowers. Sadie was sitting in a chair looking forlornly at the appalling curtains: those from her old windows would not have fitted this modern building, and a kindly neighbour, with the best of intentions, had given them drapes printed with a speed-themed pattern of horses and racing cars. It was all wrong and my first move was to change them for velvet ones in Sadie's favourite colour, dusty pink. Photos of their grandsons were soon up on the wall and in no time flat I had bought my mother a new dress, kitchen towels and a tiny pillow impregnated with lavender. Oh, I was a busy little guilt-laden daughter! Since my old bedroom was no more, Solly arranged for me to have the guest room Limewood so thoughtfully provided for visiting 'rellies'.

Sadie and the 'wheelie', 1990

Mobility was really the biggest of my mother's problems, so my father and I took her to a local shop that sold equipment for the disabled. In this way we were able to change Sadie's final years dramatically with the purchase of a wheeled walker that came with a basket and small seat for resting on whilst doing the shopping. She fairly ran out of the shop with it and of course I had my camera ready. As I select, trim, copy and paste the photograph, I look at the little figure in the red raincoat and salute her courage; she was ninety-six years old. After she died Solly brought Sadie's 'wheelie' with him when he visited us.

CHAPTER 23
'LULLABY OF BROADWAY'

Solly and Sadie were rather out of place in Laura Ashley-land after Ashurst Drive, but doing their best to acclimatise to communal living: sing-alongs in the lounge room, school kids entertaining the oldies with Christmas carols, swapping photos of their grandchildren, and talking over old times with some of the other Jewish residents. Back in Melbourne, Alan and I also moved to a new home, just half a kilometre from Poet's Corner, where we had started our married life thirty-one years before. We had sold the small cottage we'd originally bought for our retirement (it would have been too costly to renovate) and planned to sell the family home in Box Hill North. This would give us a kitty with which to go shopping, but it wasn't enough for the rising property market. Each weekend we'd mark up the classified ads and drive from one Elwood street to the next, only to find that our maximum was usually the starting price for any place we fancied. On a rainy Saturday, after yet another dispiriting auction, we decided on one last throw of the dice before heading home. So it was that on 2 May 1987 we bought the house on Broadway, Elwood.

The house has history. In 1928 there were trams in Broadway. A lucky driver had won the lottery and spent his winnings on building three small Californian bungalows, ours being the middle one, and probably now the most authentic. Alan and I were over sixty when we found our ideal home. We discarded the Box Hill past with great ease and looked forward with optimism, not back with nostalgia for the good old days. The house in Elwood was – and still is – immensely important. Alan said he'd only leave if he was 'carried out feet first', and indeed when the time came, that was pretty much how Peter and I got him to the car. I feel the same way. I make a joke out of the idea that I'm 'nesting'; it's not a bad description.

Broadway, Elwood, c1987

The huge Japanese maple tree I used to look at from the window by my desk has been cut down. It was well over fifty years old and a glorious sight, but it died. I've kept part of the main trunk decorated with the horseshoe from Sadie and Solly's kitchen. Each year hundreds of tiny self-seeded maples appear in the garden beds and I'm trying to grow another tree because I want to remember. It seems to be part of this regeneration, this foolish nesting notion I have. Where does all that come from? I'm really not *into* nature, and for the most part am terrified of insects and small scurrying things, but I save the hair I brush out of my dog's coat and put it on a shrub for birds to find and use for their nests.

We left Currie Street, Box Hill North (Alan's 'gulag'), without a backward glance. Today when I revisit the suburb I feel no pang; it's almost as though my entire time there were just an interlude whilst we waited to return to Elwood.

Collins Advertising business card, c1987

Collins Advertising moved with us, and Alan's new business card says it all. 'We're down by the sea!' announces an ecstatic dolphin. The card reveals so much more than a mere change of address: Al was coming home to the beach, spiritually as well as physically, together with his wife, dog, woodworking tools and bench, and as many bits of 'might be useful someday' stuff that he could transfer from his old workshop. The little ad agency was really winding down and he was thinking more about writing. I was engrossed in running the library and the boys were soon to come to live nearby. In September 1988 Alan celebrated his sixtieth birthday and we had a party in our new house. It was going to be good.

Back near the heart of Jewish Melbourne we were able to resume friendships that had lapsed due to geography, and also meet new people. It was a growing list that would keep expanding with my Beth Weizmann friends, Alan's fellow students and teachers at the Melton Jewish Adult Education Course, and the congregation at Kehilat Nitzan. The move did have its downside insofar as we no longer lived close to our friends on the other side of the River Yarra. But Liz, in particular, is one who travelled well. She and Alan originally met in 1985 or 1986 through a Melbourne writers' group and she soon became another close friend, always supportive and concerned for our welfare.

In 1989 the Isabella Lazarus Children's Home had a first reunion of former residents. The *Australian Jewish News* ran a picture of children in the 1940s standing on the porch of the Home. The photograph belonged to Hilda Zinner (I think Ruth in *The Boys from Bondi* is modelled on her). Hilda was hoping some readers would recognise the photograph and contact the people at the Montefiore Homes who were organising the event. Alan's shock at seeing his twelve-year-old self in the newspaper was profound. His description of life in the Home from the short story 'The Sunday Cupboard' gives me a clue as to the memories that were invoked:

Children at the Isabella Lazarus Home, c1941. Alan is at the end of the back row on the left. Photograph from the late Hilda Zinner, reprinted courtesy of the Australian Jewish News

> Sunday afternoon, from two o'clock precisely, was visitors' afternoon at the Abraham Samuelson Memorial Home for Children. On that day, once a fortnight, parents, relatives, guardians or anyone who could establish a *bona fide* relationship with a child was allowed, but not actively encouraged, to inspect the stock.
>
> Like merchandise on a store shelf the children were arranged along the verandah in descending order of age, their toes making a military line while their varying heights gave the impression of a freshly painted but broken picket fence.

Alan was sixty-one and I was fifty-nine. We'd been married thirty -two years and he had never talked much about any of the 'homes' he'd known. The reunion was an eye-opener. On display were early records showing that Alan had been the very first resident, rattling about alone in a big old mansion converted into a home for reffo kids yet to come from Europe.

He arrived on 8 December 1939, aged eleven, and left the Home in January 1944. Matron kept meticulous records and on a 1942 chart headed Schooling and Hobbies. Alan is listed as being in his second year at Crows Nest Central School. He was destined to have just one more year of education, and might have found work as an electrician or in the building trade. These reports the matron and her husband made on all the children, outlining their expected futures, tore at my heart. The reffos, exiled but educated, were all upwardly mobile and if, like Marianna in the short story, they were lucky enough to have one or two parents willing to work their fingers to the bone to give their offspring a good chance in this new land, they'd be off to university. No such luck for my boy from Bondi; he would be apprenticed as soon as it was legal, and at fifteen be cast out into a world of boarding houses and prostitutes and have no further contact with Jewish welfare authorities.

For the reunion Alan was asked to make the speech in reply on behalf of the former residents. With his hand on his heart he spoke passionately, saying the Home had 'saved him from the gutter', given him stability and a sense of Jewish identity. It's all true, but I was angry. I told the man who organised the event that it was disgraceful there had never been any after-care and that Alan had been left to sink or swim in the rough and tumble of 1940s Sydney. When we fostered Joel, Jewish Welfare in Melbourne was extremely helpful. In the 1930s, Sydney was the home base for Dr Fanny Reading, the founder of the National Council of Jewish Women. She was an advocate for child welfare and had consulting rooms in Bondi. As the Council's New South Wales leadership told me when I launched

Alva's Boy in Sydney, 'Dr Fanny would have been very upset if she'd known about Alan.' I don't doubt it.

The Association of Jewish Librarians, predominantly American, put on an annual conference. For their silver anniversary in 1990 they planned to join with their Israeli colleagues and hold the event in Jerusalem. I asked if I might attend, and the State Zionist Council of Victoria, realising this was an important meeting at which Australia should be represented, agreed to assist with some funding. I also planned to see Sadie and Solly in London. The most useful session I attended was one given by a librarian from Montreal who spoke about their Jewish library, the Bibliothèque Publique Juive, which had been officially launched in 1914. As an inspirational example for a multicultural society such as ours, it's worth quoting from that library's history:

> ... it became the first 'folks', or 'people's', library created to serve the public at large rather than catering to a small group of individuals of shared ideological convictions. The first clause of the 'Founding Principles' of the Folks-biblyotek, ratified in 1916, reads: 'The People's Library is a People's Institution, founded by the People for the People.

I was the only Australian among the mostly American delegates and had to fax home to Alan for the words to 'Waltzing Matilda' so I might sing it at the end of the conference dinner. I came back to Makor very enthusiastic to replicate something like the Montreal library in Melbourne.

The trip was to be the last time I saw Sadie. On my departure, as she and Solly entered a service lift at Heathrow Airport so that she would not have to negotiate escalators or stairs, I took a picture. They're both smiling and waving goodbye, but the image is blurred; maybe I was already crying and didn't hold the camera steady. A better farewell photo is of Sadie as she stood by her china cabinet in the Limewood flat a few days earlier. For once I'd caught her without a 'pinny' and, as she looks at me quizzically with just a little smile, I see myself.

Sadie, age 97, in the flat at Limewood Court, 1990

In late 1989 our boys had moved to a rented house in Elwood; I like to think they came to be near Alan and me. Daniel, who is tidy and organised, became exasperated with his brothers who, on the whole, are not tidy and organised. He moved into a flat of his own where he could continue to be tidy and organised, and the other two were left short of one-third of the rent. Toby, at that time working at a patisserie in neighbouring Brighton, invited Rhonda, the new baker from Perth, to come and share. Soon they became a lot more than colleagues at work; it wasn't long before we were contemplating a wedding. Western Australia, where Rhonda comes from, was a 'foreign' land, and her heritage was different from ours. We were unsure how to plan the celebration. Toby and Rhonda insisted on simplicity.

The wedding was planned for March 1991. A few weeks before the event I was booked to make a presentation at a Jewish educational conference in Sydney and was staying in Double Bay. The program had me scheduled to speak on two consecutive days, and after the first I went to bed very tired and took a sleeping pill. The less-than-two-star hotel didn't boast a *concierge* at night, so it was alarming when two large New South Wales policemen knocked on the door. My mind flew back to the accident in 1979 and I feared terrible news. The police told me to phone Alan urgently. (There had been no other way for him to get in touch with me as we didn't have mobiles then.) Sadie had died in hospital, aged ninety-seven, and my father wanted to know whether to delay her funeral until I could get there. I flew home to repack a suitcase for March in England. Cousin Maurice must have picked me up at Heathrow and Solly was waiting for me at the flat in Limewood Court, his face already unshaven as a sign of mourning.

Both Sadie and (later) Solly are buried in a large Jewish cemetery at Waltham Abbey, a market town in Essex. Epping Forest surrounds the area and when we buried Sadie daffodils were in bloom. She was only four feet ten inches tall and her plain pine coffin was filled out with prayer books that had become unusable. It is a custom often observed because, according to Jewish law, prayer books may never be destroyed, only buried in the earth. I don't recall what Solly said in his eulogy but it has always been enough for me to have the poems he wrote for her and the abundant evidence of his love. Afterwards we went back to the flat to sit *shiva* very quietly. There were prayers recited at the evening *minyan*, and people came to express condolences. Solly was a shy man and not very good at intimate communication. I could never ask him questions of a personal nature; I couldn't really say anything much at the time. I'd been away so long there was no conversational space for me to ask him whether he remembered this or that thing about Sadie. It was just terribly sad.

Always tolerant and flexible, my father broke all the rules of Orthodoxy and said that he and I should have an outing, unthinkable when we were in mourning. We went to Greenwich to see the *Cutty Sark* sailing ship. It was the first time Solly had been on the light railway and seen the developments that had taken place in the old Docklands area. We both knew that Toby and Rhonda's wedding was to take place within a week and that I would have to leave him and go back. Farewells over the years had always been hard, but Sadie and Solly could stand together and wave me off. This time it was agreed that Solly wouldn't come to Heathrow and we'd say our goodbyes in the front garden of Limewood Court. It wasn't yet light; I think he was wearing the orange fleecy-lined pullover he had so daringly bought in Australia, and I was probably wearing a grey tracksuit. He was all alone and I wept in the mini-cab on the way to the airport. I'd been with him for ten days.

CHAPTER 24
AUTHOR, AUTHOR

The wedding was on 24 March 1991. Toby's one and only big romantic gesture might well have been when he and Rhonda travelled to and from the lovely gardens at Ripponlea, the Victorian era mansion, in a horse-drawn carriage. It was the prettiest sight. They were wed by the lake, and the party was in our back garden. Definitely no elaborate reception rooms with blue and white balloons, either in honour of Israel or the Carlton Football Club. Rhonda's family all came from Western Australia and Solly sent a loving message. Alan made a speech too, emphasising our family's Jewish heritage.

Rhonda and Toby's wedding at Ripponlea, 24 March 1991.
L–R: Ros, Toby, Rhonda, Alan

Toby and Rhonda opened a small patisserie of their own in a nearby suburb, and Alan and I were able to give a little financial help, though not as much as we'd have liked. They worked terribly hard – it's that kind of business – and customers responded well to Rhonda's excellent retail skills and the products she and Toby made during the dark hours when the rest of us were fast asleep. With Toby and Rhonda married and Daniel in a flat of his own, Peter had no choice but to relinquish the rented house and find himself a new home. He bought a flat nearby and Alan and I liked to think his choice was influenced by affection for us.

Alan's first novel, the fictionalised autobiography *The Boys from Bondi*, was so well received that the University of Queensland Press thought he should write a sequel and perhaps make a trilogy out of the story of Jacob Kaiser, aka Alan Collins. This time around, courtesy of Peter, we were well equipped with a better computer, and Alan set up his desk in the family room overlooking the back garden. (Now that space is mine.) It being the busiest room in the house, I tried, unsuccessfully, to suggest what I thought would resemble a real writer's study. I offered the spare bedroom, or even the little summer house in the garden, but he wanted to be in the thick of things where he could listen to a CD or the radio, watch the birds squabbling, talk to the dog, phone me at the library, wander to the kitchen and make tea. He had no authorial pretensions, not even a cardigan with leather elbow patches. *Going Home*, the second volume of the trilogy appeared in 1993 and was mostly set in British Mandated Palestine. *Joshua*, the third volume, was published in 1995 and brought the story up to the Vietnam War period. It was set in Bathurst, Sydney and Israel

Alan was often invited to talk at schools and thoroughly enjoyed the opportunity to connect with younger readers. Sometimes he came home with amusing accounts of what the children had said: 'Do you write with a pencil, a pen or a typewriter? How long does it take to write a book? Where do your ideas come from?' One of the most memorable encounters was with students in grades two and three at a Jewish primary school. 'What did you do after you left school?' was the question. When Alan replied that he was 'put to a trade', there was dead silence. 'Does anyone know what a trade is?' asked the teacher. After a long pause one little bloke waved his hand in the air. 'I know, Miss, I know! A trade is when you buy and sell shares,' he offered triumphantly. Alan, ex-apprentice, maker of wooden toys, a man with a shed and a workbench smiled ruefully. A migrant teenager in an outer suburban state school told Alan, who was their visiting author for Children's Book Week, that *The Boys from Bondi* was the 'first fucking book' he'd actually enjoyed and he thought, 'that Jew boy had a fucking rotten time'. Indeed.

However, back in 1991 Alan was still writing *Going Home*; I was battling to keep the library afloat with no money; Daniel and Peter were working in their respective jobs; Toby and Rhonda were making progress in the little patisserie; and Bessie, our beloved Border collie, was getting very elderly, but still bravely stepping it out along the Elwood beachfront with Alan every morning. In Limewood Court, London, Solly was as cheerful as ever, though we had to start thinking about a stone-setting for Sadie's grave. My father needed to see his family, and it was decided he should come to Melbourne; we thought it might be his last visit. Alan and I would then accompany him back to the UK and be present for the setting of Sadie's gravestone.

It was a remarkable sight when Solly literally ran out of the arrival hall at Melbourne Airport in January 1992. It had been a long time since he'd seen Alan or the boys, and he'd never met Rhonda. After so many years of being Sadie's carer it seemed as though Solly had taken on a new lease of life; he was full of 'get up and go.' Whatever we suggested he was keen to do. He went on picnics with us, walked along the foreshore at St Kilda with Bessie, whose pace now matched his, visited our friends, explored the funky shops in Chapel Street

and had a wonderful time. Daniel took him to Canberra, where he was hugely moved by the Australian War Memorial. Alan took him to Sydney, where he gingerly tried his very first Chinese meal. He visited Toby and Rhonda's shop, inspected the bakery, posed with his arms around them both and told them he was immensely proud of what they had achieved. Rhonda's parents, Laurie and Rae Chatley, came

Solly arriving at Melbourne Airport in 1992

Solly and Ros in Elwood, 1992

Solly in Elwood, 1992

L–R: Laurie and Rae Chatley, Solly, Ros, Alan, in Elwood, 1992

over from Perth and we had photographs taken to mark the first occasion when both families were able to meet.

On 21 February 1992, Solly, Al and I left for the UK. We would attend the bar mitzvah of my cousin Gina's son, Mark, stand together at Sadie's grave and, just for old time's sake, borrow a car to take a sentimental journey through south-west England where we'd toured with *La Cigale* in 1957.

Too soon Alan and I had to return to Melbourne. Push, pull. Although Collins Advertising was on the wane, I couldn't take more time away from Makor. Most importantly, we were expectant grandparents – Sadie and Solly's first great-grandchild was on the way. Joshua Samuel Collins arrived on 22 August 1992 and we were ecstatic. Toby and Rhonda took him to work with them in the bakery and he slept in his little carry-cot on the end of the long stainless steel bench where they rolled out the dough for croissants and Danish pastries. Now he is an adult, a chef, and has a black belt in karate.

Solly, whose health had been quite good, began to suffer from eye problems – cataracts. He was due to enter hospital later in the year so I took my annual leave in October and November 1992 to be with him. Before he went in for the procedure he and I had some outings, and the best one of all was to the Science Museum in Kensington. In my photograph he is sitting on the little seat of Sadie's 'wheelie' looking at a computer screen and listening entranced to an explanation of digital technology. What an inquisitive open mind he had! What a pity he never had more time with his grandsons. I think Eli, his second great-grandson, has inherited Solly's curiosity about the world and also some of his inventiveness.

The eye operation was successful and he was a model patient. Back at Limewood I tried to help with the eye drops, but Solly said that he really would have to learn to do it for himself – and in my mind, I added the word 'alone.' The little flat was neat and tidy, our photographs on every surface and wall, but the carpet was stained and needed replacing. I helped him choose a tweedy pattern in pink and mauve heather-like tones that Sadie would have approved; also it wouldn't show too much if he spilled anything. We arranged that when he went away to the kosher guest house for his *Pesach* holiday, the carpet layers would do their work and all would be back in place for his return. Solly was already determined to make one more trip to Australia to meet his great-grandson and celebrate his own ninetieth birthday with us.

Back in Melbourne I turned my attention to the task of moving the library to a new home. The old Beth Weizmann building in St Kilda Road was well past its prime and far too small. The State Zionist Council of Victoria had acquired and renovated a much more modern building in South Caulfield, and I was lobbying vigorously for our library to be located on the ground floor where the community would have easy access.

As an indication of just how well the library had developed, the State Zionist Council agreed to give us a space right by the front entrance, with proper library shelving and equipment. This was something more significant than merely moving a small Jewish library from two nondescript office rooms into a purpose-built area where we would have a visible presence. The expanding library facility needed additional staff and I was able to hire another trained librarian, Ruth Leonards. (As the library continued to grow, additional staff was added.) It was a turning point, not only in the role of the Zionist Council, but also in the life of Melbourne's Jewish community. Makor had grown up, and although there were to be difficult times ahead, I think the staff believed that we were there to stay and, if necessary, would fight for our existence. Reflecting on my own part in all this, I think that in my long career as a librarian, the most important decision I ever made was my refusal to shut Makor's doors for lack of funds.

The new building had a meeting hall capable of seating 300 people and was soon in demand for functions. I booked it for the launch in August 1993 of Alan's second novel about Jacob Kaiser, *Going Home*. It was thoroughly appropriate that the late Clyde Holding, a former leader of the Victorian Labor Party and Alan's friend, agreed to launch the book. He remarked that the book 'is deeply relevant to the kind of Australia we want to have, not least because of the issues of social justice that so concerned the author'. Alan's response included the following:

> I think that in *Going Home* have done an honest job as much as any tradesman. I did not set out to be an apologist for any particular viewpoint. Indeed, in dealing with the Arab/Jewish Palestine of 1947–48 I have taken an objective stance not maligning any group at the expense of the other.

In November 1993 my father made what was to be his last visit to Melbourne. It was similar to the previous year's trip but slower, for Solly was getting tired. Our friends came to the little afternoon tea party we made for his ninetieth birthday. I scoured the sweet shops to find him Fox's Glacier Mints, which he had always liked (maybe the name was the big attraction), but the stand-out event of this visit was meeting his great-grandson, Joshua. I can imagine how Solly must have

Solly and his great-grandson Joshua, Elwood, 1993

felt holding this little boy. At that time Joshua was his only great-grandchild, so perhaps Solly saw him as the standard-bearer, taking the family's history forward – *l'dor v'dor* – from generation to generation.

Solly in the kitchen at Limewood Court, 1994

I accompanied Solly home in February 1994. The new carpet looked lovely and everything in the little flat was clean and tidy. Our photographs were in their usual places. Our last goodbye was in the pre-dawn darkness outside Limewood Court, and as always, he was cheerful, standing there in his Israeli-bought 'pinny', keys in his hand, a *kippa* on his grey curls. I left to go on to Israel for an education conference. Four months later, on 25 June, Solly died.

Saying goodbye to Solly for the last time, in the dawn outside Limewood Court, 1994

My cousin Maurice phoned us with the news and promised to leave the flat exactly as it was until I got there. When I walked in on a beautiful sunny morning, Solly seemed to be there too. The *challah* was on its special plate; the *Shabbat* candles were still on the table;

his book and the little leather bookmark embossed with the words 'here I fell asleep' were still in the armchair where he was sitting when his heart stopped. Sophie was the only one of the sisters left and he'd baked some biscuits to take over to her on his usual weekly visit. However, on that Saturday morning he didn't feel up to making the long journey across London, so he phoned her to cancel. I found the tin of home-made biscuits in the kitchen. Maurice said I was welcome to stay at his home whilst I made all the necessary arrangements, but I wanted to be with Solly's spirit, so I put a mattress on the floor of the living room and slept there for the next fortnight.

My cousins were all exceptionally supportive and many of them contributed to the eulogy we presented at the funeral. Solly was buried next to Sadie, both of them in graves they had paid for in advance, shilling by shilling, month by month when the '*shul* man' came around. Orthodox Jews are bound by the laws of what is and is not appropriate for women at a funeral, but as chief mourner I insisted on wheeling Solly to his grave and joining the men in shovelling the earth onto his coffin. I don't remember whether I was able to recite *Kaddish*, the mourner's prayer.

I knew it would be easier to arrange the wording for his gravestone whilst I was in London and able to liaise with the stonemasons. I chose the text 'The crown of a good name excels them all' which is from *Pirkei Avot (Ethics of the Fathers)*, a work of timeless wisdom totally appropriate for such a man. I sat on the floor in the little flat, hour after hour disposing of the neatly kept utilities bills and arranging for the sale of furniture. I packed up the things I'd ship back to Melbourne and put the flat on the market. When it was time to go, I placed the brass *hanukkiah*, Solly's silver *Kiddush* cup and the *Shabbat* candlesticks in my hand luggage. I kept them close by me on the journey, just as my ancestors must have done when they travelled across Europe with their small treasures.

When I returned I was in trauma. For the first time in my life I tried one of those supposedly calming herbal remedies that sound like a potion out of a Harry Potter story, but I don't think it was helpful. A few months later the sale of the flat in Limewood Court was finalised. Sadie had never liked the place, despite the chintz. It was too reminiscent of 'the buildings', the old East End tenements and not to be compared with a 'real' house. I repaid my cousin the loan he'd made to my parents when they bought it, and gave each of our boys an inheritance from what was left.

Births and deaths: Eli Aaron, our second grandson, was born in February 1995. Toby and Rhonda were doing well in the patisserie but two little boys were a challenge when they had to work at night. I have a lasting memory of Rhonda with Eli in a sling on her back, rolling out pastry on that long stainless steel bench. Even though they took on part-time help, the work was becoming too hard for them.

In May 1995 Alan and I had to set Solly's gravestone. For once we would be in the northern hemisphere during the warmer months, so we decided to visit Paris and Israel with a stopover in Hong Kong on the way home. We were both now orphans. I was sixty-five and Alan sixty-six.

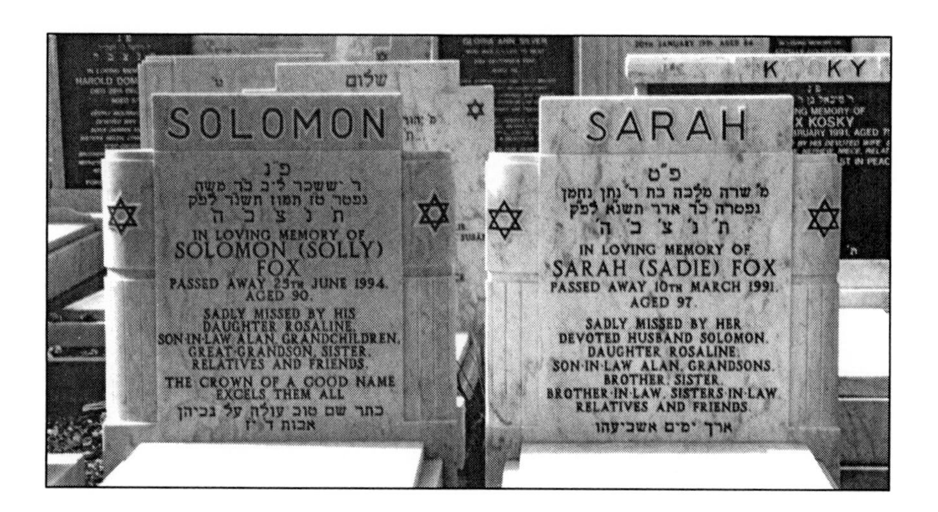

The graves of Sadie and Solly in Waltham Abbey cemetery, Essex

CHAPTER 25
ALL THE INITIALS: NT, WA, US

Bessie, our beautiful Border collie, died not long after Solly. Alan no longer had the stamina for extended walks, so we bought an eight-week-old corgi whose short legs required a lot less maintenance. We called him Bertie after King George VI, but when he accompanied Alan to the polling booth he always wore a balloon that proclaimed our republican views and Labor party allegiance.

Alan and I were having a good time playing with two grandsons and a new puppy. *Joshua*, the final part of the trilogy, was completed and I arranged the launch for October 1995 at Beth Weizmann. Sam Moshinsky, an old friend and stalwart of the Jewish community, agreed to launch the book. In his response, Alan, once again, set out his agenda:

> Do not seek in my writing the sounds and smells of the old world. What you will find though are interesting situations of the clash and ultimate blending of the two diverse Jewish cultures. What makes my work perhaps of some value is that the novels are written from the Australian Jewish viewpoint.

The year turned. The patisserie had a very successful Christmas season and Toby and Rhonda exhausted themselves making gingerbread houses and Black Forest cakes. We all tried to help out behind the counter. Alan and I had holidays in Sydney and Queensland. In February Eli was two.

In April 1996 I, along with many others, presented myself to the mayor of St Kilda and became an Australian citizen. I wonder now why it took so long for me to do it. I could have done it years earlier but maybe it was important for me to wait until Sadie and Solly had gone. We made a little supper for friends afterwards and I ceremoniously placed a Union Jack and my souvenir Silver Jubilee mug on the dining-room table. Alan insisted we play some of his favourite songs from the oh-so-British Gilbert and Sullivan; he would have given quids to have been able to write like Gilbert. I realised that when I next travelled overseas, two governments would now be charged with my safety since my new Australian passport was an added protection. This was not an idle thought, for on one of my trips our plane made a stop at Bahrain and I was hauled out of a line of passengers to be taken off for a body search. Maybe the Israeli stamps in my passport had upset the authorities but, whatever the reason, I made an enormous fuss in a very British accent and was allowed to enter the terminal untouched.

Our fortieth wedding anniversary was in February 1997, a time when Peter was working on contract in London. Generally speaking, our children are not given to making grand gestures; on this occasion they really did well. Alan and I were told to expect a car to call for us but were not informed of our destination. A fancy limousine, complete with champagne, picked us up and we were taken to a winery in the Yarra Valley where, to our intense delight, Peter, who had secretly flown in the previous day, was waiting, along with all our little family, to share a celebratory lunch. Alan and I were deeply touched and felt a great love for them all.

Collins Street sign

The patisserie was doing well, but Toby and Rhonda were seeing their youth slipping away and feeling they were not building memories other than those connected with work. They were living in a rented house so there was nothing to prevent their closing the business and taking off on an adventurous round-Australia trip in a caravan.

It was about this time that the Melbourne City Council decided to change the old metal street signs for something more modern, and they auctioned the originals for charity. Alan and Toby went along and bid, Alan for Collins Street 460–534 and Toby, naturally, for Little Collins Street 156–180. Our sign is over Alan's workshop in the garden and Toby's was bolted to their caravan and later to their house. Their year-long trip ended in Perth, Rhonda's home town. They found work and bought a modest house not far from Fremantle, where our third grandson, Isaac Joseph, was born in 2003. By the time they returned to Melbourne in 2005 we had lived through seven lonely years of long-distance grandparenting.

But when Toby and Rhonda were six months into their journey in the caravan and had reached Darwin we joined them for a holiday in Kakadu National Park. We stopped at camping sites next to motels or cabins where Alan and I could find accommodation. On the eve of *Rosh Hashanah* we were somewhere near Katharine. Toby and Rhonda, dearly wanting to catch barramundi and cook it for a festive supper, took us to the evil-looking Alligator River. It was frightening to stand on the banks, holding the hands of the little boys and watching their parents wading out beneath a sign that clearly warned of crocodiles. I imagined that Alan and I would be raising the orphans. There were no barramundi to be caught and it was unbearably hot, yet it turned out to be an unforgettable occasion. Toby was reduced to buying his fish in a shop. Whilst he was in town looking vainly for a *challah* – in central Australia? – Rhonda, equally determined to honour a celebration about which she knew very little, made an apple pie in the hot caravan. Alan had packed *Kiddush* cups and candlesticks and we celebrated *Rosh Hashanah* sitting around a deserted swimming pool in a caravan park in the Northern Territory. The traditional meal in a suburban Jewish family home

– snowy white tablecloth, shining silver and glass – would also have included fish and apples, but I don't think I've ever enjoyed a festival so much: Toby cooking his 'barras' at the barbecue, Rhonda and our grandsons, very brown in their bathers, the candles like little mirrors of the stars in a vast mysterious sky, cans of beer and bottles of lemonade to wash down the pie. We were very happy and the memory is precious.

Rosh Hashanah in the Northern Territory, 1998;
L–R: Alan, Rhonda, Eli, Toby, Joshua holding Solly's Kiddush cup

The Alligator River,
Northern Territory

Eventually we parted ways: Toby and Rhonda pushing on to the west, and Alan and I going east to Queensland. It was very hard to watch their van disappear down the road and I dissolved. Solly and Sadie waving me goodbye with smiles had shown far more courage. Alan was seventy in 1998 and it was a quiet celebration without Toby, Rhonda and the little boys.

Makor was still struggling financially, and my working life was consumed with chasing grant money, a soul-destroying task. I have never envied wealth but I knew envy at a professional level. I read about the Jewish community of Montreal, whose library blossomed with funds from the city itself, the state of Quebec, and from major philanthropists. Even more exciting was the Center for Jewish History in New York: the collections of five of the largest and most disparate Jewish libraries in the world had been brought together under one roof and the centre enjoys mouth-watering grants authorised by state and federal governments. I wanted such things for Australia and bored our friends with endless descriptions of networking Jewish resources across the country and expanding cultural programs that would reflect all shades of Jewishness.

Woman Achiever of the Year, 1999, award from the National Council of Jewish Women

There was excitement when I was awarded Woman Achiever of the Year 1999 by the National Council of Jewish Women. I look back on the interviews I had with the panel of judges with real pleasure. These women, most of them high-flyers in the business and philanthropic worlds, quickly grasped the concept of a national Australian Jewish library and understood that sharing information would lead to sharing values and promoting tolerance. Makor had established the ground-breaking memoir publishing program, Write Your Story; other Melbourne Jewish libraries were co-operating effectively in a digital network and we were providing an Australia-wide lending service – but there was so much more we could be doing. However, I was ready for a slower pace. In 2000 I would celebrate my seventieth birthday and it seemed an appropriate time to retire. Leonie Fleiszig, who had joined Makor in 1987 and had so loyally fought all the battles with me over thirteen years, would take over. I chose the February anniversary of the date on which I'd started the job. To use up accrued leave, Alan and I decided to visit America during the 1999–2000 summer holiday season. It would be a finale to our formal working lives.

Young Israel of Santa Monica shul on Venice Beach, California

My cousin Jonathan met us at Los Angeles airport and made us very welcome. We stayed in Santa Monica, and quoted Raymond Chandler to each other. An early morning walk along Venice Beach – performers, fortune-tellers, artists and market stalls – brought us a surprising slant on Judaism. Alan kept a diary and here's his entry:

> There it was right on the beach front – a hall with the doors open to the breeze and a Shabbat service in progress. Outside on the walls were murals – sort of half Chagall, half dream world, 'The Young Israel of Santa Monica', *Frum but Funky*. I stood in the doorway and the *gabbai* came out and grabbed me, asked me did I want to hold the Torah? I declined so then he asked me if I wanted an *aliyah*. I agreed and told them my Hebrew name and that I was a Cohen. Wow, big deal! I had to stay for a while and they even got Ros in to sit in a separate section of the hall. They were really very cordial and welcoming.

America: the Lincoln Memorial, the Kennedy graves, touching moon-rock, eating at the table where Harry met Sally, the Met, *Guernica* at the Museum of Modern Art, Lennon's memorial in Central Park – it's endless, so let me be personal. I'm a librarian, so for me mecca is the Library of Congress, the world's largest collection of knowledge, culture and creativity. I walked in and was overwhelmed: the scope, the scale, the beauty of the building. It was thrilling beyond anything I could have imagined. Public access computers were already available in 1999 to search the vast collections. Very shyly, Alan and I looked up *The Boys from Bondi* and found it, along with its American edition, *Jacob's Ladder*. The Holocaust Museum, the Smithsonian, the National Air and Space Museum were all quite amazing, but the LC was my Washington highlight. In New York there was the New York Public Library with the two stone lions, Patience and Fortitude, keeping guard at the entrance. But it was the plaque in the centre of the foyer floor that did it for me. Surrounded by huge marble columns inscribed with the names of donors, many very illustrious, lies a simple memorial to Martin Radtke, a penniless Jewish refugee from Eastern Europe who made good – very good – in the *goldene medine* and gave his estate to the library in humble gratitude for the education he had acquired through its freely accessible collections. That makes me feel intense pride in my profession, and have faith in the potential it has to make a difference.

We visited the Lubavitch Synagogue at 770 Eastern Parkway in Brooklyn. It was *Simchat Torah* and we anticipated an interesting experience. It was a short subway ride from where we were staying on the Upper West Side, but it was a world apart and I felt totally alienated in this strange environment. Crowds spilled out onto the pavement and we were encouraged to go inside. Whilst Alan braved the downstairs area, where black-garbed men and boys were chanting and dancing for joy, I was directed to the balcony, where women in head-scarves lifted me bodily over the seats to the front row where I could look down and search vainly for my husband in the throng of ecstatics below.

Our visit to America was also memorable because we were able to see Manfred, our dear friend from the 1950s. We found him and his wife, Judy, in Bergenfield, New Jersey, in a little weatherboard house crammed with Jewish memorabilia collected over a lifetime. In 2007 he donated his Theodor Herzl collection to an archive in Jerusalem, and I like to think that the name of the young reffo from Dinkelsbühl will be remembered in Israel.

From the New World to the Old: Alan had suggested we visit Prague as part of this holiday, though it was a big cultural stretch from JFK to Kafka and stories of the mysterious *Golem*, the clay monster of Yiddish folklore. For most Jewish visitors, Prague also means visiting Theresienstadt concentration camp, but Alan and I didn't go there; perhaps we just wanted to have a good time and not tear ourselves apart with the horror. It was a much easier conclusion to our holiday: listening to buskers playing jazz in the squares or watching an hilarious puppet performance of *Don Giovanni* featuring a blind-drunk Mozart.

We went back to London to say our goodbyes to my family and to fix a small brass plaque we had brought with us from Melbourne on the graves of Solly and Sadie. It was to acknowledge their Australian family, now including two great-grandsons, Joshua and Eli.

CHAPTER 26
KADIMAH

I officially retired as Director of Makor Jewish Community Library in February 2000, the month of my seventieth birthday. Alan was seventy-two. Our sons were forty-two, forty-one and thirty-eight and our grandsons were eight and five.

Makor Library logo

Kadimah Library logo

My farewell, including a huge party most generously hosted by Sonia and Malcolm Slonim, and presentations from the State Zionist Council of Victoria, as well as from Makor staff, was like a great family occasion. I was touched by the speeches of genuine appreciation for what I had achieved. There were beautiful gifts: an engraved silver tray with *challah* board inset which we use every *Shabbat*; a silver rose bowl and certificates of honour; the framed collage that my staff member Ruth made was filled with pictures to remind me of my thirteen years at Makor; it is a treasure.

A retirement speech is often the moment to acknowledge one's colleagues 'without whom ...' and I'm sure I said something appropriate about the way that the staff and volunteers had supported me, embraced my ideas and made considerable sacrifices to keep the doors open. Getting ready for work each day had always been a huge adrenalin rush. My enthusiastic true-believer approach had been right for Makor at that time. In more recent years, the library has benefited from Leonie's diplomatic management style and she has continued to foster warmth and growth in a modern digital environment.

Ros's retirement party at the home of Sonia and Malcolm Slonim, February 2007. L–R: Ruth Leonards, Ros

We had always had dreams, even at bleak periods when closure seemed inevitable. In September 1994 Professor Louis Waller AO spoke about the library at the annual assembly of the State Zionist Council of Victoria, and said:

> [Makor is] an active library, not a passive repository. It reaches out to those who seek to use it. It's Catholic in the very best sense, in its regimes ... Above everything, Makor has that almost indefinable but instantly recognisable characteristic – it has its own style. It is a living, lively entity.

Ros's retirement party.
Makor staff L–R: Naomi Saporta, Leonie Fleiszig, Ros, Ruth Leonards, Sonia Slonim, Mary Lavi

Professor Waller's description is just as true today with the Lamm Jewish Library of Australia. It has many surprising offerings. I think of study, soup and singing; mind, body and soul all coming together in one exuberant hub of activity. Modern technology underpins it, but never intimidates. In 2013 they celebrated the opening of their Yiddish collection, a selection on loan from the Kadimah Library. I look at a photograph of Alex Dafner, Leonie and myself on that occasion and appreciate what it signifies: the past, present and future,

In the Lamm Jewish Library of Australia. L–R: Alex Dafner, President of Kadimah, Leonie and Ros, 2013

Hebrew and Yiddish, co-operation, inclusivity; and the 'living, lively entity' that is this library.

My thirteen years as director of Makor had changed me profoundly. They had made me a much more thoughtful Jew. I was no more Orthodox than I'd ever been and was not passionate about the direction of Israeli politics; I hadn't mastered Modern Hebrew, and for that matter couldn't speak Yiddish, but I had embraced my heritage – a problematic concept difficult for me to explain. My colleagues in the Jewish community came from across the spectrum of Jewish life – from the very observant to the completely secular; identifying my place in this rich mix proved quite challenging. Obscure, arcane customs from darkest eighteenth-century Poland, or a retreat into mysticism, were not for me; neither did I describe myself as 'traditional', that catch-all word that always seems slightly apologetic ('We keep kosher but eat oysters in restaurants'). I think, too, that I shall always remain distant from the *Ba'al Teshuva*, the religious movement that first took off in the 1960s to bring hippies back into the fold, and has since blossomed so vigorously into a search for spirituality in our confusing world; it's not me.

In many ways, the next phase of my professional life was reminiscent of that earlier occasion when my friend Freda had asked me sternly what I intended to do with my life once the little boys all started school. In 2000 Alan and I were anticipating new activities: he was writing short pieces and poems and thinking about a memoir of his Bondi childhood; I was becoming interested in gardening. However, no more than a couple of weeks into my retirement Rachel from the

Kadimah became insistent.

'Librarian Ros Collins explores the riches of the Kadimah library'. Photograph by Nigel Clements, reprinted courtesy of the Australian Jewish News

Kadimah is the heart of Yiddish culture in Melbourne, if not Australia. This community cultural centre established a library in an upstairs room at 59 Bourke Street, Melbourne in 1911. By 1915 the Kadimah had moved to Drummond Street, Carlton, and by 1933 to a new building in Lygon Street. In 1967 it moved to Selwyn Street, Elsternwick. In true Jewish family fashion, a motion to amalgamate with the Beth Weizmann Community Centre in 1966 was rejected. Feuds between the various cultural strands – Hebrew and Yiddish, Zionist and Bundist, secular and Orthodox, reffos and Anglos – went on for years. All this was long before I became a Ten Pound Pom. I had no background whatsoever in Yiddish culture, the history of the secular Yiddishist Bund (or Jewish Labor Bund socialist movement), the endless controversies over just about everything. My interest was in libraries. In the years since I first became involved, Kadimah has changed greatly. Today there are digitised archives, a searchable on-line catalogue, a world-wide reference service and a great variety of programs. But it wasn't always that way.

Back in 1995 Kadimah's vice-president and library co-ordinator, Rachel Kalman, OAM, had come to see me. She wanted to discuss networking the cataloguing data for their extremely large, historic and disorganised Yiddish library collection with Makor's computerised system. It would entail moving the mindset of a mostly senior group of passionate Yiddishists whose knowledge of digital technology was minimal. It would also mean some financial contribution from the Kadimah. In view of the fact that both libraries were – and still are – only able to keep afloat with the aid of volunteers and donations from philanthropists, this was going to be awkward. Minds were massaged; egos within this fractious family of Jews soothed, and a deal was done. A donor bought the Kadimah a computer and printer, and their board agreed to contribute to the maintenance of the digital system. I allocated a few hours of time for a member of Makor's staff to catalogue a handful of Yiddish books, which someone would pick up and deliver each week. It was incredibly slow work, for none of us was proficient with Yiddish. I had no choice but to give the work to a Hebrew-speaker who patiently explained to me that whilst the alphabets were identical, the two languages were quite different.

In 2000 my dreams of retirement evaporated. Rachel told me that as I had 'nothing much to do now' I should get on with cataloguing the Kadimah library myself. From my home computer I would be able to access the Makor network, which by this time had expanded to include the libraries of the Holocaust Museum, the Sephardi Synagogue, the Australian Jewish Historical Society and the Australian Jewish Genealogical Society. I really had no choice. For the next twelve years I spent about twenty hours a week (Jewish and summer holidays excluded) cataloguing and on Wednesday mornings delivered and picked up a seemingly never-ending stream of bags and boxes of old Yiddish books. It was an education and taught me much more about my heritage.

At Beth Weizmann I had worked in an English and Modern Hebrew environment, but at the Kadimah I was transported back to Europe, to my family's roots and the Yiddish culture of my ancestors. Professionally, it was a huge challenge, for I didn't understand the language and had to master the alphabet. The elderly volunteers, who all had Yiddish as their *mama loshn* (mother tongue), and European politics and history in their bloodstream, were amused by my efforts and provided me with translations and transliterations so

I might make coherent catalogue entries. On the other hand, they didn't know much about modern library practices. If I mentioned that I'd been searching for information on the Library of Congress database, they really were unable to visualise it.

Most of the books in the Kadimah collection were brought to Australia by immigrants who then donated them. Many items are fragile but have great historic importance. I learned, with surprise, that poetry is the largest section. It was fascinating to discover that Yiddish women writers in earlier times ran into the same sort of discrimination as their counterparts in America and England, using pseudonyms or initials in order to get their work on to a publisher's desk. I found books on politics of every shade – anarchism, socialism, communism – and the history and fate of most European Jewish communities.

There were many other surprises in those boxes of shabby books. Sometimes I was delighted and amused. Gilbert and Sullivan's *The Pirates of Penzance* becomes *Die Yom Bonditten (The Sea Bandits)* in Yiddish – indeed a treasure – but often I was in tears. I discovered dilapidated little booklets, without a proper binding or English translation, that are eye-witness accounts of the destruction of a village somewhere in Eastern Europe – slim fragile records on cheap, crumbling paper, held together with rusty staples. Sometimes it took me hours of searching to locate a village that had been destroyed, for place names as well as communities have been erased, and the modern atlas is unsympathetic. It seemed imperative to get it right, to make a statement, to record the correct name. *Zachor!* Occasionally there was a grey, grainy photograph of the author into whose eyes I stared, musing about his or her life.

There were also books representative of the flowering of Yiddish theatre, so cruelly cut off by the rise of fascism. The religious books were relatively scarce, for the liturgy is in Hebrew; the Yiddish language was only used to print easy-reading texts for Orthodox women. Fiction publishing flourished and I was amazed to find Yiddish stories published not only in Poland and Russia, but also in Buenos Aires, Mexico City, Johannesburg and Melbourne. The classics from other European languages were there too. I found Yiddish editions of Dickens, Dumas, Tolstoy and 'Viliam Shakspir'. Writers who expressed strong humanitarian values and social consciences were particular favourites among the Jews of the *Haskalah* as they emerged from the claustrophobic *shtetl* environment. All of this was such a long way away from my personal experiences. The 'old-timers' at Kadimah could actually remember when Yiddish culture was so vibrant and were philosophical about it, but I was fresh to the history and appalled at the destruction of a way of life

I worked at home at all hours of the day and night, tripping over the boxes of old books that littered our floors. I didn't spend a lot of time actually in the Kadimah, but the homely atmosphere there touched a chord. In old-world environments, like the Holocaust Museum or the Kadimah, personal history is of great importance. Hospitality and providing an ancestry go hand in hand: 'Have a cup of tea. So tell me about your family.' Bono, a stalwart Yiddishist, was gruff and abrasive but had twinkling eyes. He had seen much misery in Europe, was left-wing in his politics and aggravated many of the community's conservative luminaries. Early in the piece he met me one day in the Kadimah library. I must have stuck out as being someone 'other', for he demanded, 'Where are *you* from?' I told Bono what I was doing and proffered the information that I came from London. 'No, no, no! Where is your *family* from?' he said, brushing aside the possibility that I might have had a respectable British background. My paternal grandparents, Morris and Regina, came to mind and I tentatively suggested Lemberg (Lvov, Lviv). There was an explosion, a snort of derision. *'Galitsyaners!'* he roared. 'Horse thieves from Galicia!' Nathan and Eva, my maternal grandparents from further east, were received a little better and gave me a touch more edge in the ancestry stakes. I found the whole atmosphere enchanting, quaint and very warm.

The Melbourne Chronicle, a bi-lingual cultural and literary journal, had been published by the Kadimah since 1968, and Alan contributed stories and poems throughout the 1990s. *Generation,* another Jewish cultural journal published in the same period and beautifully produced, unfortunately ceased publication for lack of funds. Its editors also accepted Alan's work and he was awarded the Manuel Gelman prize for his short story 'The Plot'.

The short story genre was really Alan's strength but I find the small handful of his poems interesting. 'The Ballad of Sid' is a dark poem. Alan is remembering Sam Collins and is terrified of becoming like his ill-fated father. I might have used this dreadful piece as an opening to a cleansing conversation with Alan, but I never did. In it he has caught Sam's turn of phrase, his pseudo-Yiddish mixed with 1930s Australian slang, as he peers into the mirror in fear:

> 'How do I look, son?
> I mean for a man of me age
> I've seen a bit of trouble
> In me time but always kept
> meself lookin' neat yer never know what's around the corner.
> Get me drift, son?'
>
> He preens and primps and winks
> at his image. He steps back,
> strikes a pose and leers like Mo.
> 'Ish Kebibble' he sings. He thinks
> it means in Yiddish 'I should worry'.
> He's got it on a scratchy Parlophone.
> 'Wind it up for me, son.'

And so it continues to the last lines:

My hair is wispy, my face is gaunt. His lips laugh
Where mine can hold no humour. His eyes draw me on:
'I'm waitin' for you, son.'

Sam Collins, c1927

Sam Collins, 1930s

During this period Alan was invited to speak at the Holocaust Museum at the time of the year when the community pays respect to the memory of the six million Jews who perished in the *Shoah*. Six writers had been asked to contribute their thoughts, and apart from Alan, all had strong family connections with Jewish Europe. He phoned the museum to double check that they really understood where he was coming from, but the organisers were quite clear that they wanted to hear his views. On the night, I sat on the end seat of the front row, ready to run if Alan said a word out of place. I knew very well how the other speakers would share horrific experiences with a sympathetic audience and explain the influence of the Holocaust on their work, and was sure Alan would be booed off the stage. He began:

> I tell you what, it's lonely up here. I am to be pitied – a Jew without the baggage that a Jew is expected to *shlep* around with him. A Jewish alien, that's what I am – not even the nomenclature of Jewish identity. Not a 'stein'

> not a 'ski', not a 'vich' to tack on to my terribly ordinary name – which would do more credit to a lad from Londonderry than you lucky folk from Lvov, with exotic names redolent of schnapps, kartoffel, cream cakes and schnitzel.

He concluded:

> … I have written of characters who experienced the Holocaust but totally different to my colleagues here tonight. I would not dare deal with matters that they have intimate knowledge of and a passion borne of that knowledge. Mine is the writer from the outside looking in. They in turn have left the telling of Jewish life in Australia from the Anglo-Jewish viewpoint to me … These writers carry with them the terrible overburden of history. They visit a country I sometimes feel I have only glimpsed from the window of a fast moving train. Maybe too, I don't want the train to stop at those stations with the strange sounding names. Not nice places, Alan, you wouldn't speak their language even though they might welcome you as a fellow Jew. So I write about what I know which is what it is like growing up and living and dying in this country where, thank God, patriotism and zealotry are negligible, and when a letter arrives with OHMS on the envelope it doesn't contain an imperative to pack your bags.

The audience thought about it for a minute and then applauded. I didn't run away. Quite a few people came to tell Alan that it was about time they heard his point of view.

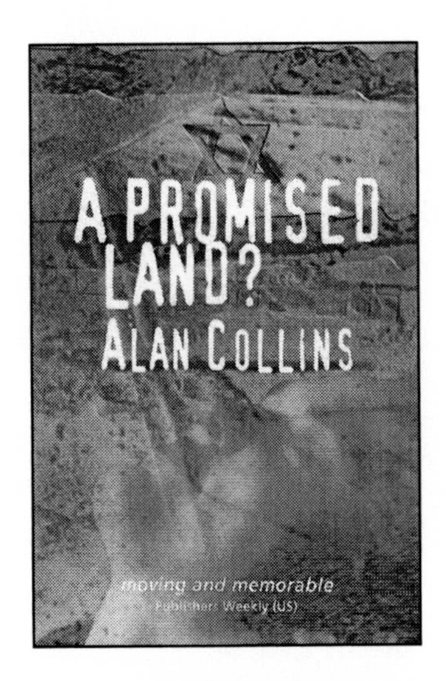

A Promised Land?
One-volume edition of the Jacob Kaiser trilogy

In 2001 the University of Queensland Press decided to issue Alan's three short novels as one 400-page volume with a new title, *A Promised Land?* (The question mark was deliberately chosen by Alan.) 'Promised land' turns up frequently in book titles: *Our Promised Land, The Promised Land, My Promised Land,* but Alan's question mark is unusual and carries a lot of weight. Do we stay or do we go? For Australian Jews will it be Bondi or Beersheba?

It always amuses me that whilst Alan's books are well reviewed, Orthodox Jewish schools and bookshops do not put them on their shelves. Well, think about it. The novels deal with neglected Jewish children and a black-marketeer uncle running just this side of the law; a Jewish orphanage where the reffo kids get most of the breaks and the local street boy is a poor runner-up; a hero, Jacob, who goes off in 1947 to live on a kibbutz with Peg, a non-Jewish nurse from Sydney's St Vincent's Hospital; a rabbi (!) who marries them; Peg, now Pnina, dying a heroine in the crossfire of an Arab raid on the kibbutz; broken-hearted Jacob more or less saying 'a pox on both your houses' and returning with an adopted baby to the haven of Bondi. Where's Jacob's 'promised land'? Twenty years on and the adopted baby, Joshua, becomes a draft-dodger in the Vietnam ballot. The story ends with him discovering his true identity in the archives at Yad Vashem in Jerusalem. Looking at our family's real-life history, it's easy to detect where many of Alan's themes originated; but a suitable book for Orthodox Jewish children?

When the editor of the Australian Jewish Historical Society journal asked me to write an article on the history of Makor ('before all the people involved, like yourself, have passed away' was the undiplomatic request), I jumped at the chance to write a definitive account. I did a good job of it, with research, footnotes and acknowledgements, and the piece appeared in Vol. XVI, 2002, Part 3, pp 328-340. I was still very connected with Makor. Every Wednesday, after I'd made my weekly visit to the Kadimah, I had lunch with the director, Leonie Fleiszig. It was all too obvious that our network of libraries, the largest public access collection of Jewish literature in Australia, needed much more support. I still dreamed of replicating the Jewish libraries of Montreal and New York on a smaller scale here in Melbourne.

My friend Danielle Charak, a stalwart of the National Council of Jewish Women, a university lecturer in Yiddish and regular borrower at both Makor and Kadimah, would sometimes help me with difficult Yiddish transcriptions. Perhaps 'difficult' is the wrong word; try 'idiosyncratic'. Unlike Modern Hebrew speakers, and despite the best efforts of academics, Yiddishists tend to be individualistic, tasting different spellings, arguing the toss about Ashkenazi and Sephardi variations (You know how it is – two Jews, three opinions!). When we were not wandering through the intricacies of *mentsh/mentsch, Shabbos/Shabbes,* Sholem Aleichem/Sholem-Aleykhem, I would discuss the future of our Jewish libraries with Danielle. 'You must put your ideas down in a discussion paper so that people with influence have something to talk about,' she said. So I spent the summer of 2004/05 writing a proposal for a Jewish Library of Australia, which I called 'Are we the People of the Book?' It was all pretty heady stuff, and I wrote quite forcefully about the policies of the libraries in the network we'd built up and what I believed should be done to develop a truly national Jewish library. The paper was well received by the various organisations charged with the responsibility for a library, but after the initial enthusiasm, matters stalled for a few years whilst the Australian economy and philanthropy faltered.

The cards Alan made for my desk

I was busy cataloguing for Kadimah. Alan made two little cards with ironic texts: the first reads, 'Retirement – like bloody hell I am!' and the second, 'Yiddish cataloguing today, tomorrow the world!' It's how he saw me.

Meanwhile, he was beginning work on the memoir of his terrible childhood. The composition was very painful and there were many stops and starts. In the evening when we'd sit down for our meal Alan would shyly give me a couple of pages to read, but 'only if you're not too busy'. I would encourage him to keep going, apprehensive in case he gave up; I knew he was writing it for me. There on the pages was all the suffering of the neglected child, all the things we probably should have talked about long before. Then he hit a block, and the writing stopped because Alan didn't know how to resolve the differences between events in the autobiographical fiction *The Boys from Bondi* and the real-life world of the new book, *Alva's Boy*. He talked about the problem with Alex Skovron, who would eventually edit his work.

Alva's Boy is probably a psychological minefield, but 'leave your mind alone' was Alan's leit-motif. The story is as powerful as *Angela's Ashes,* but Australian-Jewish instead of Irish-Catholic. The book stands, as Jan Epstein has said, as 'a tale of redemption', 'the stuff of Dickens and Victor Hugo'. It's Bondi, not Belsen, but misery is misery, a child is a child, and this one became the man I knew, just as Sadie and Solly's golden-haired girl, with her ringlets and bows, became me. 'Loving and large in spirit,' said Jan Epstein of Alan; I wonder how shall I be described?

Alan with his grandmother, Rebecca Davis, at Ashfield Infants' Home, c1929

Ashfield Infants' Home – October 1928. Matron's entry in her day book reads:

Mr Sampson Collins of 1 Belvedere Mansions, Bondi, was interviewed: Religion, Jewish, traveller by profession. Wants to place baby six weeks old in Infants' Home. Baby born at home, but mother died shortly afterwards; baby's name Alan Alva; Mr Collins willing to pay £1 a week; will bring baby Saturday afternoon.

At seventy-nine Alan remembered the bars of the cot, the smells of the food and the damp washing. Ashfield Infants' Home was 'home' for four years and Grandma Rebecca Davis only came once to visit. Ashfield Infants' Home and Ashurst Drive are worlds apart but just eighteen months later in North East Ham, London, Solly registered the birth of his daughter, Rosaline, on 19 February 1930. She was recorded as the child of Solomon Leon Fox a 'tailor's machiner' and Sadie Millie Fox, formerly Samuels, and would be going home to 36 Ashurst Drive, Ilford.

Ros in the garden with Solly and Sadie, 1930

CHAPTER 27
U.K. BYE, BYE

Alan and I had long neglected Tasmania, but we did get there in 2003. We drove along the east coast and in Hobart stayed in old-fashioned cottage accommodation that had a little suite devoted to *Titanic* memorabilia. Alan revelled in the make-believe, dressed up in the uniform conveniently provided and entered an iceberg warning in the pretend log book. But his health was not good and walking was painful, even with a walking stick.

Titanic 'make-believe' in Hobart, 2003

The following year Alan was scheduled for an orthopaedic procedure. We were shocked when the specialist told him he might as well stay put since he needed urgent triple by-pass heart surgery. Increasingly he suffered with back and leg problems and a facial neuralgia that was difficult to control. In 2004 we celebrated our forty-seventh wedding anniversary in Cabrini Hospital rehab after an arm operation. Diabetes emerged as well; altogether, Alan's health became an issue that he just hated to acknowledge. His diet in childhood – fish and chips on the run and boarding-house slops – contained nothing guaranteed to grow good bones, and he didn't have a strong physique. He had also pushed himself far too hard 'proving' himself a good Aussie father to his boys.

In sympathy, our little corgi, Bertie, 'did his back'. His spine just collapsed and the vet at the sophisticated animal hospital told us it would cost more than $3,500 for the operation. There was no way we would have had him euthanised, and with help from the family we paid up in instalments. Bertie convalesced inside a playpen that I decorated with ribbons to give his spirits a lift.

In 2005 our family was reunited when Toby, Rhonda, three boys (Isaac now two) and Rosie, their Border collie, returned to Melbourne. Alan and I had missed some crucial growing years, particularly with Joshua, but we promised ourselves that we'd catch up.

An orthopaedic surgeon suggested I could do with new hips. I had always walked hurriedly, just like Sadie used to, and like her, just wore the bones away. So in January 2006 the operation was done on the left side and I convalesced on crutches quite successfully. Our house was now acquiring grab rails in the bathroom, aids to help with putting on socks and shoes, pick-up sticks to save bending down, and special gardening equipment to assist with weeding. Alan was a sucker for kitchen gadgets that guaranteed pain-free jar-opening, but really it was easier to ask one of the boys. At seventy-eight and seventy-six we were becoming more and more reliant on our children.

Reluctantly Alan had to abandon two long-standing dreams. He would have loved us to become 'grey nomads', spending idyllic moments gazing at sunsets in remote Australian beauty spots whilst a delicious meal cooked on a portable barbecue. In his heart he always knew this was never going to happen because I wouldn't have gone with him.

The other dream was his wish to have another motor scooter like *La Cigale*, and to relive his youth. But scooters are quite heavy, and the boys and I were doubtful because he was already struggling with a modest pushbike. A compromise was reached, and Alan bought a pale blue electric-powered bike that looked just a little like the real thing and gave him a taste of the freedom he remembered from the 1950s. He really was a very modest man and completely

Al with his blue scooter, c2007.
The jacket is the one he wore in 1956

unselfconscious as he rode around Elwood doing the messages and chatting to the shop-keepers. There was no chance of me riding pillion, but I'm glad there was another motor scooter in Alan's life.

When my convalescence was over we had a holiday in Sydney; it was to be the last one. That was when he showed me the house in Francis Street, Bondi. Even though it's the scene of Alan's early misery, there's a cleansing feeling for me to go there, a sense of triumph that there was happiness for him eventually and that I was part of it. Although it makes me cry, particularly walking down to Campbell Parade, where he used to risk life and limb jumping on and off the trams selling newspapers, or race across the sand to hide in the rocks at Ben Buckler, nonetheless I can mentally raise two fingers defiantly to beautiful Sydney, buy an ice cream on Bondi Beach and know that with all our mistakes, we made it.

My second hip operation was scheduled for January 2007 and this meant that by 17 February, the date of our golden wedding anniversary, I'd still be on crutches. We didn't plan a party of any kind until very late in the piece – almost as an afterthought. We waited until March so that I'd be a little stronger, and it was a perfect day for afternoon tea in our back garden with family and friends; it was totally relaxed and happy. Alan was too overjoyed to make a speech and so I thanked our guests and told some anecdotes. I ended with:

So…let's have another party in ten years' time on our diamond wedding. For all of us may there be good health, and happy times – and as they say in Yiddish *'biz hundert un tsvantsig yor'* – for one hundred and twenty years!

Alan and Ros in the garden at our golden wedding anniversary party, March 2007

Our god-daughter, Rosie, who is a talented violinist, was a young teenager at the time and she chose to play for us Schumann's *Träumerei* ('Dreaming'), saying she hoped that Alan and I would have many more years of dreaming together. But it didn't happen that way.

Alan and Isaac at our golden wedding anniversary party

It seemed ominous when Bertie died in June, and we both wept for the little dog whose lovely red coat never grew back properly after his operation, and for whom I had made a beautiful tartan replacement. We agreed we would 'never have another dog' and were 'too old to train a puppy'. But we rallied and in July brought home eight-week-old Sophie, tri-coloured black, tan and white, and since the cruel practice of docking has been banned, our first corgi to be in possession of a beautiful fox-like tail.

Bertie

Sophie

The last time I left Alan was the hardest; perhaps he knew he was becoming ill. In 2007 I planned a final visit to the family in England and to Israel if the budget would allow. I felt then I would be ready for a comfortable retirement with Alan in Elwood by the beach. I decided to go in September/October when the weather would be reasonable in both places. Apart from seeing all my English cousins, I hoped to make some professional enquiries, for at that time there was not much happening in regard to the plans for an Australian national Jewish library. The only one of my cousins I wouldn't be able to see was Jonathan in Los Angeles.

I showed the video of our golden wedding anniversary party to my relatives and 'talked up' Melbourne and Australia with great enthusiasm. My cousin Maurice took me to see the graves of Solly and Sadie. I'll probably not be able to visit them again, but twice a year my cousin Gina visits all the gravesites on Solly's side of our family.

I did do some work on libraries in London. Most exciting, I made my first visit to the British Library. It's a tourist attraction in its own right and it's there in my memory with the Library of Congress and the New York Public Library. I also visited several Jewish libraries and some of the people I met struck me as envious of our plans for Melbourne. I was stressing co-operation and open access, whereas they seemed to cling to exclusivity. One library, at the Spanish and Portuguese Synagogue in Maida Vale, made me quite sad. I went there to photograph the painting of Alan's ancestor, Joseph Cortissos (1656-1742), who had come to London from Barcelona. The library is in a pretty, panelled room and the librarian was very courteous. I mentioned the books of Rabbi John Levi AM, who has done such wonderful work documenting Australian-Jewish history and genealogy, and she was interested in acquiring copies. We were both crestfallen when it turned out that the synagogue board was unlikely to approve the purchase of books, no matter how important, by a rabbi from the Progressive branch of Judaism.

Bauhaus architecture in Rehov Mendeli (Mendele Street), Tel Aviv, Israel

I made it to Israel for a week and stayed in Tel Aviv, a city I thoroughly enjoyed. I walked along the promenade beside the Mediterranean right up to Jaffa. I might have lived there if I'd taken the offers from the Jaffa Orange Company or Marks and Spencer all those years ago. Heritage was everywhere and I smiled at Rehov Mendeli (Mendele Street) named for the 'father' of Yiddish fiction, Mendele Moycher Sforim, whose works I had catalogued at Kadimah. I admired the 1920s Bauhaus buildings, gleaming in their restored whiteness, and in the older parts of the city wandered through a jumble of oriental cast-iron balconies festooned with bougainvillea. In Jerusalem it gave me a lot of pleasure to visit the Israel National Library in the Hebrew University and inform the directors of the excellent work being done in far-off Australia.

Whilst I was away saying my goodbyes to England, Alan had taken himself off to Sydney, on what I subsequently discovered was a similar journey. Much later, when I went there to launch *Alva's Boy*, I met a group of old friends from his youth, mostly women whose instincts were keen. They told me that at the time they had the distinct impression he was saying farewell to them and to the city. He was certainly unwell, but at that stage no diagnosis had been made and he and I believed he was merely getting older. When I left Heathrow for the journey back to Melbourne I knew I was going 'home'. The boys wouldn't allow Alan to come to the airport so early in the morning, and they brought me back to Elwood, where I was greeted by a framed message on the dining room table:

Welcome Home Ros!

...make my bed,
Light a light,
I'll be home
Late tonight
U.K. bye, bye!

The welcome home message, 2007

Obviously to be sung to the tune of 'Bye Bye Blackbird'.

Alva's Boy: an unsentimental memoir was almost finished. I was still reading the day's output over our evening meal, and there was a strange moment when Alan asked me if I thought he was going mad. It was a shock, and of course I stoutly rejected any such idea, but now I think it was 'cancer talk'. We didn't know what was wrong, but his mind was guessing. And of course there was the constant cigarette cough – even though he'd quit thirty years earlier.

The last outing we had with all the family was over the summer holiday period when we went for lunch to the Bridge Hotel, where we sat on the deck overlooking Mordialloc Creek. Alan could hardly walk and looks gaunt in the photographs. But he still attended the Kehilat Nitzan service each *Shabbat*. When he could no longer get his sore feet into shoes, he wore sandals and, like a schoolboy, took a note to Rabbi Bandel apologising for his unsuitable footwear.

At the beginning of 2008, in the midst of all the preliminary tests, I took us to the offices of Hybrid where Louis de Vries offered a contract to publish *Alva's Boy*. As we drove home Alan said, 'Well, I've finished with Sydney now,' and I said, 'Well then, it's time to start writing about Melbourne,' and as we went down North Road we started to plan how he might do it. But he would not have time to write about our lives together – it fell to me.

Alan's last outing with the family. The pub at Mordialloc, December 2007

CHAPTER 28
FIVE SEAGULLS

The progress of an illness is a miserable journey to record. It was a cancer on Alan's oesophagus; probably something connected with smoking since he was a twelve-year-old street kid. Yet the oncologist was optimistic and said the survival rate was not totally black. He thought Alan would recover.

Chemotherapy requires a strong constitution and an equally strong will; Alan had neither. There were many setbacks: late night trips by ambulance for blood transfusions, sores in his mouth, swollen feet, and weakness throughout his slight body. On one particularly bad night Peter and I carried him to the car for a final journey to hospital.

There are some things I'm not prepared to do, such as delving into medical records to find the exact dates for this or that procedure. I don't want to go there, just as I won't look at the photographs of the Cortina car in which Peter and Toby nearly died. I am searching for words to describe how we were during the period of Alan's treatment and death and am not at all happy with terms like 'surreal', 'trauma' or 'shock'. I return to the theme of *zachor*, remembering and will let my memories run free.

I'll start with Sophie, a small six-month-old corgi, for whom the park was strange and big and a little frightening. The park is within walking distance if one is strong enough, but it was too far for Sophie's short legs and Alan's weak ones, so I would drive us there. He would sit on a seat under a tree and watch as the little puppy played. When I walk there now I always look at the tree and the seat.

The cancer damaged his larynx; he lost his voice and we couldn't communicate. How ironic that we'd always had problems with the 'deep and meaningful' and here it was manifesting in the most

'Alan's seat' in Elsternwick Park

horrible way. No longer was it an option for Alan to crack a joke or make a pun. Later Peter transferred from the old answering machine a faint recording in which Alan is struggling to leave me a message: 'Please bring me new batteries for my radio'. It was terribly difficult for him to make the words, and the metaphor is heartbreaking.

I would sit by the bed and we'd hold hands. Alex Skovron, Danielle Charak and Frankie Slonim would come and read to him. Alex read some of his own short stories and Alan loved them. He had so much respect for this friend who, unknown to him, would later edit his book. Anna Blay at Hybrid had sent me a disc with the first page proofs for *Alva's Boy.* I printed them off and brought them in for him to hold. Alex was there that day, and when Peter arrived Alan asked our son to read aloud from the book; I could see he was proud for Alex to hear his work and happy in the knowledge it was going to be published.

Depression: So much is written about it now. In hospital Alan fell into a severe depression and tried to starve himself. It was 'a shit of a life' he told the oncologist and he didn't want to live as an invalid. There are medications that help, and I should be grateful that late in his hospitalisation he was given treatment that finally raised his spirits a little. Shimon, an old friend, came to visit him and we took Alan out into the sunshine in a wheelchair. He requested a cup of tea. In the photographs my false *bonhomie* seems dreadful. I won't print them here. On our last day I sat on the bed and put Alan's hand under my t-shirt so that he might hold my breast – he was always happy to do that – and he was smiling. I went down to the gift shop to buy a birthday card for Toby so that we could both sign. As I left his room, decorated with flowers and the notices I'd made exhorting him to be strong and positive, he waved a cheery goodbye.

The nurse phoned about three in the morning on Thursday 27 March. I remember saying, 'you're not telling me this,' as though I could make the news go away. Toby, Rhonda and Daniel came with me to the hospital. Peter would not go; he and Joel stayed at home to make the phone calls. Cabrini is a large Catholic hospital and they deal with death very compassionately. There's a special suite where they lay out the dead, and I could stroke Alan's forehead and kiss his face. He was still warm.

The Jewish community deals with funerals so efficiently. Alan and I had already bought plots in the Jewish Memorial Rose Garden at Springvale. As members of Kehilat Nitzan we called our rabbi, Ehud Bandel, to officiate at the funeral; we also wanted the Chevra Kadisha, the Jewish Burial Society, to treat our bodies in the traditional manner. It wasn't long before the men arrived to take Alan to the their building in Inkerman Street, St Kilda – not that far from where we had lived in 1958. Here Alan would be washed and prepared for burial.

The family left the hospital and gathered in the office of the Chevra Kadisha with Ehud, a former member of the Israeli parachute forces and now a rabbi, and the director, Ephraim Finch, a convert to Orthodox Judaism, as 'ocker' as a kangaroo. We sat amazed at how well they worked together and how wonderfully they dealt with us. Ephraim, of the white beard and twinkling eyes, phoned the carpenter with the measurements for Alan's plain pine coffin. Ehud gently explained how we were to conduct ourselves over the next few days. When I asked where Al was, Ephraim said he was safe in the back room and wouldn't be lonely as he'd visit now and then to crack a joke. We went home to write eulogies.

With such a small family we had little first-hand experience of funeral customs. Providing meals for the bereaved is a *mitzvah,* and we were astonished and grateful when members of Kehilat Nitzan quietly arrived, packed the fridge with food and just as quietly left. We sat and wrote.

Jewish burials are always conducted as soon as possible after death, and the mourning customs are well designed to emphasise life over death. There were a lot of people in the Rose Garden for Alan's funeral the next day at 11.15 am, Friday 28 March. The hearse from the Chevra Kadisha brought Alan to us and the birds in the gum trees made a wonderful racket as Ehud conducted the traditional burial service. His eulogy was from the heart and he spoke no platitudes:

> His sons told me yesterday that Alan was not a religious person. But perhaps we should redefine what is a religious person, because Alan – *Avraham ben Alva v'Shimshon HaCohen* … was for me a role model and an inspiration … Alan – the boy from Bondi, you are going home now, to the rest and the peace of your promised land – the Promised Land without a question mark. From the second book of your trilogy, *Going Home*, I learned that the Australian 'cobber' comes from the Hebrew word *chaver* and that it was brought by the Australian soldiers who fought in Palestine in the First World War who could not pronounce *chaver* and changed it to 'cobber'.
>
> So, like Bill Clinton in his farewell to Yitzchak Rabin I end this eulogy with the simple and sincere words: *Shalom chaver* – Goodbye cobber.

Ehud has now returned to his home in Jerusalem, but we will always remember his compassion. I have arranged for a flowering Grevillea ('Wendy Sunshine'), to be planted in the garden at Kehilat Nitzan, and a plaque bears Ehud's name and Alan's and the Hebrew word *chaverim* – friends.

Ehud involved all the boys, including Joel, in the recitation of Psalms and invited each to say a few words about their father. I didn't realise at the time that it was not so usual for widows to make a speech, but when Ehud invited me, I said this:

> I want to thank you all for coming today to farewell my dearest love. Most of you here are not family and we were, and indeed are, so glad you chose to be our friends. Alan never actually had a real family until we made one together. His love for his boys, Dan, Pete, Toby and Joel, and for his wonderful daughter-in-law, Rhonda, and for his grandsons, Josh, Eli and Isaac was deep and rich and full of hopes for their happiness. They are his future and his life continues through them. I will care for them on his behalf, but it won't be the same at all.
>
> He told me every single day how much he loved me and it was no glib platitude – he really meant it with all his heart. We had fifty-one years together and I treasure every moment. It was my lucky day when Al agreed to marry me. I had him imprisoned in a London telephone box at the time so he didn't have much choice, but I think he was glad to have his mind made up for him. I continued to make up his mind for him for fifty-one years, but of course I always let him decide the big issues like who should lead the ALP. In 1957 *Oklahoma!* was the hit musical and he always loved it. Somewhere in there is the line 'a heart as big as all outdoors' – how very true of my Alan. And Doris Day was singing a very soppy song *'Que sera, sera'* (what will be, will be) How true this is today.
>
> We were so lucky that we could share so much, and literature featured enormously in our lives. I'm so very proud of what he has achieved and it gave us both such a thrill when letters came from people who'd read his work with pleasure. Alan always said his books were 'ordinary' – that's not so. I am so proud to see them listed on databases from places such as the Library of Congress and the British Library. We were hoping he'd write about his life in

Melbourne but that can't happen now. However, his new book, *Alva's Boy*, will be published later this year.

Alva was Alan's mother and she died at his birth. She was named for Alan's Spanish ancestor who served the famous Duke of Alba at the time of the Inquisition. Al was astonished when I found the details of his family. Was it really true that he had such an interesting and colourful ancestry – that he wasn't just a nobody from the streets of Bondi?

His terrible childhood and adolescence are well known to most of you. I think that as his illness took away his strength he started to reflect more and more on his early years. He saw himself as Alva's boy and he enjoyed me telling him that his mother would have been very proud of her son.

The ragged little boy from Bondi, the young man with the 'sad eyes', the hopeful traveller who landed in England and found me; these are gone. To the children and me he wasn't any of those persons - he was just Al. The family he created will always love and treasure his memory and try to do him honour.

His cardiac surgeon said recently that Alan had 'a very nice little heart'. He didn't understand how big and loving a heart it was.

After we had filled in his grave, as is the custom, and recited *Kaddish*, a simple wooden temporary marker was put in place. We left native Australian flowers and seashells, rather than the traditional stones, which always seem too hard and forbidding.

Sitting *shiva* involves seven days of mourning, staying at home, sitting on low chairs and receiving condolences; a *minyan*, apart from its meaning of ten Jewish adults, also refers to the prayers that are recited in the evening at the house of the bereaved. We were not quite so observant as to sit for the entire *shiva* period and only held two *minyanim*: on Sunday and Monday. Both were so crowded that the people spilled out into our garden. I think it was Rhonda's idea, but we decided it would be a comfort if all the family slept in our house for a few nights, so sleeping bags and blankets covered couches and floors whilst we grieved together.

The boys and I set about some of the more immediate tasks, and Toby was particularly practical in getting rid of those most horrible of mementos – medications. I went through the clothes and was delighted when the boys took some of Alan's shirts, jackets and sweaters. Even our eldest grandsons sometimes turn up in a familiar item and it gives me much pleasure. Our friend Tony Heselev, a man of great empathy and compassion and a fine journalist, worked with me on obituaries for *The Age* and the *Australian Jewish News*.

All this activity was conducted on auto-pilot, as I was quite unable to find consolation, equilibrium or acceptance. A friend gave me meditation tapes and recommended I keep a diary, but I couldn't sustain any of it. I walked Sophie along Elwood beach fantasising that Alan's spirit in the shape of a seagull sitting on the broken-down old jetty was communicating with me. If five seagulls were sitting in a group I identified them as our family, one for each of us – Alan, me and the three boys.

Seagulls on the old jetty at Elwood Beach, 2008

CHAPTER 29
YEAR ONE

Each year, the Jewish Community Council of Victoria publishes a directory/diary including both English and Hebrew dates, information about when to light candles, where to find any Jewish organisation, Jewish school holidays and a reminder for every anniversary, from the most relatively minor such as the phases of the moon, to the commemoration of the Warsaw Ghetto revolt. I have kept the editions since Alan died and they are great triggers for my memory.

The 2008 (or, if you prefer, 5768) edition records an exhausting year and I now speculate on what I was feeling. There's no doubt that I was driven, obsessed and compulsive, particularly where Alan's work was concerned.

The grief was very raw and for a couple of months I did not wish to live. Two dear friends, Beryl and Norma, phoned every day like clockwork; I called them my 'two shoes', for I was like a flat dweller waiting for the people upstairs to undress: first one shoe hits the floor and then the other. March is autumn in Melbourne, and the leaves were starting to fall. Winter crept along and so did I. Walking home with shopping in the late afternoon dusk, I wept because Alan would not be there. The beach was unbearable; I just shoved the 'unheld' hand into my pocket as Sophie and I trudged along beside the grey bay, and mentally marked off his favourite places. I slept deeply and soundly without dreaming, and the weak sleeping tablets prescribed then have become a harmless habit. All the frenzied activity of that year amazes me; work was my antidote for sorrow.

A few weeks after the funeral, Alex Skovron came to see me. He was concerned that the manuscript for *Alva's Boy* was not edited, and the publishers, Louis and Anna at Hybrid, were anxious to have the book finalised. Alex is a highly regarded poet and professional editor. With kindness and compassion he suggested we work together to get *Alva* ready for publication. Alan's book is set in the Sydney of the 1940s and 1950s, and his historical allusions all needed to be verified: the wording of advertisements, Australian slang of the period, the dates of major events such as the opening of the Harbour Bridge, the Japanese submarines in Sydney Harbour, newspaper headlines. It was a suitable task for a librarian.

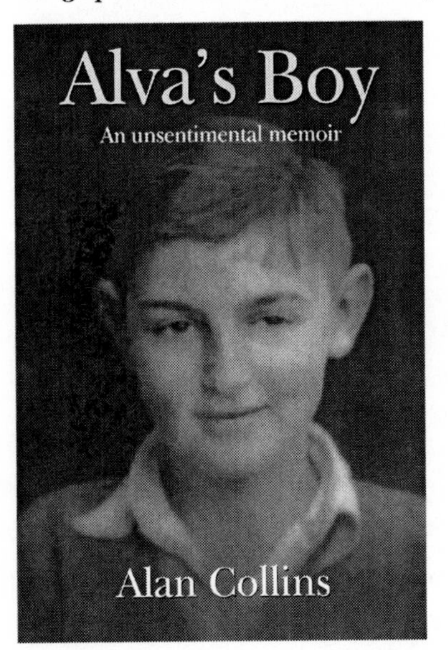

Choosing a book cover was a challenge; I wanted a picture of young Alan, but few were ever taken of him as a child. A tiny photograph of an eleven-year-old boy was made into a haunting front cover and we decided that Alva and Bondi Beach would be the perfect complement for the back:

Alan and I had already agreed on the title. He had also written the dedication:

For Rosaline
and the family
I never thought
I would have

It's the last two lines that say it all. His other books are also dedicated to me and the boys, but here in absolute nakedness is the core of his being. Alan had never dared hope for a family, and as a child he was known as 'poor Alva's boy'. The phrase must have burned his soul.

Alan's last Valentine, 2008

It's not Belsen or Auschwitz, no turnips or Siberian prison camp, no fleeing across Europe, but who are we to judge pain? Manfred once told Alan that although the reffo kids had suffered unimaginable torments and deprivations, and many had lost their parents, they all knew that, unlike him, they had once been loved. At the launch, Joanne Govendir, who knew Alan from her childhood, sang a lullaby because, as she said, 'Alva had never had the chance to sing for her boy.'

As the year progressed, so the anniversaries came around. For fifty-one years Alan would make me cards for Valentine's Day, our anniversary, my birthday and Mothers' Day – witty, full of puns and excruciating doggerel – and I have kept them all. In the early days they would be cut and paste jobs, just as advertising used to be. In later years Alan would personalise the sentimental verses in the pre-packaged computer programs. Back in February 2008 he was very weak and the last Valentine is a tiny message, ten centimetres square, on unevenly cut photocopy paper. He must have struggled to compose it in secret when I was out shopping.

In the diary, February is a busy month, and a week later Alan bravely tried to manipulate the computer to make me a birthday/wedding anniversary card; the puns are missing, some of the lettering didn't print correctly and he must have been feeling very ill. He chose to illustrate his greeting with pictures of *La Cigale* and the 1927 Chevy. I imagine his thoughts were all of 1957 rather than 2008. I, on the other hand, chose a shop card with a bright red motor scooter – I changed Vespa to Lambretta – and my message was determinedly optimistic:

Ah, they were fun days weren't they!
But there's lots more 'goodies' in store
You're getting better
We'll launch Alva's Boy
Eli will be 13
Isaac will be 5
Josh will be 16
You'll be …
We'll have a holiday, etc. etc.
Oh, and you will write the NEXT book!

My community diary throws up some odd items. On Monday 31 March Alan and I had been scheduled to enjoy a very special occasion. Our financial advisors had given us a voucher (on account of our golden wedding) for afternoon tea at that most prestigious of Melbourne's hotels, the historic Victorian era Hotel Windsor, where cakes come on beautiful tiered stands and tea (leaf, of course) is poured into the finest china cups. We'd had the impressive card for over a year, unused because Alan was not well enough, and I begged for an extension of time, hoping that we'd make it one day. The voucher sits in the 2008 diary, a red card with gold lettering, but the invitation has expired.

Tribute evening at the Jewish Museum, 2008.
L–R: Rabbi Ehud Bandel, Judy Becher, Stan Marks, Alex Skovron, Leah Justin, Paul Forgasz, Ros

Alan's enthusiasm for the Melton Adult Education Program was legendary, and the teachers were very fond of him with his provocative questions about Jewish philosophy, history and culture. Judy Becher, the president, asked me whether I felt strong enough to participate in a tribute evening they wished to organise in June, and although it was difficult, I agreed. The Jewish Museum put on a great evening to a packed hall. The director of Melton, Leah Justin, with whom Alan loved to flirt, gave an introduction full of wit and loving memories, and Alex Skovron read from *Alva's Boy*. Our old friend Stan Marks read Alan's short story 'Marianna's Father', Rabbi Ehud Bandel spoke from the heart, and Paul Forgasz, one of his most perceptive teachers, gave a mini-Melton lesson taken from a text by Maimonides, and focused on Alan's innate humility. As Alan so often quipped, he was 'a modest man, with a lot to be modest about'. He really had 'no tickets on himself' and it was an endearing quality.

The family all had a busy year in 2008. Dan went off for a trip to Central America and Cuba; Peter bought a new flat and Toby got a new job. I was cataloguing Yiddish, editing Alan's book, arranging the launch and finalising the wording for Alan's gravestone which was to be consecrated on Sunday, 12 October, a little over two weeks after what would have been his eightieth birthday, and two weeks before his memoir was to be launched.

Hebrew is not the easiest alphabet for the engraver, and I made many journeys to see Ehud and verify the letters. In transliteration, Alan's Hebrew name reads *Avraham ben Alva v'Shimshon ha-Cohen*. In translation it means 'Abraham son of Alva and Sampson the Cohen'. All the gravestones in the Rose Garden are of uniform size; there is limited space for names and I wanted to be inclusive. No doubt it may confuse genealogists that Joel is there too, but I could never have left him out.

The Jewish lunar-based calendar doesn't match the Gregorian one we use in everyday life. By coincidence, the day before the consecration was the anniversary of Alan's bar mitzvah and I chose to attend the synagogue service. The designated *parsha* that Alan had chanted so long ago in Sydney's Great Synagogue, is called *Ha'azinu*, the Hebrew word for 'listen'. It is also known as the Song of Moses, delivered to the Israelites on the last day of his life. I never delve into Midrash, textual exposition or interpretation; however, I can't help but think of the prophet climbing to the top of Mount Nebo and looking at the Promised Land that he would never have the opportunity of visiting.

Alan's grave in the Jewish Memorial Rose Garden, Springvale

There were not as many people at the consecration as there had been at the funeral. Ehud recited the prayers and after we had said *Kaddish* we came home with a few of our nearest friends for bagels and coffee. I brought back the wooden marker from Alan's grave and placed it next to a lavender bush in the garden bed by our front door.

My memories of the launch of *Alva's Boy* are dominated by the atmosphere in the hall at Beth Weizmann. Looking from the lectern to see a sea of friends, many in tears, made it difficult for me to retain equilibrium, even though I tried to keep my speech light-hearted. I had planned a proper program with musical interludes. Our god-daughter, Rosie, reprised *Träumerei*, which she had played for us in the garden at our golden wedding party. Joanne from Sydney sang, unaccompanied, a Ladino (Spanish-Jewish) lullaby. Nichaud Fitzgibbon, an old friend of ours, is a well-known musician and had agreed to perform. The classic American songbook (Gershwin, Rogers and Hammerstein, Porter, et al) includes many of Alan's favourites and I wanted the afternoon to end on an upbeat note. I had left Nichaud to make the choice and when she came onto the stage in her white satin tuxedo and announced that she would sing Gershwin's 'Someone to watch over me', it was hard for me to bear – and still is. I sat in the front row next to Jeanne Pratt, and as Nichaud began the pensive introduction to Gershwin's lovely song, Jeanne instinctively held my hand and I will always be grateful.

The main speakers were Alex Skovron, who launched the book, and I. Alex spoke very kindly about me. It seems immodest, but his words so accurately reflect the turmoil I was experiencing – the 'bittersweetness':

> In these past months, Ros has been on the emotional roller-coaster ride of her life. After the traumas of Alan's illness and death, she was hurtled into a grieving that was coloured so intensely by the bittersweetness of the emerging book and the intricacies of the editorial process. Ros's tireless and painstaking involvement in that process helped to ensure that Alan's aspirations for his unique memoir, from the integrity of the text to the impact and atmosphere of the cover, could be fully realized. Her coordination of the launch arrangements was equally exacting. Through it all, Ros's strength of spirit and her devotion to Alan's legacy have been truly inspirational.

The 'busy-ness' of that first year was not yet ended. The Jewish Museum wanted to build an audio-visual archive of Australian-Jewish life and asked me to participate. Would I be willing to allow a cameraman and interviewer to film me at home? It was a scramble to put together a suitable family history with appropriate visuals. They suggested I start with my own grandparents and go on from there, but I said they'd have to have Alan's history too since we came as a double act.

The family felt I should organise a Sydney launch because Alan's memoir is so focused on that city, and thus in December I spent four days arranging a week of engagements for the following March, to culminate in a function at Waverley (Bondi) Library. Two important memories remain from that visit: Firstly, I saw 48 Francis Street, Bondi, again. The outside of the house is virtually unchanged since the 1940s. Alan had taken me there in 2006, before he had written *Alva's Boy*, and when Lyn and Joanne Govendir drove me there I was overwhelmed to look again at the scene of Alan's childhood misery. I sat on the old gas box as he had done and thought about it all. Secondly, I met Trudie Schneider. In the book, Trudie is the little girl up the street who was feisty and strong and had stood up for Alan when things were bad. I tracked down this sprightly eighty-year-old and she told me all she remembered of him. I promised she'd be able to attend the launch in March.

48 Francis Street, Bondi, Sydney

The 2008 diary entries conclude with appointments for something called Calma. Back in February, Toby and Rhonda had given me a birthday gift voucher for one of those places that pamper the body, soothe the mind and leave you smelling of delicious perfumes – all aches, pains, worries and troubles massaged right away. If ever there was a moment to use such a treat, it was surely then and I was grateful.

CHAPTER 30
YEAR TWO (2009–2010)

The Sydney launch had a very different feel from the one in Melbourne. Of course it was held in city of the book, with all the beauty, the misery and the redemption of its ending. The glorious location was Alan's home, just as suburban Ilford had been mine. When we came to Australia in 1957 he said we would make our lives in Melbourne because 'it would be hard to be serious in Sydney. I'd always be at the beach'. There were other reasons, too, other memories that he didn't discuss until he wrote *Alva's Boy*.

It was Scott Whitmont, the best of Sydney booksellers, who approached Barry O'Farrell, then the leader of the New South Wales Opposition, to launch the book. Barry gave a superlative speech about this raggedy little Jewish street kid in 1940s Bondi who survived and triumphed over an abusive childhood. He spoke movingly about the reffos and how well Alan had caught the spirit of the times:

> While we were slow to offer refuge to European Jews – despite the urgings of people like Stanley Melbourne Bruce – thousands made their home here before and after the war. Along with peoples from many countries, they helped set this country on the path for success. Their legacy is felt today.
>
> And in Alan Collins' *Alva's Boy* their first, tentative, difficult steps are detailed, their reception captured. He describes a period that is as much a part of this nation's history as Cook's voyage of discovery or the arrival of the First Fleet.

Barry ended his speech by quoting from Leonard Cohen's 'Anthem':

> Ring the bells that still can ring
> Forget your perfect offering
> There is a crack in everything
> That's how the light gets in.

Somehow that reminds me of Alan's own phrase,

> Yet I grew like a weed between the cracks in the pavement, not roly-poly as over-cosseted Jewish children were supposed to be but thin and wiry.

Sydney launch of Alva's Boy.
L–R, back row: Sally Betts, Mayor of Waverley, Barry O'Farrell, MP, (former) leader of the NSW Opposition, Tony Reed (former) General Manager, Waverley Council; front row: Ros, Trudie Schneider

The Mayor of Waverley made a good speech too, stressing that if a film was ever made of any of Alan's works the première would definitely have to be in Bondi. The photographs were taken, and I was delighted that Trudie was there to link the 'now' and the 'then' with a happy smile. There were no tears.

I was in a heightened state after the Sydney launch and threw myself into the promotion of all Alan's work. I corresponded with overseas publishers, film producers, television stations and literary journals. *Alva's Boy* received very favourable reviews and the University of Queensland Press advised they would be producing an e-book edition of *A Promised Land?*

A film was something Alan and I had always wanted. When *The Boys from Bondi* was first published, a small production company took an option, long since lapsed, to make a television series. My friend Zelda, a film producer, and I tried to revive interest in the project but the fashion of late has been for gritty, urban dramas, preferably with much heaving and panting. However, perceptive reviews of *A Promised Land?* give me hope that one day this Dickensian story of a Jewish orphan in 1940s Sydney will make it to the screen.

There were also short stories in Alan's computer, some already published in *Troubles*, some unpublished, and I knew how much he had wanted to see a new edition of his first book. His publishers, Hybrid, were not able to finance it alone, but I had a solution. When Alan became sick, Manfred, his old friend from 1950s Melbourne, then living in New Jersey, had been very distressed. The day after the funeral a letter came with a cheque enclosed. Manfred understood how badly Alan had wanted to be at home, but appreciated that I wouldn't be able to care for him properly. The cheque was to pay for a nurse. I sent it back but it was returned, this time with my name on it and the instruction to use the money as I thought fit. *A Thousand Nights at the Ritz and Other Stories*, my title for the new collection, seemed the ideal way to use the gift and commemorate the friendship between the reffo from Dinkelsbühl and the boy from Bondi.

Anna, Managing Editor at Hybrid, ensured that the stories in *Ritz* looked just right and I found the edit a much easier task than the heart-break of *Alva*. Arnold Zable wrote a wonderful introduction and I was delighted with the cover design, the lettering and the whole upbeat tone of the production.

I did not want another book launch at Beth Weizmann, where there would have been overtones of sadness. *Ritz* was going to be a fun event, so I booked the upstairs oval foyer of the lovely old Art Deco cinema,

Arnold Zable launching A Thousand Nights at the Ritz. L–R: Mark Fitzgibbon at the piano, Arnold Zable, Ros

the Astor, for 20 February 2010.

In my introductory speech I said:

> The thought of standing on a stage and once again addressing a sea of solemn faces just didn't fit easily with *A Thousand Nights at the Ritz*. Alan was a humorist, and I think he would have loved the informality and nostalgia of this place which is perhaps closer in spirit to the man whose view of life was so quirky, off-beat, subversive and generally outrageous.

Arnold launched the book with his inimitable flair and enthusiasm and some of the phrases from his published introduction to the collection are spot on:

> [The characters are] a gallery of larrikins and rogues, shysters and hawkers, loners and newly arrived reffos … parvenus and social climbers.
>
> [Alan Collins has] an ear for the vernacular, and a visceral understanding of the physical world, its smells and textures, its grit and sensuousness.
>
> [The] writing is distinguished by a wicked sense of humour and a sense of the absurd that borders on the bizarre.
>
> [There is a] humanist vision that permeates the author's work.
>
> Collins' work was driven by a lifelong hatred of injustice and racism, religious bigotry and conformity, and the humiliations that derive from privilege and class. He could not abide exploitation and inequality, and

understood the crucial role class continues to play in shaping people's lives.

The faded plush décor, the chandeliers, Nichaud's brother Mark at the piano, Alan's favourite cakes – lamingtons – for afternoon tea, balloons, ice-cream and old cinema posters; it was the perfect send-off.

My passion for promotion was undiminished and *Ritz* was a real spirit raiser. We are told that there are stages of grief; denial and anger come before acceptance. My underlying emotion was anger – not so much because Alan had died, but because he had been denied so much in childhood and now, unfairly, was not able to enjoy seeing all his books in print. I wanted to put it all right for him, ride out in his defence, a Jewish Joan of Arc.

Limmud is a Jewish festival of learning and culture which features very high-powered, overseas speakers and local luminaries. Anna at Hybrid suggested I offer a session on Alan's life and work and I decided to turn the selection of slides I'd prepared for the Sydney launch of *Alva* into a Power Point presentation called 'The Boy from Bondi and the Ten Pound Pom'. Limmud is structured so that audiences always have a choice among as many as six different sessions each hour, and competition is fierce. I was scheduled at the same time as a hot-shot academic from New York who was talking about Sholem Aleichem, so boys from Bondi – or indeed from anywhere else in Australia – didn't really have a chance, and I presented my masterpiece to about twenty people. However, I did get to use the material at the Sydney Jewish Writers' Festival later in the year. But I find literary festivals, Jewish or otherwise, a mixed blessing. There are a lot of people doing a great deal of air-kissing, angling for a good spot where a photographer might find them, promoting their latest book or fronting up to pontificate with a panel – all often rather pointless.

Much more interesting was my introduction to the world of the literary blog. Until 2010 I didn't know what a blog was, let alone the literary variety. I found ANZLitLovers by accident and soon realised it had quality criticism that offered me cultural stimulation far removed from the expensive tickets and cheap wine of the festivals. I contacted Lisa Hill, the creator of this wonderful resource, and she agreed to look at *A Promised Land?*, *Alva's Boy* and *A Thousand Nights at the Ritz*. In due course the reviews appeared and they were comprehensive, thoughtful and perceptive. ANZLitLovers often uses guest reviewers and Karenlee Thompson, an author from Queensland, contributed an evaluation of *Ritz* that delighted me:

> As I read some of the stories in this anthology I easily imagined myself sharing a glass of wine and a few tall stories with a writer who Arnold Zable describes in his introduction to this posthumously published work … as a 'classic Australian yarn spinner'.

There were flow-on effects from ANZLitLovers, as another quality blog, Reading Matters from London, reviewed *A Promised Land?* in similar terms: Kim Forrester wrote:

> From the very first page, I was swept away by the tale of Jacob's troubled life. Collins has an amazing gift for story-telling. The three novels are filled with drama, intrigue, adventure, grief and joy. There's plenty of warmth, humour and poignancy too.
>
> In Jacob's struggle to reconcile the Jewish and Gentile aspects of his life, we see that where we come from influences who we are and where we are going. In many ways this is a book as much about Australian identity as it is about Jewish identity – and some of it, including the bigotry, prejudice and ignorance, makes for uncomfortable reading.

Ros receiving an award from the Zionist Council of Victoria, 2010

At their annual conference in November 2010, the Zionist Council of Victoria gave me an award 'for outstanding services'. I was very proud; the boys came to watch and I just wished Alan had been there. With the generous support of the Lamm family and a grant from the government of Victoria, my dream of a Jewish Library of Australia looked set to become a reality. The Lamm Jewish Library of Australia was officially opened in 2012. Leonie and I still lunch and marvel at how far we've come since the Makor Library of 1987. Neither of us is as shy as we once were, and we've learned how to deploy *chutzpah* to achieve our goals.

CHAPTER 31
MERRY WIDOWS

Our story began with Solly's girl and then moved into Alan, Ros and the boys. Now it's just Ros: Old-age pensioner, widow lady, small corgi dog, pretty front garden, nicely kept house. 'She's got three sons, you know; they keep an eye on her'.

Dear Reader, believe me, when I asked you in my introduction to 'let me entertain you', I really only remembered the title and tune of the song, not the context. It's from Sondheim, a tribute to old-time burlesque and the stripper Gypsy Rose Lee. Revealing all? Well maybe not, but we *are* coming to the last act.

Popular music and familiar songs can bring out the memories that inform a memoir. Years ago, a talkback host on ABC radio chose Dean Martin singing 'That's Amore' (or it might have been 'Volare') as a musical interlude. She said the studio crew had scoffed at such old-fashioned stuff, but when the song began they all started to dance. So did Alan and I. We bought the CD *The Best of Dino* and each Friday as we worked together preparing *Shabbat* dinner for our family we'd delight in the wit and musicality the crooner brought to his romantic lyrics. I still dance but by myself – nostalgia and noodles.

A Noel Coward character in *Private Lives* comments on the potency of 'cheap' popular music. For Alan and me the great American musicals were not 'cheap' but often serious social commentary. When he was too sick to get about much we gathered a collection of the best, from *The Pyjama Game* (trade unions) to *Cabaret* (anti-Semitism), and found pleasure in the music that had punctuated our journey. For Solly and Sadie too, musicals of a much earlier time had great meaning. She'd melt at memories of *Rose Marie* and *The Maid of the Mountains* and they'd look at each other and smile shyly. They remembered meeting up in the 'gods' in 1926 just as Alan and I remembered *Oklahoma!* in 1956.

The *Oxford Book of Quotations* has over a column of entries about wives, but only a smattering on widows – perhaps an indication of how the world sees us. I don't much care for stage widows: Widow Twankey, the pantomime dame, Nellie Lovett in *Sweeney Todd,* Queen Gertrude in *Hamlet* – a dreary lot. Hanna Glawari, the eponymous *Merry Widow*, was a great favourite with Sadie and Solly. She's a feisty piece of work, but there are not many like her, either on the boards or in literature. In religious traditions widows are figures of pathos: there's the widow's mite in St Luke and poor widows like Naomi for whom the farmers in the Book of Ruth are obligated to leave 'gleanings'. Even in typesetting 'widows and orphans' refers to words or phrases left dangling at the end of a page. It's a miserable catalogue.

On the whole, I like best the Jewish jokes where the protagonists are so earthy and real. For example:

> It's the *yartzeit [yortsayt]* of Herman Mendelbaum's death and his widow decides to make a pilgrimage to the cemetery to recite a prayer over his grave and place a small stone, as is the tradition, to show that the deceased is remembered.
>
> She arrives at the cemetery, but it being a while since she had been there, she is confused and cannot find poor Herman's grave site. Finally, she comes across a grounds-keeper who escorts her to a small chapel on the cemetery grounds where the records are kept. Poring over large maps and lists, he finally turns to the widow and says, 'I

can find no record of a Herman Mendelbaum buried here. The closest I can find is a Sadie Mendelbaum.'

'That's him!' she exclaims. 'He always put everything in my name.'

(Source: http://www.zipple.com/jokes/jewishwidow.shtml)

I'm finding ending the memoir is not that easy. Starting it was also difficult, until Alex Skovron suggested I leave my grandparents to enter the story when they will, and begin with the departure from my wedding on the back of Alan's Lambretta motor scooter. That worked well. But a satisfying conclusion is elusive, perhaps because the genre itself, by its very nature, is open-ended.

Sally Spalding, our friend in WA, journalist, teacher and critic, who reviewed *Alva's Boy* so perceptively, writes:

> A memoir is not an easy thing to write. It clamps its feet firmly between two camps - one of which is the history of a life lived and the other of an experience remembered. So the memoir, unlike a novel, wears two hats. It is on the one hand an historical document and on the other, a personal narrative. It sits somewhere between experience and fact, memory and truth, reality and imagination. Alan Collins' memoir, *Alva's Boy*, successfully straddles both history and literature.

I was embarrassed when she insisted on seeing how *Solly's Girl* was shaping up. 'Hey, where's some hope at the end?' she asked. On the other hand, Karenlee Thompson in Queensland read my final chapters quietly over a bottle of wine and wept (but then so did I as I wrote them). My editor, Adele, said, 'It's *your* book – think about the readers for whom you wrote it.' At the beginning I thought I was writing for my children and grandchildren. Then it seemed I might be completing what Alan started in *Alva's Boy* – albeit not in the same style. It's hard to tell. Family history might seem pretty straightforward but it isn't: opinion and memory, 'embroidered' history, anecdote and fact, the way it was and the way we prefer to think it was. Sally Spalding summed it up perfectly.

Nomenclature is a case in point. We never knew Alan's mother, Alva; and my mother, Sadie, was always called Nana. I'm Grandma or, my preference, Ros. The last *Buba* in either my family or Alan's was Regina, my paternal grandmother, who died in 1939, nearly eighty years ago. And what of *Zeyde*? Alan insisted on being called Al by his children and grandchildren. With our Anglo-Australian names and backgrounds did we lose the plot, break the thread, forsake the *shtetl*, sever the link?

I have many problems understanding poetry and T S Eliot's 'Love Song of J. Alfred Prufrock' is challenging: 'I grow old … I grow old … I shall wear the bottoms of my trousers rolled.' It's the rolled trousers that make the pictures for me. My father, Solly, rolled his trousers when he braved the sea in the UK or Australia, and now I'm doing the same down at Elwood Beach because I'm too vain about the veins behind my knees to show my legs. Prufrock is a pessimist – the mermaids won't sing for him – but I opt for optimism because it's so much easier to live with.

I am, as Alan would have said, 'busier than a one-armed paperhanger', or 'flat out like a lizard drinking'. Death is not really a problem to me; hopefully mine will be pain-free. It is very much easier to contemplate since I decided, and it *was* a decision, to believe that Alan and I will somehow reconnect. Judaism is ambiguous about an afterlife – it seems to have 'a bob each way'. Walking along the beach wondering about the transmigration of souls – I'm ok with mysteries.

About a year ago, Peter was talking with a man in a restaurant. Parked outside was a Lambretta scooter and Peter commented, 'I think my dad had one like that.' His table companion turned out to be the president of the Lambretta Association of Australia and he was very keen to hear more of Alan and me and *La Cigale.* Did we have photographs of her? Would I write an article for their newsletter? How wonderful it would be, he said, if she turned up in some farmer's barn.

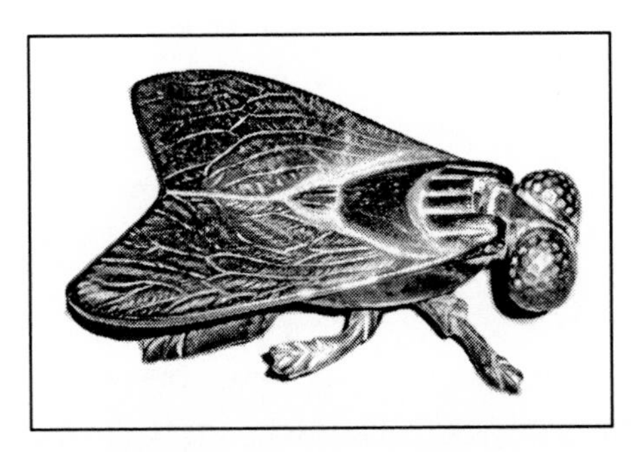

The mascot from La Cigale

The family in February 2014.
L-R, back row: Daniel, Rebecca, Peter, Joshua, Eli, Toby, Rhonda;
front row: Eli Alva, Isaac, Ros. Photograph by Nigel Clements

EPILOGUE – ELWOOD

I walk down Vautier Street and see the old-fashioned Californian bungalow where Alan found lodgings when he fled Sydney for Melbourne. I speculate about which room was his, about the hopes and dreams of the 'boy with the hungry eyes'. In Southey Street a striped awning and security grille now guard the entrance to our 'studio' where I displayed Chianti bottles draped with melted wax and wondered about my new life at the bottom of the world. I have seen the house in Francis Street, Sydney, and wept over the childhood of Alva's boy. When I visited London I went back to Daleham Gardens to look at the chilly attic where Alan and I had dreamed about the four children we might one day have. I have stood outside 36 Ashurst Drive, probably for the last time, and looked up at the window of the little box room that was mine. The house was a haven for Sadie and Solly, but not so for me. There is also suburban Currie Street, Box Hill – twenty-eight years, our children's childhood. For Alan it was 'the gulag'; for me, surprisingly, almost forgettable.

Broadway: all the charm of the 1920s, Art Deco, mansions and cottages, all bravely holding back the brutality of modern development. Elwood: beach promenades, the elders and the new aspirationals holding fast to seaside charm and ice-cream parlours. Here is where the boy from Bondi always wanted to bring his Ten Pound Pom. Not exactly a Sydney surf beach – Port Phillip Bay is more sedate and serious – but just right for who we were, for who I am.

ACKNOWLEDGEMENTS

I am deeply grateful to my sons, Daniel, Peter and Toby. They have encouraged me with technological, domestic and emotional support and, above all, with their love. They don't seem to mind being 'in Mum's book' but I have tried to be discreet. Similarly, I am grateful to 'Joel' for allowing me to tell his story. Simon Collins, the son of Leon and Wan, very kindly agreed that I might include memories of his father.

There are many friends and organisations mentioned in my manuscript. I have done my best to check facts with each one and wish to thank them all for their courtesy in allowing me to write about them. Any errors are mine.

My extended family overseas have been of great help, sharing their memories and undertaking research on my behalf. In particular, I would like to thank my cousins Gina Drew-Davis, Daphne Osen, Gerald Samuel, and Jonathan Tutleman. They have given me so much information and have taken my gentle jokes about Britain with good humour. In Australia I have been fortunate to locate the Ambor family and share their reminiscences.

I have drawn on unpublished material written by family members, most importantly my father's memoir 'As Far as I Remember' (1968) and the family tree that he compiled for us. Harriet Baskin's documentation for my mother's family, particularly the American connections, has helped me to understand the period of the family migrations.

Andy Collins' comprehensive genealogy of the Collins family has been invaluable in helping me to untangle the Dutch ancestry of Alan's paternal line. Similarly, the work of Heather Davis has shown me a way though the maternal background. *These are the names: Jewish lives in Australia 1788–1850* by Rabbi John Levi AM DD (Melbourne University Press, 2006) has been an essential reference, particularly in regard to our convict connection. My information about the Cortissos family came from the papers of the Jewish Historical Society of England (Transactions, Sessions 1970–1973: Volume XXIV & Miscellanies Part IX, 1974).

Whilst most of the photographs are from personal albums, I would like to acknowledge the courtesy of the *Australian Jewish News* and the London *Jewish Chronicle* for permission to reprint several images. I am very grateful to Marti Friedlander for her photographs of our wedding. Nigel Clements has done several photo shoots of our family and of me in a professional context. I greatly appreciate his courtesy in allowing me to use his work and, most particularly, for the cover picture. I am very indebted to my son Peter, who has scanned all the family photographs, and to my grandson Eli, who has created the map.

There have been many kind friends who have taken the time to read extracts and offer suggestions and I wish to acknowledge and thank them for their support and mentoring: Jan Epstein, film journalist; Lisa Hill, founder of ANZLitLovers; Clifford Posner of the Grumpy Swimmer Bookshop in Elwood; Alex Skovron, poet and editor; Sally Spalding, author, teacher, and journalist in Western Australia; Karenlee Thompson, author and critic in Queensland.

Danielle Charak kindly read the entire manuscript and gave advice on the Yiddish and Hebrew terms. Writing is a lonely task, and I wish to gratefully acknowledge her advice and encouragement.

Makor Publishing is an activity of the Lamm Jewish Library of Australia. The Write Your Story program is an important contribution to Australian-Jewish history and I am proud to have established it in 1998. Leonie Fleiszig is Director of the Lamm Library and has created the warm and welcoming environment in which such a program can flourish so successfully. We worked together for many years and it is a pleasure to acknowledge her achievements. Leonie sets the tone for her staff – Lauren Joffe, Mary Lavi and Hanna Yahalom – and the harmonious and helpful atmosphere of the library is a testament to her leadership.

Adele Hulse is the principal editor for Makor Publishing. Many of the Write Your Story authors are shy and diffident; some have horrendous stories to record. An editor with wisdom, empathy and compassion as well as professional skills is essential for the program to succeed as it does. I, along with many others, am grateful to Adele.

Ruth Leonards has long been associated with the library and is also my friend. We worked together for many years and I have great admiration and respect for her librarianship, and now her skills as a copy editor. The professional standards of the Write Your Story program owe a great deal to Ruth's expertise.

It has been a pleasure to work with Julie Tanner. My memoir has been designed with care and affection for the words and pictures and I am grateful for her skill and professionalism.

Throughout my book I have referred to Sophie, my small corgi, but her little life ended as I finished editing. She came with me all the way, from the beginning of Alan's final illness until the last full stop of my manuscript. *Zichrona Livracha* – May her memory be a blessing.

MAP OF THE PLACES OUR FAMILIES KNEW IN EUROPE

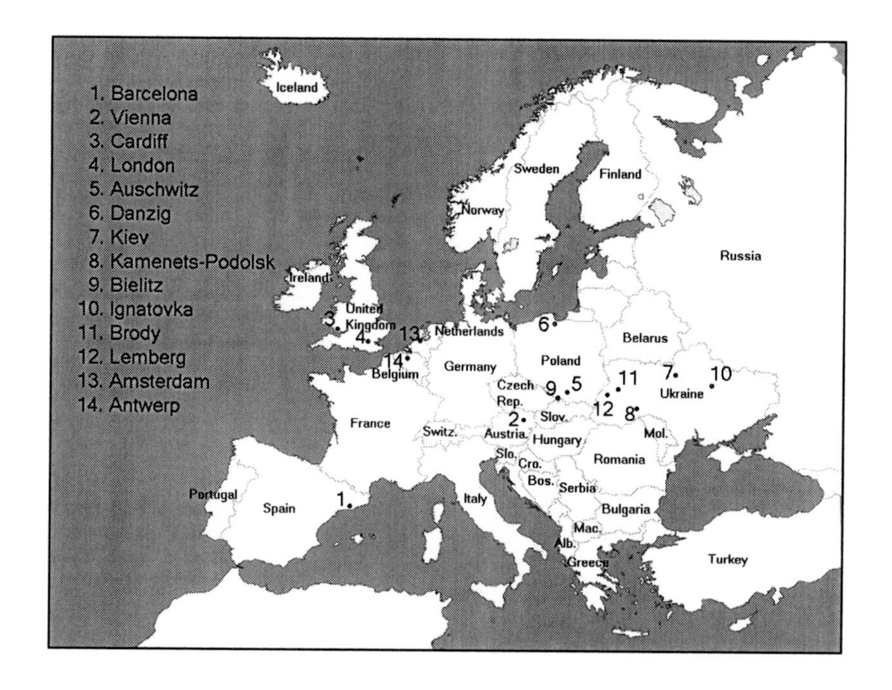

Family Tree No. 1: ANCESTORS OF ROSALINE FOX

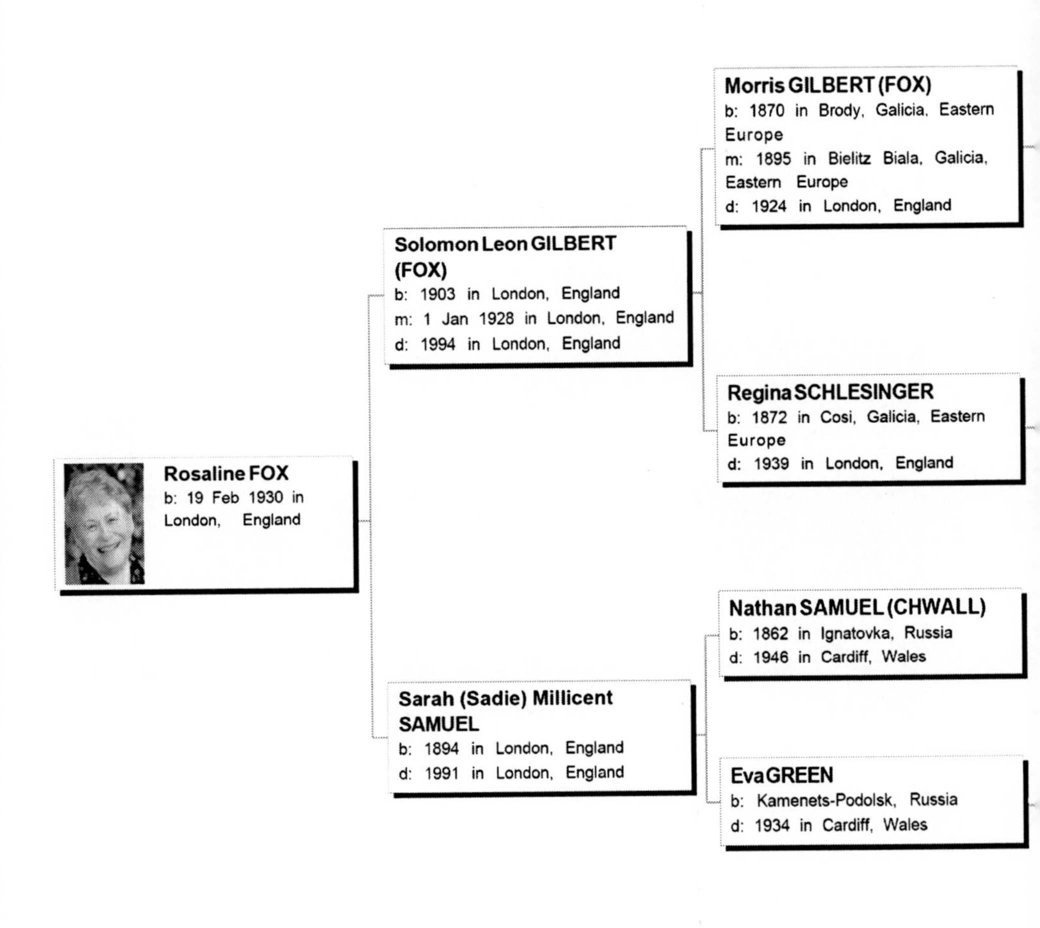

Chaim Zvi GILBERT (GELBERT)
b: Galicia, Eastern Europe
d: Galicia, Eastern Europe

Socha Leah LEIMSEIDER
b: Galicia, Eastern Europe
d: Galicia, Eastern Europe

"Zaida" LEIMSEIDER
b: 1806 in Galicia, Eastern Europe
d: 1910 in Galicia, Eastern Europe

Herman SCHLESINGER
b: 1839 in Galicia, Eastern Europe
d: 1909 in Bielitz-Biala, Galicia, Eastern Europe

Rosa KNOEBEL
b: Galicia, Eastern Europe
d: Galicia, Eastern Europe

Seidel CHWALL
b: Russia
d: Russia

David (Dov) GREEN
b: Russia
d: London, England

Sybil Rose ?

Family Tree No. 2: DESCENDANTS OF ROSALINE FOX

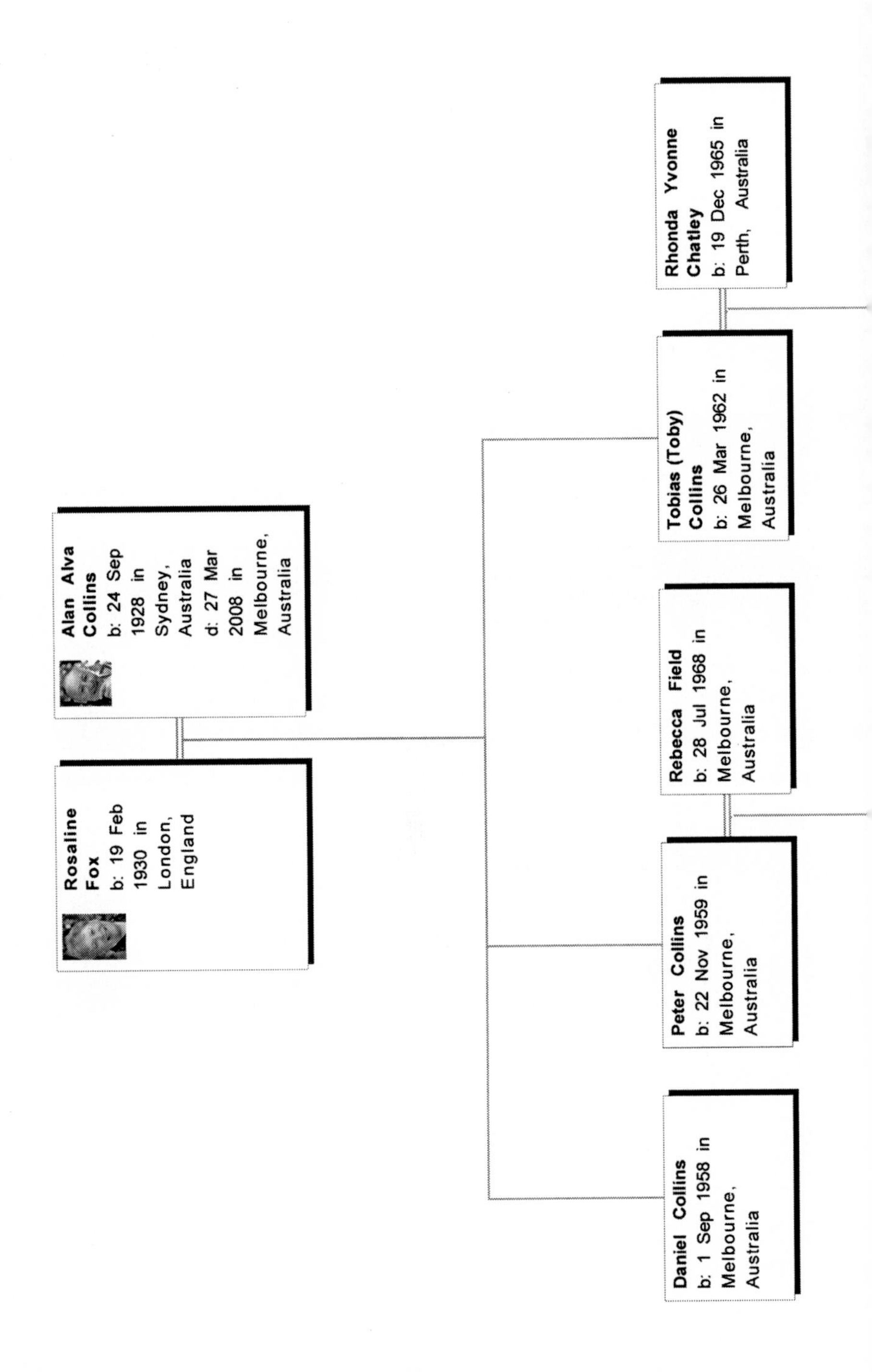

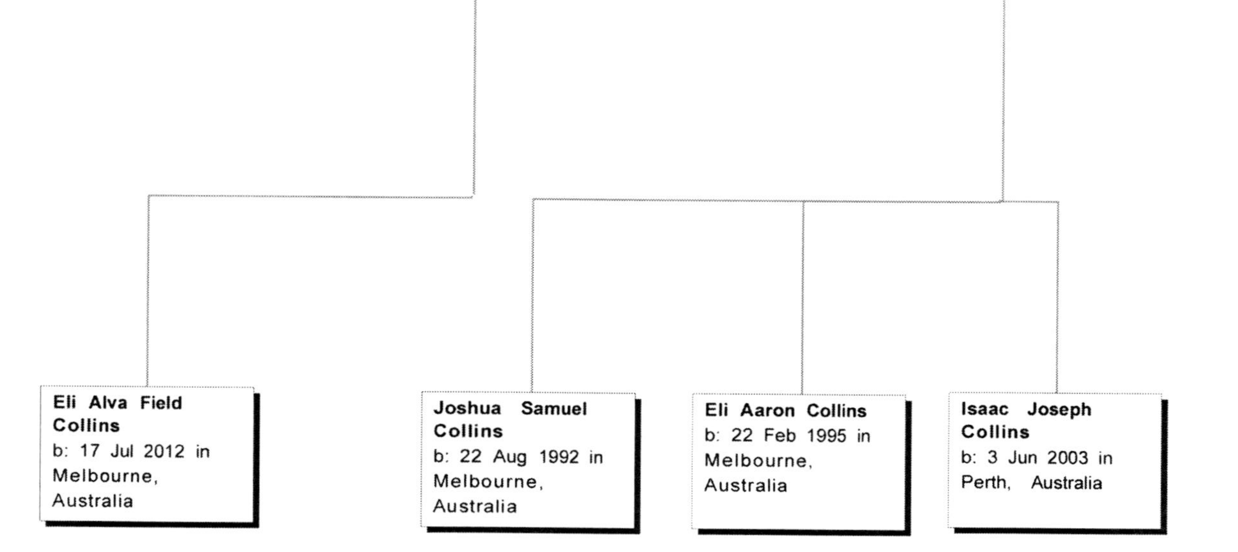
Eli Alva Field Collins
b: 17 Jul 2012 in Melbourne, Australia
Joshua Samuel Collins
b: 22 Aug 1992 in Melbourne, Australia
Eli Aaron Collins
b: 22 Feb 1995 in Melbourne, Australia
Isaac Joseph Collins
b: 3 Jun 2003 in Perth, Australia

Family Tree No. 3: THE LEIMSEIDER / GILBERT FAMILY

Note: The names Gilbert (Gelbert) and Leimseider were used irregularly. Fox was a name 'adopted' by Morris Gilbert. However, the birth certificate for Rosaline Fox clearly states that she is the daughter of Solomon Leon Fox and Sadie Millie Fox, formerly Samuels (Samuel).

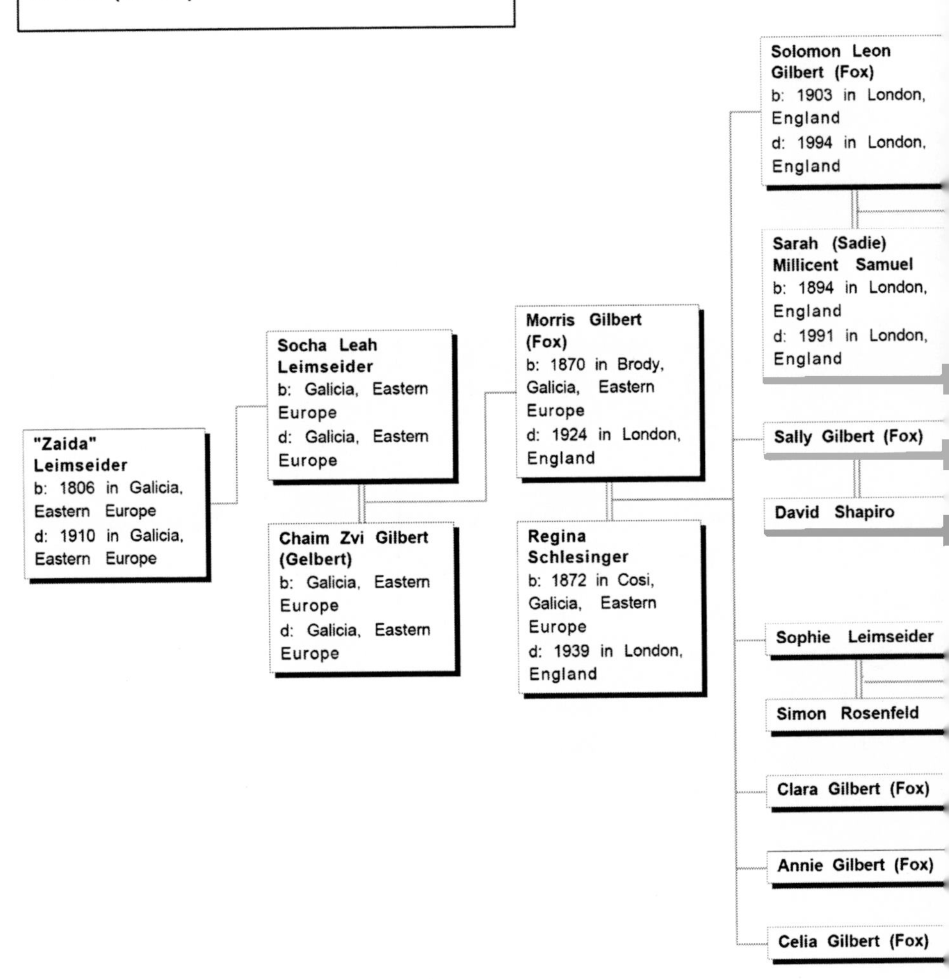

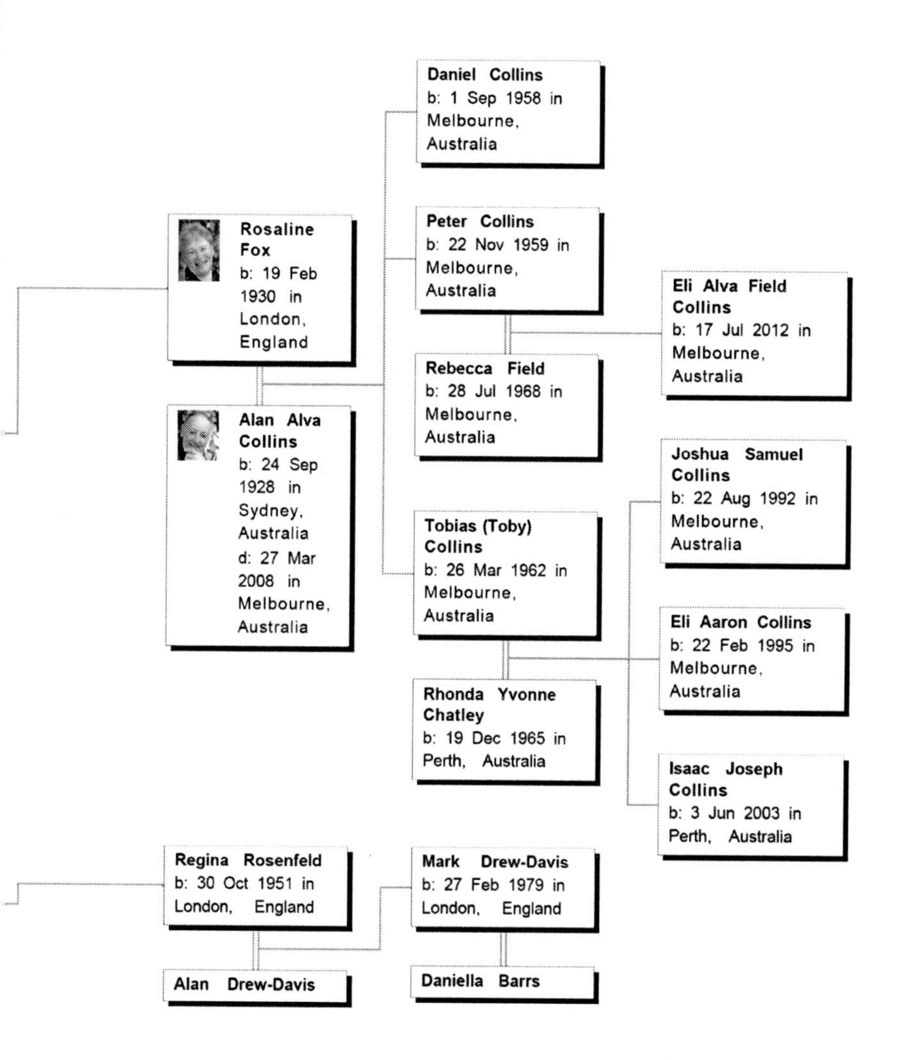

Daniel Collins
b: 1 Sep 1958 in Melbourne, Australia
Rosaline Fox
b: 19 Feb 1930 in London, England
Peter Collins
b: 22 Nov 1959 in Melbourne, Australia
Eli Alva Field Collins
b: 17 Jul 2012 in Melbourne, Australia
Rebecca Field
b: 28 Jul 1968 in Melbourne, Australia
Alan Alva Collins
b: 24 Sep 1928 in Sydney, Australia
d: 27 Mar 2008 in Melbourne, Australia
Joshua Samuel Collins
b: 22 Aug 1992 in Melbourne, Australia
Tobias (Toby) Collins
b: 26 Mar 1962 in Melbourne, Australia
Eli Aaron Collins
b: 22 Feb 1995 in Melbourne, Australia
Rhonda Yvonne Chatley
b: 19 Dec 1965 in Perth, Australia
Isaac Joseph Collins
b: 3 Jun 2003 in Perth, Australia
Regina Rosenfeld
b: 30 Oct 1951 in London, England
Mark Drew-Davis
b: 27 Feb 1979 in London, England
Alan Drew-Davis
Daniella Barrs

Family Tree No. 4: THE SCHLESINGER FAMILY

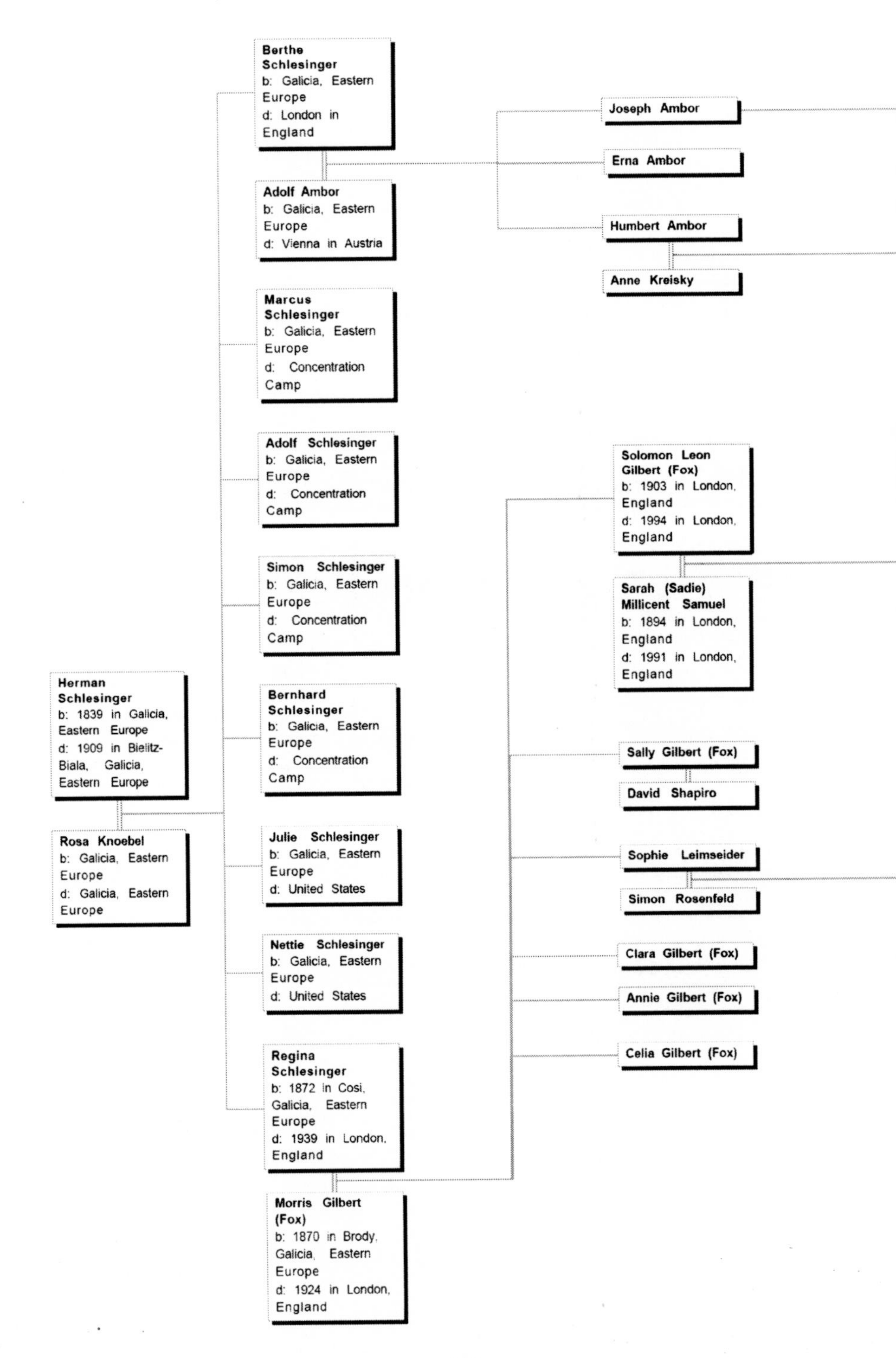

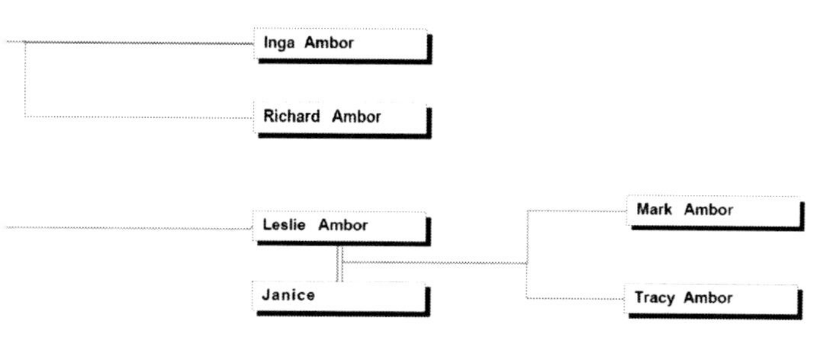

Note: Marcus, Adolf, Simon and Bernhard Schlesinger, my great-uncles, were murdered in a concentration camp, probably Auschwitz. Julie and Nettie Schlesinger, my great-aunts, emigrated to America.

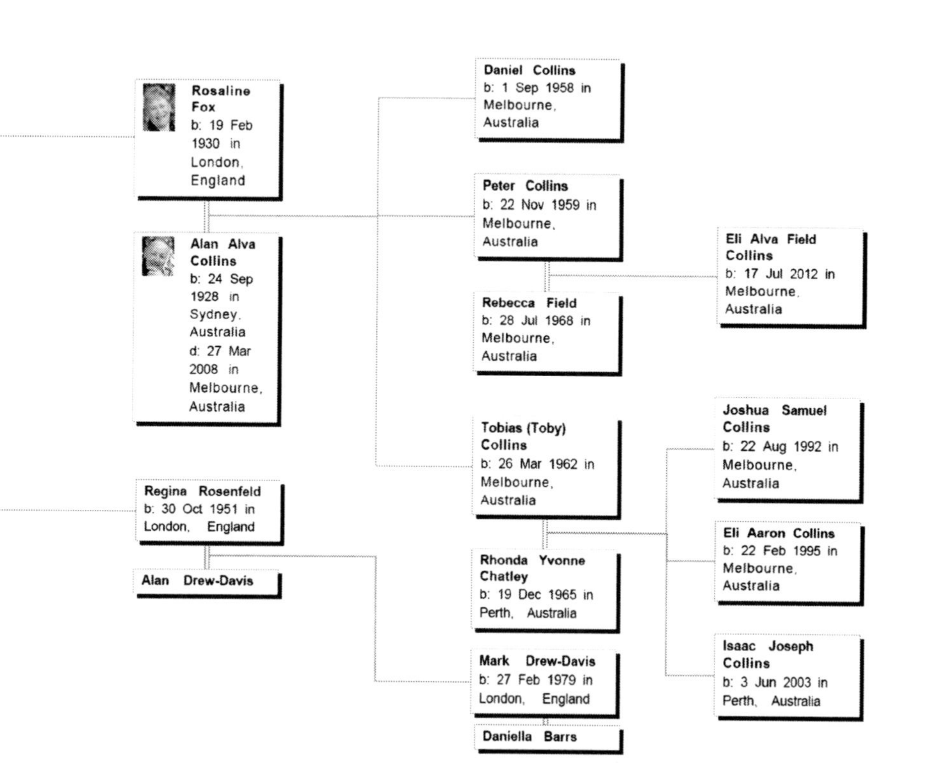

Family Tree No. 5: THE GREEN / SAMUEL FAMILY

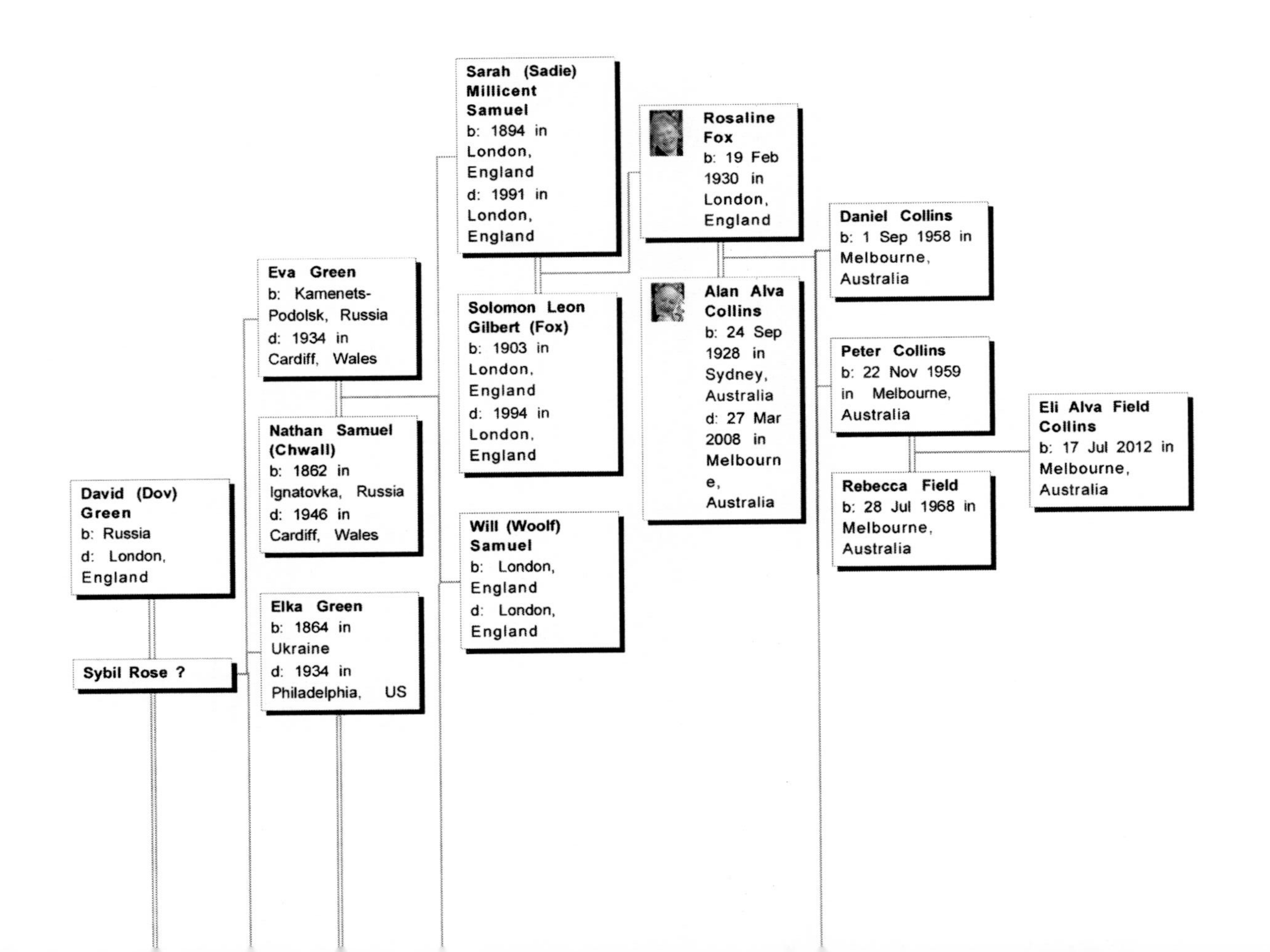

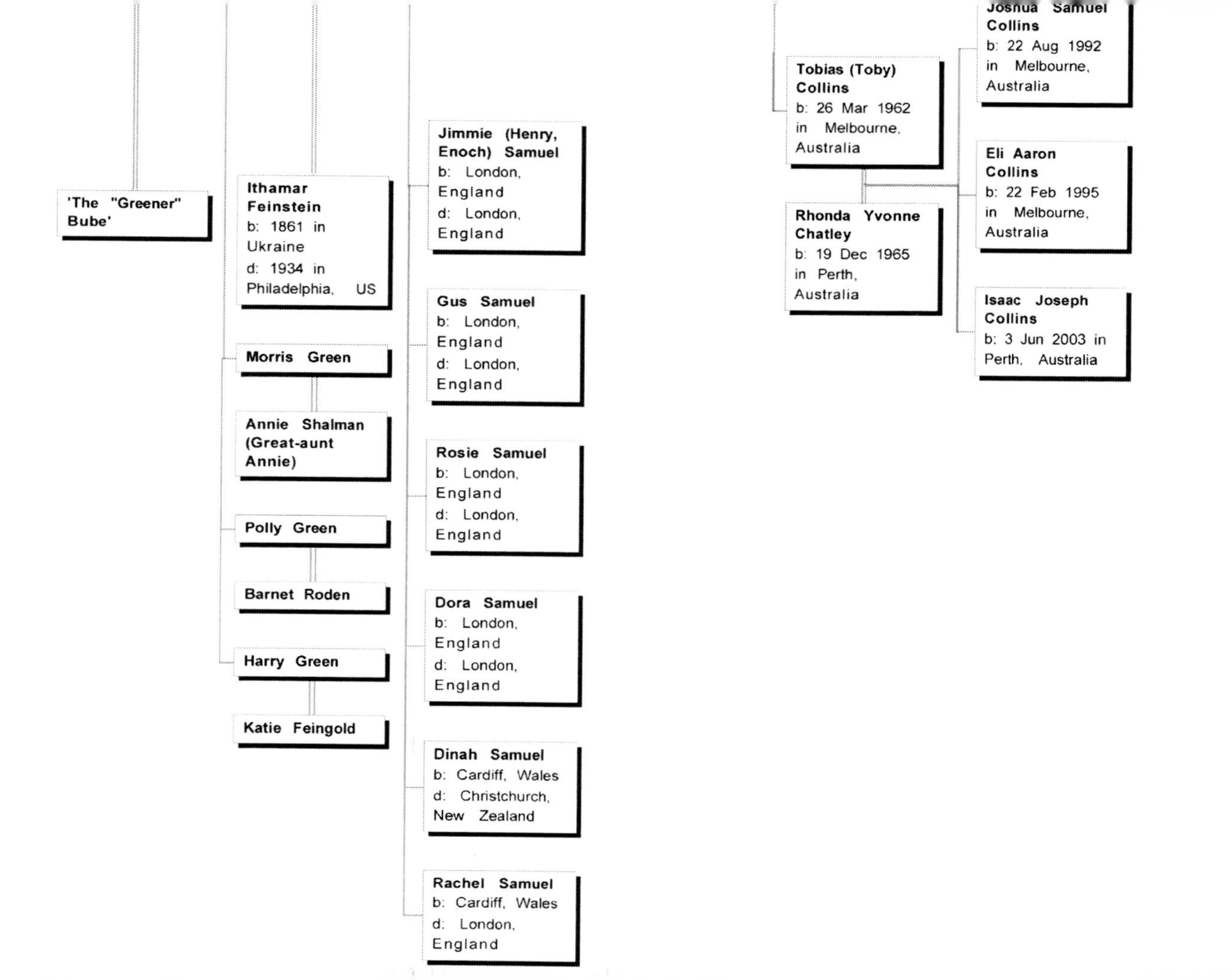

'The "Greener" Bube'
Ithamar Feinstein
b: 1861 in Ukraine
d: 1934 in Philadelphia, US
Morris Green
Annie Shalman (Great-aunt Annie)
Polly Green
Barnet Roden
Harry Green
Katie Feingold
Jimmie (Henry, Enoch) Samuel
b: London, England
d: London, England
Gus Samuel
b: London, England
d: London, England
Rosie Samuel
b: London, England
d: London, England
Dora Samuel
b: London, England
d: London, England
Dinah Samuel
b: Cardiff, Wales
d: Christchurch, New Zealand
Rachel Samuel
b: Cardiff, Wales
d: London, England
Tobias (Toby) Collins
b: 26 Mar 1962 in Melbourne, Australia
Rhonda Yvonne Chatley
b: 19 Dec 1965 in Perth, Australia
Joshua Samuel Collins
b: 22 Aug 1992 in Melbourne, Australia
Eli Aaron Collins
b: 22 Feb 1995 in Melbourne, Australia
Isaac Joseph Collins
b: 3 Jun 2003 in Perth, Australia

Family Tree No. 6: THE COLLINS FAMILY IN THE NETHERLANDS

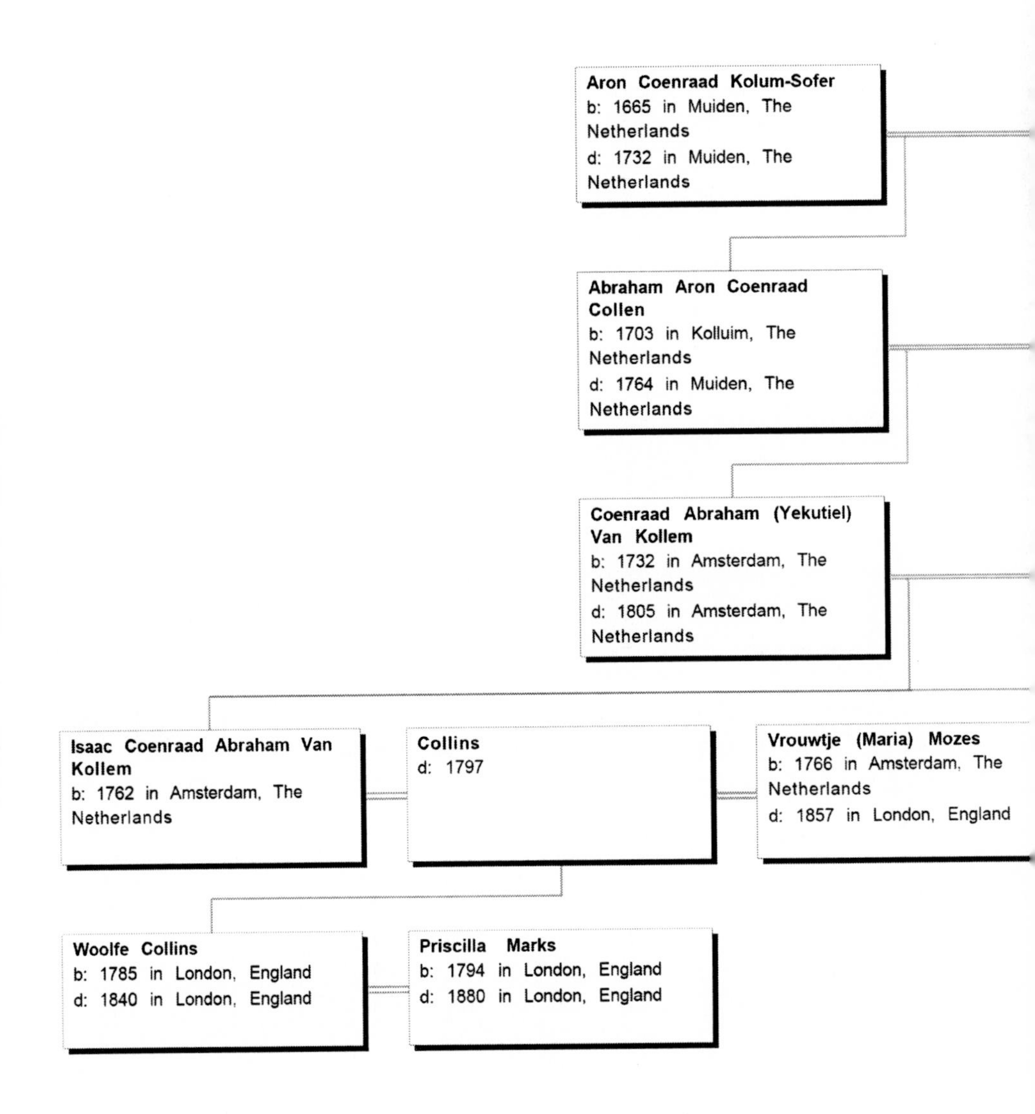

Esther Phillip Levy
b: 1666 in Muiden, The Netherlands
d: 1754 in Muiden, The Netherlands

Note: Sophia Collins and Isaac Coenraad Abraham Van Kollem were siblings. Their children, Woolfe Collins and Priscilla Marks were thus first cousins.

Sara Joseph Jacob de Mets
b: 1704 in Amsterdam, The Netherlands
d: 1785 in Amsterdam, The Netherlands

Bloeme Hartog Isaac de Vries Jaffe
b: 1730 in Amsterdam, The Netherlands
d: 1807 in Amsterdam, The Netherlands

Sophia (Feijle) Collins (Van Kollem)
b: 1766 in Amsterdam, The Netherlands
d: 1861 in London, England

Samuel Marks
d: 1822 in London, England

Priscilla Marks
b: 1794 in London, England
d: 1880 in London, England
(Duplicated)

Woolfe Collins
b: 1785 in London, England
d: 1840 in London, England

Family Tree No. 7: THE COLLINS FAMILY IN ENGLAND AND AUSTRALIA

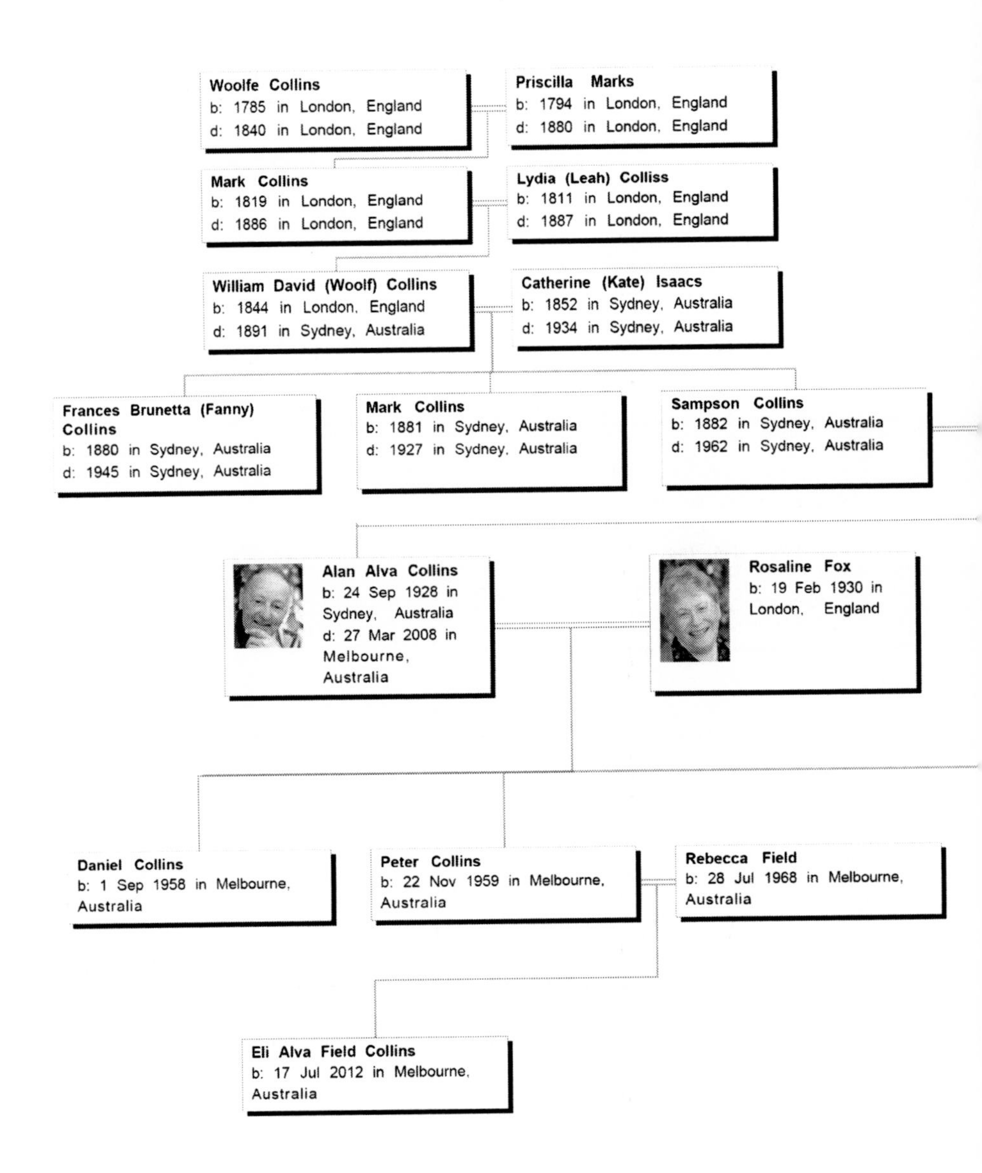

Sampson Collins had four wives. He married Camelia Truegold in 1909. They were divorced c1925. He married Viva Rachael Israel in 1925; she died in 1926. He married Alva Poebe Davis in 1927; she died in 1928. In 1933 he married Lillian A. Goodacre and they were divorced. Sampson had two sons: Alan Alva, son of Alva, and Leon, son of Lillian.

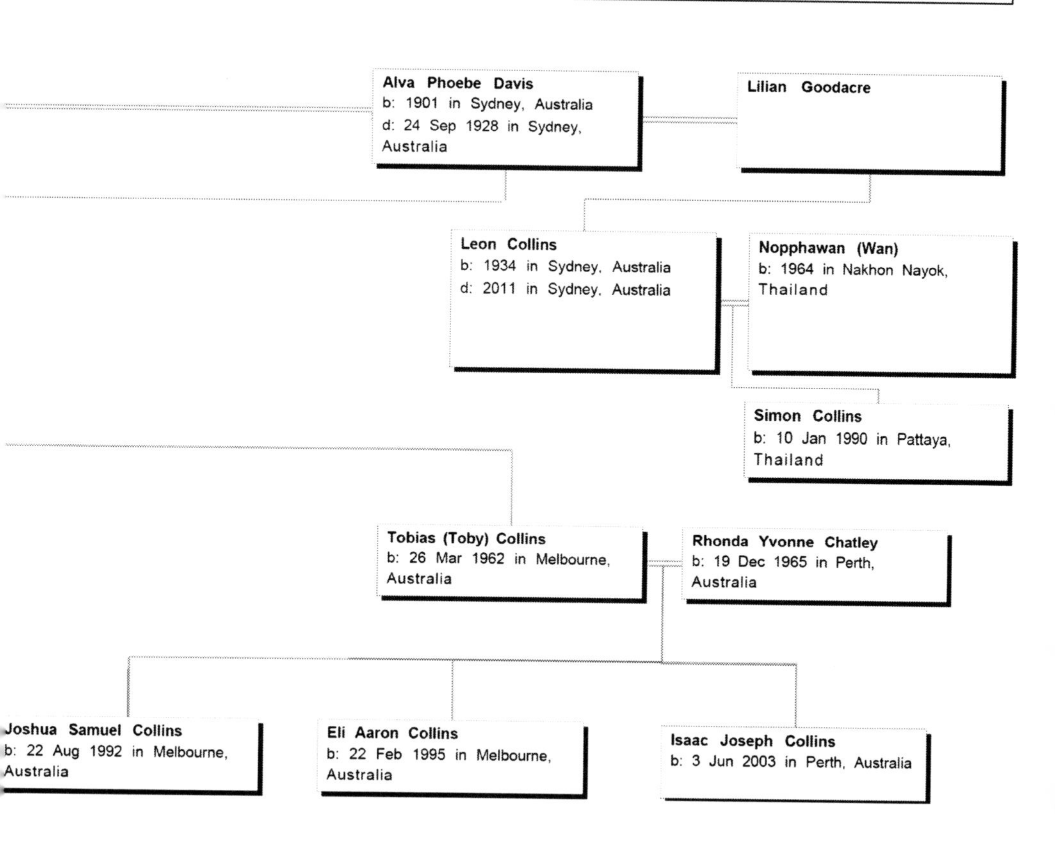

Family Tree No. 8: THE CORTISSOS FAMILY

Note: The Cortissos family originated in Spain and/or Portugal. In the 15th century, at the time of the Spanish Inquisition, Emanuel Jose (Joseph) Cortissos, Marquis de Villa, gave his three sons Spanish as well as Hebrew names. His eldest son (Abraham?) went to Barcelona and a descendant, Don Emanuel, served the Duke of Alba whose name is commemorated in Alan Collins' mother, Alva Phoebe Davis.

Joseph Cortissos (1656-1742) was a commissary (contractor) for the armies of England and Portugal. He died in London and his portrait is in the Spanish and Portuguese Synagogue. His grandson, also Joseph, documented the family history c1780.

Elias Cortissos
b: Spain ?

Mark Davis
b: 1856 in Sydney, Australia
d: 1908 in Sydney, Australia

Alva Phoebe Davis
b: 1901 in Sydney, Australia
d: 24 Sep 1928 in Sydney, Australia

Alan Alva Collins
b: 24 Sep 1928 in Sydney, Australia
d: 27 Mar 2008 in Melbourne, Australia

Daniel Collins
b: 1 Sep 1958 in Melbourne, Australia

Peter Collins
b: 22 Nov 1959 in Melbourne, Australia

Rebecca Field
b: 28 Jul 1968 in Melbourne, Australia

Eli Alva Field Collins
b: 17 Jul 2012 in Melbourne, Australia

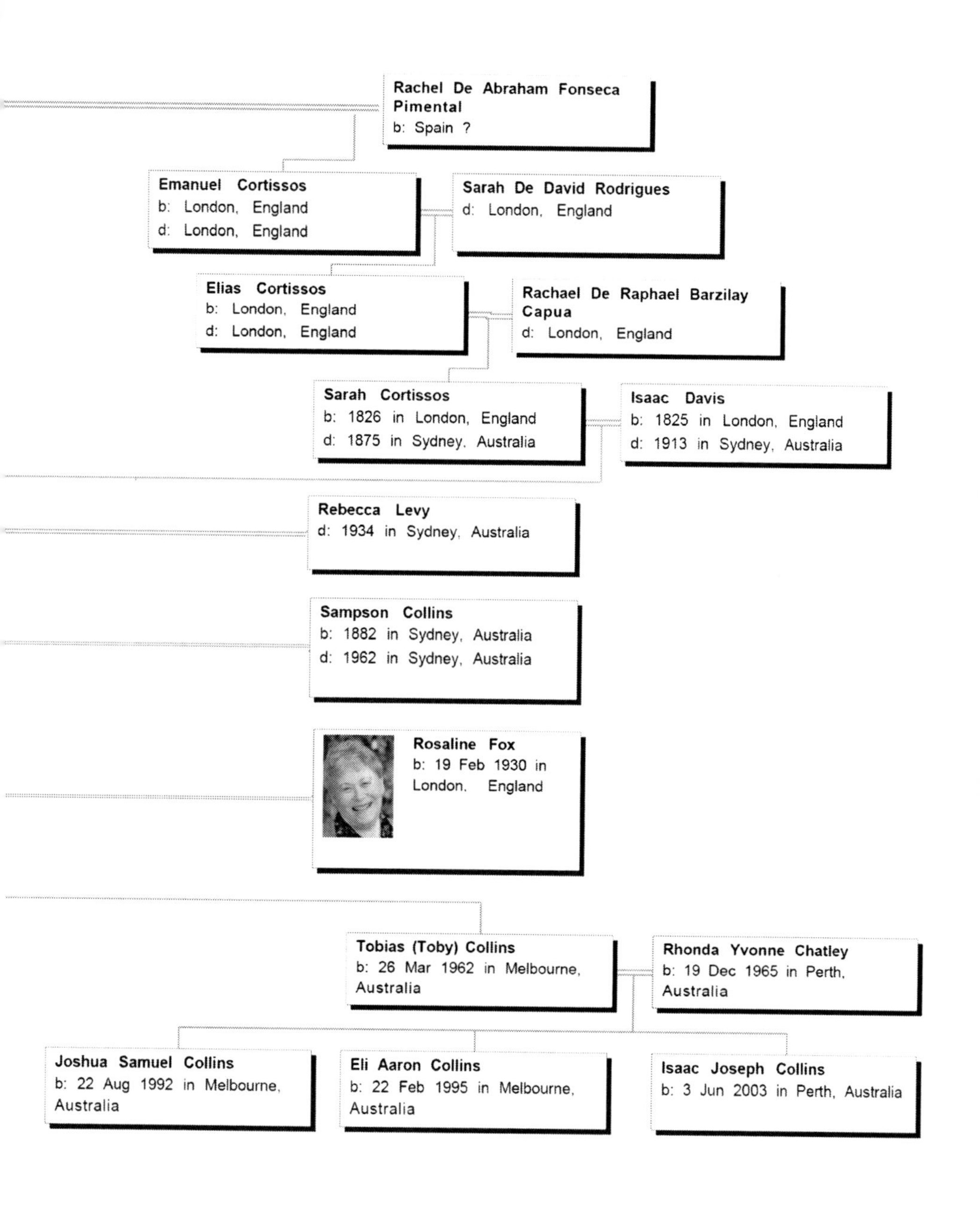
Rachel De Abraham Fonseca Pimental
b: Spain ?
Emanuel Cortissos
b: London, England
d: London, England
Sarah De David Rodrigues
d: London, England
Elias Cortissos
b: London, England
d: London, England
Rachael De Raphael Barzilay Capua
d: London, England
Sarah Cortissos
b: 1826 in London, England
d: 1875 in Sydney, Australia
Isaac Davis
b: 1825 in London, England
d: 1913 in Sydney, Australia
Rebecca Levy
d: 1934 in Sydney, Australia
Sampson Collins
b: 1882 in Sydney, Australia
d: 1962 in Sydney, Australia
Rosaline Fox
b: 19 Feb 1930 in London, England
Tobias (Toby) Collins
b: 26 Mar 1962 in Melbourne, Australia
Rhonda Yvonne Chatley
b: 19 Dec 1965 in Perth, Australia
Joshua Samuel Collins
b: 22 Aug 1992 in Melbourne, Australia
Eli Aaron Collins
b: 22 Feb 1995 in Melbourne, Australia
Isaac Joseph Collins
b: 3 Jun 2003 in Perth, Australia

Family Tree No. 9: THE DAVIS FAMILY

Note: The convict Samuel Davis (1813-1892) was a son of John Jacob Davis and Maria Joel who had twelve children. He was transported to Australia in 1831 at the age of seventeen. Samuel was the brother of Mark Davis (1793-1869) who became a great-great-grandfather of Alan Alva Collins.

David Davis

John Jacob Davis
b: 1751 in London, England
d: 1842 in London, England

Isaac Davis
b: 1825 in London, England
d: 1913 in Sydney, Australia

Alva Phoebe Davis
b: 1901 in Sydney, Australia
d: 24 Sep 1928 in Sydney, Australia

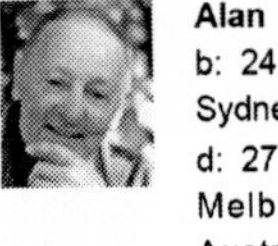

Alan Alva Collins
b: 24 Sep 1928 in Sydney, Australia
d: 27 Mar 2008 in Melbourne, Australia

Daniel Collins
b: 1 Sep 1958 in Melbourne, Australia

Peter Collins
b: 22 Nov 1959 in Melbourne, Australia

Rebecca Field
b: 28 Jul 1968 in Melbourne, Australia

Eli Alva Field Collins
b: 17 Jul 2012 in Melbourne, Australia

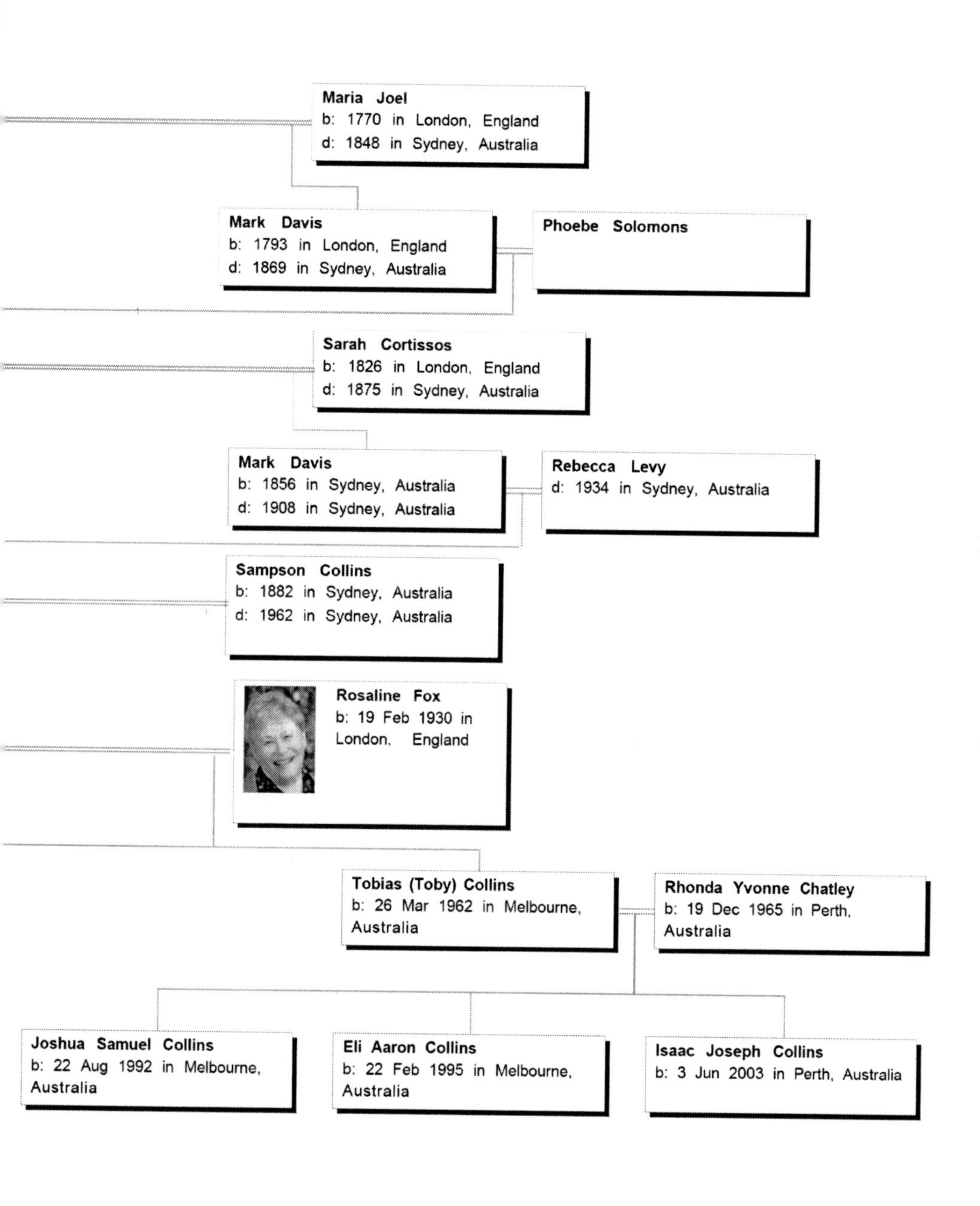
Maria Joel
b: 1770 in London, England
d: 1848 in Sydney, Australia
Mark Davis
b: 1793 in London, England
d: 1869 in Sydney, Australia
Phoebe Solomons
Sarah Cortissos
b: 1826 in London, England
d: 1875 in Sydney, Australia
Mark Davis
b: 1856 in Sydney, Australia
d: 1908 in Sydney, Australia
Rebecca Levy
d: 1934 in Sydney, Australia
Sampson Collins
b: 1882 in Sydney, Australia
d: 1962 in Sydney, Australia
Rosaline Fox
b: 19 Feb 1930 in London, England
Tobias (Toby) Collins
b: 26 Mar 1962 in Melbourne, Australia
Rhonda Yvonne Chatley
b: 19 Dec 1965 in Perth, Australia
Joshua Samuel Collins
b: 22 Aug 1992 in Melbourne, Australia
Eli Aaron Collins
b: 22 Feb 1995 in Melbourne, Australia
Isaac Joseph Collins
b: 3 Jun 2003 in Perth, Australia